The World of Malgudi:

A Study of R.K. Narayan's Novels

In the same series

Fiction of the Nineties
Veena Noble Dass and R.K. Dhawan, ed.

Indian Literature Today, 2 vol.s.
R.K. Dhawan, ed.

Recent Indian Fiction
R.S. Pathak, ed.

Five Indian Novelists
V.V.N. Rajendra Prasad

Major Indian Novelists
K. Venkata Reddy

Indian Women Novelists, Set I (Vols. I-V); Set II (Vol.VI-XI)
R.K. Dhawan, ed.

The Novels of Mulk Raj Anand
R.K. Dhawan, ed.

The Novels of Arun Joshi
R.K. Dhawan, ed.

The Novels of Salman Rushdie
G.R. Taneja and R.K. Dhawan, ed.

The Novels of Raja Rao
Esha Dey

The Novels of Bhabani Bhattacharya
Balram Sorot

The Novels of Anita Desai
Usha Bande

Nayantara Sahgal and Doris Lessing: A Feminist Study in Comparison
Neena Arora

The Novels of Shashi Deshpande
Sarabjit K. Sandhu

Comparative Perspectives on Indian Literature
A. Ramakrishna Rao, ed.

Studies in Indian Writing in English
P. Bayapa Reddy

The Novels of Manohar Malgonkar
M. Rajagopalachari

Virginia Woolf and Anita Desai: A Comparative Study
Asha Kanwar

The Novels of Kamala Markandaya and Ruth Jhabvala
Rekha Jha

The World of Malgudi

A Study of R.K. Narayan's Novels

A. Hariprasanna

PRESTIGE

Published by
Prestige Books
New Delhi 110 008

ISBN: 81-85218-93-5
1994
Reprint 1998

Photo Typesetting by
Pivot Computers
Delhi 110 006
Ph. 2918404

Printed at
Mehra Offset Press
New Delhi 110 002

Contents

Preface

The present inquiry deals with the world of Malgudi as reflected in the novels of R.K. Narayan. Interestingly, Narayan has been writing fiction for more than five decades. His reputation has become international over the years. He has been extensively praised by eminent novelists including Graham Greene, V.S. Naipaul and John Updike. Fortunately the octogenarian novelist is still active as a creative artist and has been adding to his fictional corpus from time to time. Recently, he has been awarded the Yatra award of one lakh rupees, instituted by Rupa and Harper Collins, for presenting 'a graceful and profoundly human vision of life' in his works.

Malgudi, an imaginary town, is the chosen fictional locale for all the novels and most of the short stories of Narayan. It is essentially Indian in spirit and is made a living presence in his works. Malgudi can be said to be the "short and long" of India, a microcosm of the Indian society. It is through the world of Malgudi that Narayan tries to present his view of the world and vision of life—the triumph and timelessness and permanence of the age-old traditional values of the society to which he belongs. The present study makes a modest attempt to recapture the Malgudi world in its essence.

Such an effort to depict the Malgudi world as this one owes to many scholars whose work I have drawn upon, which will be found mentioned in the references cited. If I have adopted or adapted something inadvertently, I hope it will be excused as oversight.

I cannot close these prefatory remarks without expressing my gratitude to those who helped me in undertaking the present project. My thanks are due to Sri R.A. Jayantha, who suggested the topic of research and instilled in me the quest for a better understanding of Narayan; to the Research Council of the Department of English, S.V. University,

Tirupati, that gave me permission to undertake the present research. I must express my gratitude to Prestige Books for bringing out the present book so elegantly and expeditiously. Finally I would like to place on record my thanks to my parents and my brother, who have always been a sustained strength and constant encouragement in all my academic pursuits.

Tirupati **A. Hariprasanna**

Something of What Follows

R.K. Narayan regarded as one of the "Big three"[1] among the Indian novelists in English has been justly admired for his remarkable gift for telling stories, for portraying memorably people of small oddities and eccentricities, and for his humour. Haydn Moore Williams makes the following interesting observation on Narayan: "R.K. Narayan always has a good story to tell, like the bazaar story-teller of immemorial tradition. George Steiner, writing of the decline of story-telling in the modern novel, says that few of our modern idols . . . could have kept a railway-carriage entertained on a long journey. Narayan certainly could."[2] To tell a story engagingly is no mean gift for a novelist. However, there are other aspects of Narayan's work such as his artistic integrity, his themes, his narrative art and craftsmanship, and his moral vision presented through the comic mode. Every one of them deserves to be studied separately with reference to his individual novels as well as his total corpus. As yet it would seem that these have not been given the attention and emphasis they deserve, although the critical attention given to Narayan's works cannot be said to be negligible.

Certain themes recur in the novels of Narayan. But as they are not particularly topical or provocative, they are not likely to attract attention to themselves. Narayan has deliberately avoided politics and polemics of any kind. All the same, the themes he chooses for his novels will seem to be of perennial interest especially to a sensitive mind interested in human beings. One of them is man's susceptibility to self-deception due to entertaining illusions. It is the most recurrent and it provides an excellent field for Narayan's comedy. The other themes are: the renunciation, generational disaffiliation, conflict between tradition and modernity; the East-West encounter, education, etc. Narayan's method is to treat his themes, not in abstract or in didactic terms but in terms of individuals in flesh and blood and their experiences. And hence the universal appeal of his novels, although they confine themselves to a narrow region in South India. The themes of Narayan are all inter-related and inter-dependent. But for purposes of study and analysis one may have to isolate them.

On more than one occasion Narayan has said that his primary interest is in character: "My focus is all on character. If his personality comes alive, the rest is easy for me."[3] Again on another occasion in an interview to William Walsh he is reported to have said: "My main concern is with human character—a central character from whose point of view the world is seen and who tries to get over a difficult situation or succumbs to it or fights it in his own setting."[4]

In yet another interview Narayan has reportedly said: "I value human relationship very much, very intensely. It makes one's existence worthwhile—human relationship, in any and every form, whether at home or outside."[5] These and other statements of Narayan stress the primacy of character, human individuals and human relationships in his fiction.

Preoccupation with human character in one's fiction, somewhat old-fashioned and conventional as it might seem, is no negligible or unimportant aspect of fiction. On the contrary, it is one of the basic and the necessary elements of all fiction at all times. It is through character and conflict that a novelist explores his chosen theme or themes. David Madden and Virgil Scott point out: "The elements of conflict and character are as important as that of theme, and the writer who fails to handle these elements skilfully will have written a poor story regardless of his profound or significant meaning."[6] Therefore there is no need to be apologetic about Narayan's interest in character. He is preoccupied with, as M.K. Naik puts it, "What man can make of himself and of the entire business of living."[7] Therefore an examination of Narayan's fiction, no matter what the aspect chosen for analysis is, necessarily involves an analysis of his characters, particularly his protagonists.

The mainspring of Narayan's fictional art is his abiding, humane and responsible interest in varieties of people, especially the vast majority of the average and the ordinary, and in the limitless possibilities of their lives. In fact Malgudi, which is a wholly imaginary suburban town and the locale of the bulk of his fiction, is a richly peopled world. Here indeed one finds "God's plenty." Along with Malgudi the family provides the novelist with a convenient and manageable context, concrete and particular, to study at close quarters human individuals and human relationships in all their variety and intricacy. It also helps him in creating the illusion of realism, so very necessary for the success of his kind of fiction in which the fabulous figures frequently.

Narayan deliberately restricts himself to and insists on matters of everyday life, and therefore chooses ordinary men and women for his fictional contemplation. His protagonists are anything but outstanding. Malgudi is peopled by average and ordinary men and women, who generally belong to the middle, and lower middle-classes of South Indian society. These he knows first-hand, in fact he himself happens to be a product of the middle-class. Therefore he can give an authentic and convincing account of them. Their world is the precise area of his creative genius. As H.M. Williams has noted, "Private life, families, the ambitions, success and frustrations of simple Indians usually of the lower middle-class. These have provided Narayan with a plethora of subject-matter."[8] Moreover as Rajeev Taranath observes, he "cherishes and explores the unnoticed, subtle possibilities of the average and unremarkable."[9] It is important to note that Narayan does not idealize or glorify them. But with remarkable truthfulness, compassion, and authorial detachment, he portrays them as they are caught in a net of illusions, deceptions, self-deceptions, and achievements.

In the novels of Narayan without exception it is the man or woman of ordinary abilities rather than the extraordinary person that seeks to realize some or the other ambition, fails or achieves a measure of success in society which is more traditional than modern. Against the background of a changing Indian society, which is reflected in the imaginary city of Malgudi, Narayan weaves his human comedy. Over the years, Malgudi experiences some swift changes, the impact of which is reflected on the traditional Indian society with its centuries-old culture, customs, beliefs and superstitions. As Graham Greene comments "the life of Malgudi—never ruffled by politics proceeds in exactly the same way as it has done for centuries, and the juxtaposition of the age-old convention and the modern character provides much of the comedy." Because of the upheaval and replacement of the traditional values of the Western and modern civilization, the various human situations depicted in the novels border on the tragi-comic. But ultimately, the tradition and the traditional values triumph. The modernity touches only the fringes of the society and is never very real and does not touch the core. After the conflict, characters manage to return to the real and solid world of Malgudi, and to a life free from "distracting illusions and hysterics."

The present study seeks to examine Narayan's portrayal of his fictional world in detail—the place and the people and all that happens to them and their way of life, how they tend to entertain certain absurd ambitions and illusions, and how they return to the society to be an integral part of it rather than be isolated, how certain individuals deliberately go out of the family fold to realize their own potential and how in doing so serve the self-same society and how some more characters remain within the warm security of the family even with all their strifes and struggles, and how yet another group of persons, realizing the time has come, renounce the world for various reasons and seek salvation, and finally, by what means and mode of treatment is Narayan able to do all this through his fiction.

The present inquiry seeks to highlight the range of the society of

Malgudi with particular reference to a good many of Narayan's novels. Though there are thematic connections between Narayan's short stories and novels, the short stories will not be considered in depth, in order to keep the present undertaking within manageable limits. Nor would it aim at being exhaustive even with regard to the novels themselves. Without adhering to the chronological order, the novels that would be taken up for consideration in this study, would be grouped into separate categories, according to their thematic affinities. Such grouping facilitates comparison and contrast of the novels concerned.

Thus this essay begins with the study of the majority of Narayan's novels, grouped together to facilitate a geographical description of the place and the socio-cultural changes that have occurred in the place as well as the way of life of the people over the years, thus drawing attention to the topography of the Malgudi world – a world where the human drama is enacted by various fictional characters – men and women of Narayan. It tries to show how Malgudi represents the society or world at large, being a microcosm of the macrocosm.

The fictional world of R.K. Narayan in its exploration of the familial relationship of the domestic world, is largely devoted to the study of the family and various family relationships in detail, as the family forms the basic unit for any society. Narayan presents his protagonists against the background of their families and familial relations. He skilfully draws particular attention to the various details of their families. Many of them are seen as rooted in the traditions, customs, beliefs, and superstitions of their families. Thus every one of the important characters is given a recognizable identity and helped to come alive.

The first two novels of Narayan, *Swami and Friends* and *The Bachelor of Arts* illustrate this point. The central theme of either novel is growth towards emotional maturity which involves a crisis involving relations with others and the growth is made possible largely by the stability, solidarity and security of their respective families. The family is a secondary but significant theme in both the novels. *The Dark Room* and *The English Teacher* appear chronologically after the first two novels and present the obverse and reverse of the theme of married life, the second of the traditional stages or the *garhasthya,* according to the Hindu way of life. While *The English Teacher* presents the song of love in marriage, *The Dark Room* offers "a study of domestic harmony."[10] These two are pre-eminently domestic novels, and sensitive studies of husband-wife relationship, and they give ample scope for comparison and contrast. *The Financial Expert* and *The Vendor of Sweets* explore the father-son relationship and the generation gap. While Margayya sheds his love of money and returns to the family fold, Jagan seeks release from the family bonds by taking to the stage of *vanaprasthya,* the third of the traditional stages. *Waiting for the Mahatma* and *The Painter of Signs* could have been included in this study for consideration, but they have been left out chiefly to keep the study within bounds. These two novels delineate the grandmother-grandson and the grandaunt-grandnephew relationship, peculiar to Indian culture and family.

Certain individuals, deliberately choose to isolate themselves from any and every form of family relationship and defy the norms and conditions of society, to seek their individual potential, only to render their services to the said society in one way or the other, though they are termed "misfits." *The Guide, The Man-Eater of Malgudi,* and *The Painter of Signs* present such characters who become estranged from the conventions, codes and mores of the family and society, who go out of the family fold either by necessity or by choice to live their lives independent of every one of the bonds. It is, as it were for them, the demands of the family and by the same token, society prove an obstacle to the development of their selves and to the full realization of their potentialities.

There are others who in spite of the obstacles, obligations and limitations placed over them by the bonds of the family and restricted by a strict social code, strive to realize their absurd aims and ambitions, irrespective of the consequences. However, it is brought home to them that society does not tolerate any such folly and finally they return to the folds of the society. For, despite their absurd follies and foibles most of the characters remain conformists and tradition-bound, if not at the first at least towards the end, like Chandran, Savitri, Margayya and a multitude of other characters, who appear absurd and pathetic in their struggle with the tradition-bound society. They are of course ultimately led to a stage where their illusions crumble and normalcy is restored. Thus they mature and are all the more wiser for their follies. For, to preserve the harmony between all individuals and society, individual ambitions have to be subdued.

The protagonists of some of the novels taken up for the analysis, feel impelled to try some form of renunciation because of frustration, disappointment, failure, irreparable loss, and failure of relationship. Here Narayan tells us of the fraudulent holyman or *guru,* ideal sainthood and about the real ascetic or *sanyasi*. To start with, *The Bachelor of Arts* and *The Dark Room* grouped together to facilitate the purposes of study, explore the premature and ignorant renunciation taken up to escape certain emotional *crises* and subsequent upheaval in their lives. *The English Teacher* which comes chronologically after the other two novels depicts Krishnan's grief at the premature death of his wife, and his coming to terms with the tragic fact. His coming into psychic contact with the spirit of his wife, enables him gradually to accept her death as well as develop an equanimity of mind and inner calm, considerable degree of non-attachment, and serenity of mind associated with the *sthitaprajna.* In *Waiting for the Mahatma* Narayan takes the risk of introducing Mahatma Gandhi as a character. The Mahatma belongs to the class of the extraordinary while the ordinary and average are Narayan's forte. The Mahatma's humanity and compassion are stressed, he is seen as the living embodiment of the very essence of renunciation – ideal sainthood. Living in the midst of people whose joys and sorrows he shares, he also cultivates at the same time an inner calm. *The Guide* presents the theme of the fraudulent holyman or *guru* from a fresh angle. The novelist makes satirical exposure of the false *sanyasi* far less important than focussing attention on the role of faith that a credulous community places in one who is believed to be a holyman, and its consequences to both the ascetic as an individual and as a public figure, and to the community. *The Vendor of Sweets* tells the amusing story of Jagan, an eccentric and obscurantist father, who can be devoted to Gandhi and the *Gita*, and also make handsome profits as a sweet-vendor, his absurd affection for his son, and his disillusionment and withdrawal from familial attachments and entering of *vanaprasthasrama. A Tiger for Malgudi*, written sixteen years after *The Vendor of Sweets*, is in many ways an unusual and challenging novel. Because under the guise of telling the apparently fantastic and improbable story of a jungle tiger attaining true enlightenment, Narayan actually tells a story whose real theme is renunciation or *sanyasa.*

Narayan renders into modern fiction various myths and legends drawn from the classical Indian traditional literature, epics and tales such as the *Mahabharata*, the *Bhagavata, Jataka* tales and the *Panchatantra*, the world famous and internationally known collection of animal stories. Taken from these various traditional sources the myths and legends are improved and improvised to suit the modern times and contemporary situation. Through these stories Narayan tries to present a view of life and a moral vision in terms of the comic mode, though never didactic or instructive anywhere. In the words of George Woodcock: "The ancient Indian myths which Narayan began to read within his middle years are not merely plots for films; his novels recreate them."[11] Therefore one can say that Narayan's view of life is essentially Indian and that his novels offer a recreation of the traditional imagination as it acts upon the individual consciousness within the contemporary society.

Narayan is a writer with a full commitment to certain spiritual and religious ideas with which Indians are normally familiar[12] and he has been able to penetrate into the core of Indian life without being hampered by problems of regionalism, religion, caste and class with which an Indian writer has to come to grips. What is characteristically great about him is that he has been able to capture the essence that is Indian.[13]

That Narayan's vision is characterized by a unique Indian sensibility is of no doubt. And his adherence to the ancient Indian tradition—(as reflected in his fictional world) a tradition which is deeply rooted in the beliefs of the transmigration of the soul, *karma,* reincarnation and renunciation, becomes clear through a perceptive study of his fiction.

Almost all his novels touch upon the above mentioned themes. The only difference being that while in some of the novels they form the major themes, in others they provide a significant and added meaning to the narration. As one of the characters in his novels comments, he always finds "some ancient model." He always comes upon an ancient myth or legend which lends itself to him to express his moral vision of life. As Wiiliam Walsh observes: "The religious sense of Indian myth is part of Narayan's grip of reality and his particular view of human life and his individual way of placing and ordering human experience."[14]

And moreover he is able to achieve what he aims at—to present his view of the world and vision of life through the comic. He is able to treat even the element of the serious and pathetic in terms of the comic. This mode of treatment seems to suit Narayan's purpose admirably—that of presenting joys and sorrows, pains and pleasures, smiles and tears through laughter. Because the world which he depicts is paradoxical in its essence. In the Malgudi world appearance and reality, individual and society, hope and despair, laughter and tears are all inseparable and interwoven.

In the depiction of his characters Narayan observes an attitude of complete detachment. "He watches their antics bemused and without a wish to alter them. Enough that they are, if not witty themselves, the cause of wit in others."[15]

Gifted with a unique zest for life he chooses for his fictional contemplation ordinary men and women and "like Chekhov has produced from their very inadequacies, from their weaknesses and shallow pretensions, a combination of sadness and comedy that is irresistibly appealing."[16]

He is a master of comedy who is not unaware of the tragedy of the human situation; he is neither an intolerant critic of Indian ways and modes nor their fanatic defender; he is on the whole content to snap Malgudi life's little ironies, knots of satiric circumstance, and tragi-comedies of mischance and misdirection. At his best he can present smiles and tears together, smiling through the tears in things and glimpsing the rainbow magnificence of life.[17]

NOTES

1. K.R.Srinivasa Iyengar, *Indian Writing in English* (New Delhi: Sterling, 1985), p. 800.
2. Haydn Moore Williams, *Studies in Modern Indian Fiction in English* vol. II (Calcutta: Writer's Workshop, 1973), p. 97.
3. Ved Mehta, "The Train Had Just Arrived at Malgudi Station," *John is Easy to Please* (London: Secker and Warburg, 1971), p. 148.
4. Cited by Perry D. Westbrook, "The Short Stories of R.K. Narayan," *The Journal of Commonwealth Literature,* No. 5, July 1968, p. 512.
5. Cited by Lakshmi Holmstrom, *The Novels of R.K. Narayan* (Calcutta: Writers Workshop, 1973), p. 124.
6. David Madden and Virgil Scott, *Studies in the Short Story* (New York: Holt, Rinehart and Winston, 1984), p.13.
7. M.K. Naik, *The Ironic Vision: A Study of the Fiction of R.K. Narayan* (New Delhi: Sterling, 1983), p.1.
8. Haydn Moore Williams, *Studies in Modern Indian Fiction in English,* Vol. I, p. 59.
9. Rajeev Taranath, "The Average as the Positive – A note on R.K. Narayan," *Critical Essays on Indian Writing in English,* ed. M.K. Naik et al (Madras: The Macmillan, 1977), p. 307.
10. K.R. Srinivasa Iyengar, p. 370.
11. George Woodcock, "Narayan, R.K," *Commonwealth Literature* (London: Macmillan, 1979), p. 176.
12. V. Panduranga Rao, "The Art of R.K. Narayan," *The Journal of Commonwealth Literature,* No. 5, July 1968, pp. 99-110.
13. William Walsh, "R.K. Narayan" Writers and their Work, No. 244. Cited by Hilda Pontes in *R.K. Narayan* (New Delhi: Concept, 1983), p. 20.
14. William Walsh, *R.K. Narayan: A Critical Appreciation* (New Delhi: Allied, 1983), pp. 166-67.
15. V.Y.Kantak, "The Achievement of R.K. Narayan," *The Indian Literature of the Past Fifty Years 1917-1970* (Mysore: University of Mysore, 1970), pp. 140-41.
16. George Woodcock, p. 176.
17. K.R. Srinivasa Iyengar, p. 384.x

This Place and These People

A novel deals with the physical features, people, life, customs, habits, manners, traditions, language etc., of a particular locale. But this does not mean that what is depicted is mere factual reporting or photographic reproduction. The novelist emphasizes the unique features of a particular locality and its uniqueness. He achieves this by constant selection and ordering of material which he uses creatively. Thus through proper selection and ordering of his material the novelist makes the place come alive. The distinctive spirit of his chosen region comes through his novels and is the same everywhere. And he also shows us that life in its essential is the same anywhere and everywhere. Whatever differences there are, they are used as a means of revealing the similarities – from the particular and the local to the general and universal. The selected place becomes a symbol of the world at large, a microcosm which reflects the great world beyond.

Narayan can be said to be a regional novelist in this higher creative sense. Narayan's stories have a fictional locale – Malgudi an imaginary world. Like Hardy's Wessex, Malgudi is the chosen locale which forms the background to the novels of Narayan. It is a typical Indian town and it has been presented in his works vividly and realistically. He portrays the individuals against this imaginary town Malgudi. All the novels and most of the short stories are set in Malgudi.

Various critics have attempted to identify the original of this mythical town. Iyengar speculates that it might be Lalgudi on the River Cauvery or Yadavagiri in Mysore.[1] Others are of the opinion that Narayan's Malgudi is Coimbatore which has many of the landmarks – a river on one side, forests on the other, the Mission School and College and, all the extensions mentioned in the novels. However, one is not likely to arrive at any definite answer as to its geographical location, even if one shifts all the references to the town in the novels, such specific allusions as that "Malgudi is almost a day's journey from Madras." The simple reason is that Narayan has not drawn any map or framework for his Malgudi as Faulkner for example, did for his Yoknapatawpha or Hardy had in mind for his Wessex novels. But others have done this for Narayan. M.K. Naik has appended a map of Malgudi in his book *The Ironic Vision*. But all efforts to identify Malgudi have remained futile, for it is a pure "country of the mind" – a dream town and not any town which exists on the map of India. It remains a dream country in which physical features of various places intimately known to Narayan fuse in single detail and are rearranged and magnified. As William Walsh observes: "The physcial geography of Malgudi is never dealt with as a set piece but allowed to reveal itself beneath and between the events. One comes to have a strong feeling for the place's identity. The detail suggests surely and economically, the special flavour of Malgudi, a blend of oriental and pre-1914 British, like an Edwardian mixture of sweet mangoes and malt vinegar."[2]

The recurrence of the same landmarks serves to put together the various novels into an organic whole. They may rightly be called *Malgudi novels* just as Hardy's novels are called *Wessex novels.* The setting or place thus constitutes the real essence of a novel being one of the most important features. The novelist creates an imaginary world which becomes the backdrop for his work and embodies his vision of life. Thus the novelist's vision gives it a distinctiveness – "a local habitation and a name." Sometimes it might even be a depiction of the real or actual world.

The "Peopled place" then is where one meets the populace of that society, "the named, identified, concrete, exact and exacting . . . gathering spot of all that has been felt."[3] Regional is a term applicable to a person who writes as an outsider. But Narayan writes about Malgudi as complete insider; (he may view the Malgudians ironically but) he shares their way of life and essential mores.[4]

The place becomes the backdrop for the customs, beliefs and the way of life of a people. It reflects certain norms and moral, social and ethical codes. It expresses the novelist's point of view. Thus place and people are inseparable. This kind of knowledge and information is essential to a writer. And that is why as a writer Narayan says elsewhere:

> I must be absolutely certain about the psychology of the character I am writing about, and I must be equally sure of the background. I know the Tamil and Kannada speaking people most. I know their background. I know how their minds work and almost as if it is happening to me, I know exactly what will happen to them in certain circumstances. And I know how they will react.[5]

Like Thomas Hardy and William Faulkner, Narayan is able to achieve this localization, a mastery of place, and Malgudi – Narayan's imaginary world becomes a living presence. And it is an everywhere in India. One can easily recognize it in his fiction and can expect at any minute to go out "into those loved and shabby streets and see with excitement and a certainty of pleasure a stranger approaching past the bank, the cinema, the haircutting saloon, a stranger who will greet us, we know, with some unexpected and revealing phrase that will open a door to yet another human existence."[6]

Unlike Hardy, Narayan's Malgudi is much more human as his interest lies in human beings. He explains: "I seek life wherever I go. I seek people, their interests, their aspirations and predicaments."[7]

One can say Narayan's chief interest is in man, man in society, living a "normal and well integrated life."[8] That is why Narayan's Malgudi is very real and alive. With an all-pervasive warmth, it enfolds and embraces us.

Narayan creates his fictional world of Malgudi as an essentially Indian society or town. The Indianness and Indian sensibility pervades the whole place. Narayan's Malgudi is also a microcosm of India. It grows and develops and expands and changes, and is full of humanity, drawing its sustenance from the human drama that is enacted in it.

Like Hardy, Arnold Bennett too writes about Five Towns, also famous as fictional places. For Bennett the Five Towns were provincial. His attitude towards them is always expository in the sense that he explains and exhibits them to an outside world.[9] But for Narayan Malgudi is anything but provincial. And in the words of Meenakshi Mukherjee: "Nothing could be more provincial and localized than the life of Malgudi town, yet R.K. Narayan successfully achieves a universal vision through it."[10]

Thus Malgudi, a small South Indian town, provides the setting for all his novels. Asked about the conception of the place, he is reported to have said: "I remember waking up with the name Malgudi on Vijayadasami, the day on which initiation of learning is celebrated."[11] It was in September 1930, he said, that the name of the town had been vouchsafed him by the divine patrons of knowledge:

> Malgudi was an earth-shaking discovery for me, because I had no mind for facts and things like that, which would be necessary in writing about Lalgudi or any real place. I first pictured not my town but just the railway station, which was a small platform with a banyan tree, a station master, and two trains a day, one coming and one going. On Vijayadasami I sat down and wrote the first sentence about my town: The train had just arrived at Malgudi Station.[12]

Thus the idea for this famous place just sprang up in Narayan's head. Malgudi is a dream town and as such is not to be found in its totality anywhere. It seemed Narayan's uncle once asked him: "What is this Malgudi? Where is it, why do you write about some vague place, not found anywhere, while there are millions of real places you can write about."[13] Narayan explains why he chose a fictional place like Malgudi: "An imaginary town like that has great possibilities. You can make anything out of it, whereas if you set your town in a real place you are bound by geography and its existing structure. But in a place like Malgudi, though the heart of the city may be fixed it can expand."[14] This then is the reason for his having chosen the imaginary world of Malgudi. But unlike Hardy, he does not endow any symbolic significance to his landscape, though it can be said to be the real hero of his novels. But he has an intimate sense of place and describes it in novel after novel and gives a real life picture of the place and the people. One can say that Narayan is not interested in the place for its own sake. His abiding interest lies in "peopled places."[15]

Narayan seems to agree with Hardy's observation that "It is better for a writer to know about a little bit of the world remarkably well than to know a great part of the world remarkably little."[16] That is why he limits himself to a small fictional region – Malgudi – and provides all the topographical details like any other regional novelist. He deals with the physical features, way of life of the people, customs, beliefs and manners. He depicts the social-cultural milieu and the changes that occur in the place over the years. He shows how the place and the people are interlinked and interdependent and how one cannot be seen without the other.

Narayan is able to capture the "spirit of the place"[17] and makes it immortal. In fact Malgudi is Narayan's "Casterbridge"[18] and is the centre of action for all his novels. There is a sense of communion between the character and the place.[19] According to Uma Parameswaran, "Malgudi is the only character that grows, changes, reacts to time and circumstance, has a spirit, a soul. Relatively other characters appear to be less dynamic."[20] It would be interesting to have an idea of its topographical or geographical details and major landmarks.

Malgudi has all modern amenities such as roads, railway, hotels, hospitals, clubs, educational institutions, printing presses, photo studios, banks and industries. There are various roads, streets and lanes such as Kabir Street, Sarayu Street, Vinayaka Mudali Street, Ellamman Street, Anderson Lane, Abu Lane, Kabir Lane, Kalighat Lane, Hospital Road, Forest Road, Mill Road and Race Course Road. The Trichy Trunk Road passes beyond Lawley Extension. There is the Market Road which intersects the Race Course Road. The Kalighat Lane cuts across the Market Road at some point westward. The Forest Road leads to the Mempi Forest. The end of the town is marked by Nallappa's mango grove, where

Swami spends most of his time playing with his friends and we come to know that Rajam is the son of the Superintendent of Police. One also comes across the District Magistrate attending the meeting organized by the Municipal Chairman to welcome Mahatma Gandhi. Thus one realizes the place is also visited by the Mahatma in the forties.

Malgudi has a court of its own. In *Swami and Friends* there is a mention of lawyers and the closing of courts as a result of the heatwave in May. In *The Dark Room*, Janamma, wife of the Public Prosecutor visits Savitri. The adjournment lawyer, whose business it is to see that a case is prolonged beyond anyone's imagination figures in *The Man-Eater of Malgudi.* The Sun Rise Pictures is inaugurated by the District Judge in *Mr. Sampath* which indicates that Malgudi is the District Headquarters.

The town has its own Municipality, a public library and a Reading Room – where Madhu, the talkative man meets Rann, a "Futurologist" in the *Talkative Man.* There is also a Taluk Office from where the gong strikes and it is heard in *Swami and Friends* and *The Vendor of Sweets.* There are two high schools and one elementary school. The Albert Mission School and the Board High School are the two schools where Swami studies in succession. Margayya of *The Financial Expert* sends his son Balu to the Elementary Town School. Then there is Albert Mission College, where Krishnan of *The English Teacher* works as a lecturer.

Numerous printing presses are also there in Malgudi. Two of them are run by Nataraj of *The Man-Eater of Malgudi* and Sampath of *Mr. Sampath.* There also comes into existence another new press in *Talkative Man.*

Malgudi has a Central Jail too. Sriram in *Waiting for the Mahatma* and Raju of *The Guide* spend their term in its Central Jail. A P.W.D. Office is also there, and one finds the Executive Engineer complaining about his outdoor activities in the heatwave, in *Swami and Friends*..

There exist several industries in Malgudi. It is in *Swami and Friends* one makes the acquaintance of mill managers Mr. Hentel and Pelty. Two weaving mills come into existence in *The Bachelor of Arts* and one hears of the Mill Road. There are various provision stores like National and Co-operative Stores.

Banks are also there in Malgudi. And Ramani of *The Dark Room* is the local manager of the branch of Englandia Insurance Company. Ramani employs a lady probationer to secure business from women which shows the town's slow awakening to modernity. Then there is also Englandia Banking Corporation in *Mr. Sampath* whose manager is Edward Shilling. There is a Fund Office which makes payment to Sriram's grandmother in the *Waiting for the Mahatma*. One also comes across the Central Co-operative Land Mortagage Bank in *The Financial Expert.*

Malgudi has its own railway station. It is from here that Margayya goes to Madras to find Balu in *The Financial Expert.* And Raju in *The Guide,* who is actually known as railway Raju, meets Rosie for the first time at the railway station. It is at this station that Swami bids farewell to Rajam. It is from here that Chandran's parents go to see off Chandran in *The Bachelor of Arts.* Once again it is here that Krishnan of *The English Teacher* waits for his wife and child. As Malgudi and Mempi Hills grow, the Malgudi station too expands and acquires more importance. That is why Raju of *The Guide* finds it more profitable to act as a tourist guide rather than be a small stall owner on the platform. It is at the railway station that the talkative man meets Commandant Sarasa, wife of Dr. Rann in *Talkative Man.*

The town has its own recreation centres like clubs and cinema houses. Swami's father and Principal Brown of *Swami and Friends* and *The Bachelor of Arts* are members of two respective clubs where they go to play tennis. Ramani of *The Dark Room* is a member of one of the clubs. He visits the Palace Talkies with his wife Savitri. And the cinema house also shows English films as is evident from *The Bachelor of Arts* where Chandran along with his friend Ramu goes to a night show. It is here that Krishnan of *The English Teacher* meets the college Principal Mr. Brown. There also springs up a night club – "Kismet" which, Tim of *The World of Nagaraj* frequents.

One also hears of the motor-cars and taxi drivers. Swami goes to the club in his father's friend's car. Ramani owns a chevrlot, Vasu owns a jeep. There are scooters and auto-rickshaws. Gaffur the taxi-driver appears in many novels. We come to know that the people get used to the taxis and auto-rickshaws more and more in *Talkative Man.* Rann always engages a taxi on his excursions with Girija, the Librarian's granddaughter.

There are hotels like the Taj, Anand Bhavan, The Boardless and Modern Lodge in Malgudi. A number of photo studios like Star Studio and others are also to be found in Malgudi.

Malgudi is a fast-growing town. And after Independence there are significant changes. The old roads, parks and colonies are renamed after national leaders such as Gandhi and Nehru. New extensions to colonies spring up. New printing presses like Empire Press, The Sun Rise, Golden Printing and Star Press come into existence, set up with modern machinery. Mempi Hills are connected with Malgudi station by means of buses and taxis. Mempi Bus Transport Corporation is also there. New picture halls, shops and new hotels spring up and Malgudi grows and develops.

Yet with all these changes it retains its landmarks which give the town, "the look of a place with a past." The river Sarayu flows to the north of the town and it is ten minutes walk from Ellamman Street. Its banks become crowded in the evenings as it is the resort of the town folk. A little down of the town lies Nallappa's Mango Grove – where the river is shallow and can be crossed easily. The Taluk Office is situated to the east of the town where the gong chimes at regular intervals. The railway station is situated on the South. To the south-west of the town are situated the new and best localities like the Lawley Extension and New Extension.

Thus the imaginary town of Malgudi becomes a real living presence which is felt in each novel. It lives and grows and develops from novel to novel, from the early thirties to the early nineties, to be more specific, from his earliest novel *Swami* and *Friends* to the latest and most recent novel *The World of Nagaraj*. With each novel Malgudi opens new vistas of life and one sees how a simple innocent traditional society undergoes changes owing to the impact of westernization and modernity. From a slumberous town it develops into a metropolitan city with modern streets, banking corporations, circus etc. It marks a movement in time which affects the geography of the place as well as the social, political and cultural contours of society, as Narayan's characters enact their own human drama.

But Malgudi also experiences some changes that leave a mark upon the traditional Indian society with its own customs and beliefs. Individuals caught up in the web of social change are seen with an ironic vision. As Graham Greene remarks, "the juxtaposition of the ageold convention and the modern character provides much of the comedy."[21]

Malgudi operates at two levels, the human and the topographical. On one level Malgudi appears to enclose the grand humanity like grandmothers and grandaunts with their oral tradition and religious rituals. While on the other there are hotels, cricket clubs, hire purchases and new extensions – in fact all modern features occur. The traditional Indian values as well as the modern have a stronghold on Swami, the protagonist of the *Swami and Friends*. Swami believes in Gods, demons and others as much as he believes in cricket.

Moreover, Malgudi also proves to be very much a part of the mainstream of the nation. The Malgudians demonstrate against the arrest of a political worker by the British Government influenced by Gandhi. Even school children like Swami boycott the classes and break the windows of their schools.

Malgudi in 1930s is at crossroads of Indian culture. It belongs to the pre-Independent era. In these years Malgudi is in transition. And this critical point of time is reflected in the place and people as well: "The old grandmother, the fire-eyed Vedanayagam, his class teacher; and the Head Master with his thin long cane,"[22] all these produce an image of intimate Indian childhood. Starting a cricket club suggests not only the growth of Swami but also the advancement of life in the town.

Various geographical, social, political, cultural, religious and economic changes occur in Malgudi. Among these the geographical changes are quite easily traceable. The banking corporations, the Sunrise Studio, The Star Press, The Regal Hair Cutting Saloon, The Englandia Insurance Company, Anand Bhavan, The Central Co-operative Land Mortgage Bank, New Extension and many other marks of modernity constitute Malgudi's phase of life. Streets and Lanes recur in each novel with all details – for instance Kabir Street, Ellamman Street, Vinayaka Mudali Street and Anderson Lane. The taxi-driver Gaffur, who remains a distinct feature of Malgudi town appears in many novels like *The Guide, The Vendor of Sweets, The Painter of Signs*, *Talkative Man* and *The World of Nagaraj.* The Mempi Forest supplies the Malgudians with all the timber they need for various purposes.

Thus one can say that Malgudi exists on two levels – the time-ripened traditional values that shaped the culture and emotional outlook and the modern way of living owing to the Western notions of progress. The younger generation are Mali, Balu and others who stand for new values. They are sharply contrasted against their conservative fathers, grandmothers and grandaunts. Malgudi seems to emerge as a combination of the old and the new, of the ancient and the modern. And it is against this backdrop that Narayan presents the life of an entire community which he knows thoroughly and first-hand, being a part and parcel of the middle-class society he portrays.

Modernity has not made much impact on the pre-Independent Malgudi. The progression from innocence to experience has not yet started and Malgudi is still relatively free of the disturbing and corrupting influence. That is why one does not come across the smugglers' den in the Market Road in *Swami and Friends,* which is to be found in *The Painter of Signs.* Yet with all modernization there are no drastic changes in Malgudi, and normalcy of life – that of an essentially Indian and traditional community prevails. Hence the strength of the grandmother's presence which Swami finds infinitely serene and soothing. As time passes Swami grows up and becomes interested in cricket and it is now his turn to play the role of an edifactor as he tries to teach his grandmother about cricket. The granny listens to the tales of cricket and tries her best to understand. The unreserved rapport and communication between these two generations reflects the serene atmosphere of Malgudi. But the same rapport is not to be seen later in the advanced years, which creates a generational gap.

In *The Bachelor of Arts,* Malgudi awakens to the modern civilization but still retains enough of its own traditional values like social taboos etc. Chandran's infatuation for Malathi can never be fruitful in tradition-bound Malgudi with its mores and customs. For, in a traditional Hindu society love-marriages are unheard of. In a traditional society marriage is always arranged by the family, one's own parents. Horoscopes must be consulted and they should match and above all castes must be considered. One sees the working influences of modernity in the life of Chandran and his friends – the night shows and cigarettes and the like. The religious life of Chandran's mother is contrasted with that of Chandran who is all for modernity. She represents the traditional Indian housewife. She sits in the back verandah, thinking of her husband and children and uttering the name of Sri Rama with the prayer beads in her hand. She refuses to budge when Chandran tries to argue with her and insists on respecting the old customs. Chandran fails to marry Malathi and in desperation becomes a *sanyasi* in rebellion against the society that prevented him from marrying Malathi. But towards the end he realizes that his renunciation is a rejection of traditional values and comes to understand that reality lies in making peace with society and all that it stands for. Hence his forsaking of his life as a fake *sanyasi*, returning home and making a conventional marriage. We get a last glimpse of him as a happily married young man which seems to be the affirmation of the traditional values.

The protagonists' deviation results in disorder and disillusionment and it is only at the end they once again come back to the folds of reality – the reality being Malgudi. Malgudi offers a refuge for outsiders too – outsiders such as Vasu and Rann, though their descent on Malgudi results only in disorder and destruction.

It is noticeable that Chandran's infatuation for Malathi and his becoming a *sanyasi* are but momentary illusions of life. That is why at the end Chandran returns to Malgudi, discarding his earlier illusions. Malgudi and the values it upholds remains to be the only reality in the midst of all illusions Chandran drops the idea of going to England and restricts himself to *The Daily Messenger* and Malgudi. The modern illusions and the Western values are cast aside and Malgudi stands for the real with its conservative way of living. Veeraswami's Resurrection Brigade is heard no more after the college. Malgudi is not a place for revolution and each of such notions would sound ridiculous.

In *Swami and Friends, The Bachelor of Arts* and *The English Teacher* there is a progress from innocence to experience, from innocent pleasures of childhood to youth and to maturity. Malgudi that is perceived in *Swami and Friends* remains virtually unchanged. Krishnan of *The English Teacher* is none other than Chandran settled down to a blissfully happy married life. The novel falls into two parts. The first confines itself to married bliss and the latter to the bereavement of the husband and his reconciliation with life and reality and his communion and achieving oneness with his wife Susila, on a transcendental plane. Here there are no upheavals, social or religious in breaking the established norms of society, but an intense personal tragedy of the protagonist.

In a traditional Indian society woman has a clearly-defined role in domestic situation. Krishnan's mother says: "unless I have cleaned the house, I can't go and bathe. After bathing, I've to worship and only after that I can go near the cows."[23] As Krishnan remembers: "House-keeping was a grand affair for her existence. The essence of her existence constituted in the thrills and pangs and the satisfaction that she derived in running a well-ordered household." (29)

Thus in Indian context women more than men represent custom and reason[24] and for every occasion whether it be a homecoming or a birth, certain rituals are to be performed. And it is woman who has the responsibility of performing these rituals. For instance, one has to decorate the threshold with mango leaves on every occasion, considered to be auspicious. And the floor and the doors are to be decorated with white floral designs. Krishnan's mother is no exception to all this. When Susila, Krishnan's wife falls ill, she attributes the illness to the influence of the evil-eye and she calls a Swamiji to remove the evil influence and "he uttered some *mantras* with closed eyes, took a pinch of sacred ash and rubbed it on her forehead, and tied to her arm a talisman strung in yellow thread." (93) The doctor also seems to have faith in the Swamiji. He says: "Ah no, don't belittle these people. There is a lot in him too, we didn't know. When we understand it fully I am sure we doctors will be able to give more complete cures." (93)

Such beliefs and customs prove to be extremely comic and yet all the more intense and serious for it. And it is towards the end that Krishnan achieves a transcendental "oneness" of spirit with his wife Susila. After attaining peace within himself Krishnan resigns his job at the Albert Mission College and takes up the vocation of teaching young innocent children.

The economic progress of Malgudi makes for the negligence of the traditional customs and beliefs and adoption of the modern Western civilization. Malgudi's awakening to modernity is first seen in *The Dark Room*. "Malgudi in 1935 suddenly came into line with the modern age by building a well-equipped theatre – Palace Talkies – which simply brushed aside the old corrugated-sheet-roofed Variety Hall, which from time immemorial had entertained the citizens of Malgudi with tattered silent films."[25]

Ramani gives the first hint of how progressive the town has become. The manager of the Englandia Insurance Company branch, he boasts of getting ten lakhs of business. There is to be witnessed a change in women's attitudes too. They come out of the bonds of the tradition and seek financial gains and economic independence. Shanta Bai is an example of this. She says: "I love unconventional things. Otherwise I should not be here, but nursing children and cooking for a husband." (79) Savitri resolves that her daughters should study upto the B.A. and not depend for their salvation on marriage. The traditional Indian family comprising husband and wife and children and other close relatives suffers with the Western influence. There arises a conflict between the old and new and the tradition and modernity. As a result the traditional housewife Savitri suffers. She tries to renounce her family but could not. She leaves her husband only to come back to him at the end. She realizes her place in the society. The traditional values of society close in on her and unlike Ibsen's Nora, Savitri couldn't bang the door on her family responsibilities. She resigns herself to her fate.

Malgudi experiences rapid social changes which one comes across in *Mr. Sampath* for the first time. One comes to know that

> the district board and the municipality had launched a feverish scheme of road development and tank building and three or four cotton mills had suddenly sprung into existence. Overnight as it were Malgudi passed from a semi-agricultural town to a semi-industrial town, with a sudden influx of population of all sorts.[26]

And the Municipal Chairman plans a grand "Malgudi extension scheme" visualizing "a garden city at the eastern end of the town with its own market, business premises, cinema, schools and perfect houses." (29) We also come to know that the District Board President is opening a bridge "Five miles from here, across the Sarayu. . . . It is going to transform our entire Malgudi district." (29) Thus Malgudi develops into a thriving commercial centre quite advanced. And the Market Road grows to be the lifeline of Malgudi. Slums spring up as a result of industrial progress. All this shows the economic and cultural advancement of Malgudi – which is epitomized in the making of the film "The Burning of Kama" with a Hollywood director. But despite all these changes it retains "its traditional middle class values intact."[27] Srinivas's wife cannot venture to go outside the house all alone. Ravi's mother thinks that her son is possessed and resorts to occult. The inhibitions regarding the dancing class and dancing girls still remain. In spite of all the inhibitions laid down, the society allows ample scope for an individual like Sampath, to play various roles like printer, film director and an actor, thus providing him an opportunity to realize his potential. But for all his vagaries Sampath too returns to the reality at the end and normalcy is restored; Ravi's madness subsides; Shanti realizes her place with her son and rejects the film career; Srinivas goes back to his even tenor of life in Malgudi.

Malgudi experiences rapid economic changes and there is a fast economic growth. Many banks and business concerns materialize and promote the financial growth of Malgudi. Margayya of *The Financial Expert* becomes a financial wizard due to the impact of Second World War. "Contractors, stockists and others have a lot of money and the town was reeking with it."[28] This leads to Margayya's spectacular rise from a street money-lender to a financial wizard until his downfall. But Malgudi does permit neither Margayya nor Pal to continue for long. Hence the sudden downfall of Margayya, who eventually comes back to the folds of the society and even the broken joint family bonds are restored and the original inevitable life of Malgudi immediately returns.[29]

The changing political scene affects Malgudi but only slightly. It is also caught in the web of the Quit India Movement. But the impact of the Gandhian movement is not felt by the entire community unlike Raja Rao's *Kanthapura.* Only the protagonist is involved in the political struggle. But the entire Malgudi community welcomes Gandhi when he visits Malgudi. It is here that the idealism of Gandhi and the hypocrisy of the Municipal Chairman are juxtaposed. In such a society Sriram's love which is non-traditional cannot flourish. The novel also shows the emergence of a modern woman. Bharati with her own ideals and identity is a person in her own right and is even able to influence Sriram and make him realize certain values in life. With the expansion of the railways Malgudi becomes a tourist centre, gains nation-wide popularity and attracts people from all over the country in *The Guide.* And that's how Raju becomes a popular tourist guide and meets Rosie.

Over the years Malgudi changes. The social, cultural and economic changes are reflected in the place as well as the people. In the lives of the individuals and their dreams and aspirations, in the way they try to achieve their ambitions, be it money or fame or salvation. The advent of modernity gives rise to a perennial conflict in Malgudi. The conflict between two sets of values – the old and the new, East and the West, tradition and modernity, illusion and reality and so on. A.N. Kaul observes the picture as one of "Domestic life versus passionate love, scholar versus Sadhu, the claims of art, an easy warm society versus a cold, but correct individualism, tradition versus modernity."[30] These are the conflicting emotions always warring with each other.

Raju of *The Guide* represents modernity and its influence. He is lured by his infatuation for Rosie, a married woman and in trying to fulfil that desire he defies the age-old ethics and conventions of Malgudi and violates the rigid social code. And it is once again the impact of modern civilization – the railway that causes Raju's doom, by bringing Rosie into his life. Ultimately he refuses to listen to his mother and pays a deaf ear to Gaffur's advice.

In the course of events Raju mistakenly comes to be taken for a saint which is not really surprising in a country like India which has its own great tradition of *yogis* and *rishis*. And it is the centuries-old tradition that helps transform a sinner into saint. As C.D. Narasimhaiah points out, "the traditional past and the changing present which with all the degradation that has come upon it still holds the possibilites for survival – some deep springs of vital energy sustaining her."[31] Here Raju's attainment of salvation is in accordance with the great Hindu tradition of *varnasramadharama* particularly that of *sanyasasrama.* Raju's redemption suggests Narayan's affirmation of the "permanent values."[32] Thus Malgudi changes and yet remains the same. Its "spirit remains the same" and it is this that sustains and restores the protagonists to their old or normal life.

In *The Man-Eater of Malgudi* Narayan depicts the conflict between good and evil and tradition and modernity. The action, as the title implies centres round Malgudi and its environs. Vasu represents all that is modern and alien and Nataraj stands for the traditional Malgudi community. There is the temple elephant Kumar – looked on as Gajendra, and there is the monosyllabic poet trying to compose his epic "Radhakalyan." And the novel once again celebrates the triumph of traditional values – good overcomes evil, thus proving that a society does not tolerate evil for too long. Nataraj's faith in God makes him think "Elephant? Who could kill an elephant" which proves to be true at the end.

Vasu, the taxidermist descends upon Malgudi and disturbs the serenity and peacefulness of the place and even tenor of life. He is seen as an extreme egoist. The traditional Malgudi frowns upon Vasu's offer of supplying stuffed eagles, regarded as sacred *garudas* to be kept in the puja to be worshipped as Vasu's action is a violation of all that is sacred. That is why Nataraj thinks that his very presence defiles his precincts. He becomes a satirical embodiment of modern Western violence and Sastri decides that "he shows all the definitions of a *rakshasa*."[33] And a *rakshasa* should perish according to the ancient Hindu mythology.

Vasu thus is equated to Bhasmasura of the ancient myth who ultimately destroys himself. He violates every sacred code of Malgudi society and the conservative Hindu society finds it unable to withstand his existence. Otherwise Malgudi society proves to be tolerant providing a place for all eccentrics except murderous violence.[34] Malgudi means reality and in the midst of this solid reality, Vasu becomes "not important but unreal"[35] and society has no place for the unreal.

The impact of modernization on a conventional society becomes clear in *The Vendor of Sweets*. The conflict between tradition and modernity and East and West is inherent here. Mali's visit to America is a symbolic representation of the East-West encounter which is the first sign of the corruption of the younger generation. After returning from America, Mali resorts to beef-eating which in itself is a violation of the social code of Malgudi. Jagan is bewildered when he is faced with all these "strange notions." He accepts Grace, the Korean-American girl as his daughter-in-law. But his real troubles start from the moment he tries to identify with Mali's fantasies. Mali's scheme to finance story-writing machines jolts Jagan from his passive existence. To him it becomes "a comic parody of the spontaneous creative process of the human mind, a kind of comic jolt, to Malgudi's natural flow of life, where the granny still tells stories to children at their bedside."[36] He realizes that a time has come for him to change his life style and to get things into right perspective. At sixty, one is reborn and enters a new *janma*.[37] He renounces the world and enters the stage of *vanaprastha,* laid down by the scriptures and thus proves once more of prevalence of the age-old values.

With the passage of time Malgudi passes from a semi-agricultural town to a semi-industrial town with a sudden influx of population of sorts and "it was the base for a hydro-electric project somewhere on the Mempi Hills and jeeps and lorries passed through the Market Road all day."[38] The town-hall verandah and the pavements around the markets, the no-man's land of Malgudi swarmed with children of all sizes, from toddlers to four footers, dust covered, ragged—a visible development over the years.

Raman in *The Painter of Signs* compares the changing Malgudi scene with that of New York. There is a marked change in the attitudes of the people too. What is more, there is a shift in values. Raman is a fair representative of this change. He is an advocate of the age of reason. His attitude is that of being scientific. "Be scientific please, scientific." (10) Despite this one can say that he stands at cultural crossroads. There rages a conflict within him between old and new values of life. He feels confused and is in a dilemma unable to decide "whether the legendary gods are real or imaginary allegories." (133) Like Raman, Daisy too is a symbol of modernization. She is the first of her kind and is a kindred spirit like Rosie of *The Guide*, and is a liberated woman. She comes out of the family fold to uphold the cause of family planning with an enormous zeal. In Raman's words she has "a sort of unmitigated antagonism to conception." (70) The very thought of having children is repulsive to her. She is a complete contrast to the women of Malgudi like Raman's aunt. The aunt is quite traditional and is unable to come to terms with Raman's passion for Daisy. She leaves for Benares, to spend the rest of her life there looking forward to a peaceful end at the feet of the Lord Viswanatha. Thus she renounces her family ties. Towards the end Daisy too leaves Raman finding it impossible to reconcile herself to the idea of playing the role of a traditional housewife. And Raman finds himself "uncomfortably poised between the two worlds."[39] He is thus divorced from the two – his traditional self represented by his aunt and his modern self represented by Daisy. The deserted Raman symbolizes "the bewilderness of the new generation of Malgudi."[40] O.P. Mathur observes that "Modernization and modernised characters were targets of irony in many of Narayan's major novels like *The Guide, The Man-Eater of Malgudi, Mr. Sampath* and *The Vendor of Sweets*. But in *The Painter of Signs,* they are viewed with marked approval."[41] But nowhere do we find this marked approval. What one finds is Malgudi – a Malgudi that is quivering between tradition and modernity, East and West inextricably mixed up[42] is that conflict which creates the "psychological and social tensions involved in the uneasy conjunction of old ways and new evolving values."[43]

Daisy symbolizes the latter and yet is unsure of her new values which is the reason why she unconsciously upholds the traditional values just like Raman. "Bring them [the gods] back to their pedestal, before you begin to feel that they resent you and are punishing you with madness. The gods, if they are there, will look into my mind and judge whether I am choosing the right path or not. If I am wrong let them strike me dead. I am prepared for it." (140) Thus we can see that Malgudi has not lost old values, and "even in those with a tendency towards modernity one is always aware under the educated speech of the profound murmur of older voices."[44] The traditional society does not permit a marriage between Raman and Daisy which in fact seems to be unusual in the sense that Daisy lays down certain conditions for her marriage with Raman – one, that they should have no children, and two, if by mischance one was born she would give the child away and keep herself free to pursue her social work and she further adds "on any day you question why or how, I'll leave you." One finds a parallel of the Ganga-Shantanu myth of the *Mahabharata* here where Ganga marries King Shantanu on the condition that he should never question her actions, whatever she may do and the moment he does she would leave him.

Although Malgudi does not encourage any of these modern perversities, it still tolerates them and ultimately accepts them into its fold if and when they choose to return as is evidenced in case of Raman.

In *Talkative Man* one sees Malgudi well into the eighties with all modern amenities such as a night club, Nalli's Hardware, a real estate office – offering its services to Malgudi citizens, the modern sanitaryware with all its porecelain stuff, innumerable studios, a hire-purchase, Swami's cottage industries, and so on. The town now populates hundred and odd thousand people. The geographical changes reflect also the attitudinal change in the people and the pace of their life. In *The World of Nagaraj* we come to know that the citizens of Malgudi now frequent the night clubs and use auto-rickshaws quite frequently instead of *jutkas*. That is why Madhu of the *Talkative Man* engages an autorickshaw from Nalli's Hardware when he ventures to take Rann on house-hunting expedition. Rann feels grateful at the sight of an auto. And Tim of *The World of Nagaraj* always uses an auto.

The acceptance of some of the modern values is seen in the changing attitudes of people toward women, regarding their education and employment and economic independence. The visions of the old librarian regarding his grand daughter Girija brings out clearly the attitudinal changes. He wants his grand-daughter to get a Degree and become an officer.

But despite all the developments Malgudi still retains its essentially Indian scene and its agricultural tradition. It never loses its old fervour entirely. The old values are still intact and very much valued. And the moral code of the society does not change all that much. Hence Madhu's abhorrence at Girija's affair with Rann. That is the reason why TM's neighbours are shocked at Commandant Sarasa's appearance in a Salwar Kameez and bobbed hair, and people stare at her. Likewise Rann also creates a stir in Malgudi with his dress and deportment. People are apt to gaze at him whenever he ventures out of TM's house, where he is a guest, in his three-piece suit, as if questioning TM about this oddity. It is only later, after all these rather unnerving experiences of being stared at that Rann adapts himself to the normal "Malgudi executive costume" of cotton pants and shirt sleeves.

In the traditional society of Malgudi one still hesitates to and cannot throw away even a calendar portrait of Gods and Goddesses. "How can anyone discard a God."[45] Even though TM does not hesitate to borrow a smuggled camera to take a photograph of Rann, he has qualms about disposing of the puja room in his ancestral home used by his elders. He retains the family meditation room even if only to retire to the room once in a while in order to think where no one dared to intrude. It is into this world of values that Rann descends and causes disruption and disorder before pursued by his wife Sarasa, the Commandant, who, to her chagrin finds husband-hunting to be a "fatiguing business." This story of a wife's attempt to retain her erratic elusive husband[46] is modelled on the Savitri-Satyavan myth of the *Mahabharata*. Varma, the proprietor of the Boardless, very much impressed with the wife's determined pursuit and capture of her husband, brings out the parallel.

A chronological study of Narayan's novels make us realize the changes that have occurred in Malgudi, over "the sleepy old community"[47] through the years and in spite of these numerous changes that have come in quick succession Malgudi has an amazing power of retaining its traditional values. The innocence still does not give way to experience. That is the reason for the innocent villagers being able to transform a sinner into a saint, that is the reason for the Master of *A Tiger for Malgudi*, renouncing the world and living in the Mempi Hills. One can say that Malgudi still holds dear the traditional values of life,[48] and remains a conservative town unused to modern life. Thus one can say Narayan celebrates the survival of permanent values, and Malgudi provides the necessary fixity of background against which is set a comedy of deviation and disturbance of the normal.

Narayan sees Malgudi as a fundamentally conservative Hindu society, changing under the impact of the West, industrialism and modern ideas. India is seen with humour and some satire, as a mixture of traditional holiness, with the comfort-loving sterility of the bourgeoisie. Modern India is seen as an inevitable but on the whole, inescapable phenomenon compounded by extreme political activism, permissive sexual morals, the breakdown of the traditional extended family system, "American" popular culture and rapid half-lunatic violence.[49] Thus Malgudi is open to the outside influences like any other society and the impact of these changes reflect in the lives of the people too. Hence, Malgudi of the *Swami and Friends* differs very much from that of *The Painter of Signs, A Tiger for Malgudi, Talkative Man* and *The World of Nagaraj*. The transformation is there. But underneath it all it remains essentially the same and we may say that "Malgudi is the real hero of the novels and many short stories and that underneath the seeming change and the human drama there is something – the 'soul' of the place – that defies, or embraces, all change and is triumphantly and unalterably itself."[50]

Thus Narayan, one can say, transforms the actual world in which he lives into the imaginary world of Malgudi. He writes of people and places about whom he knows and amongst whom he lives,[51] because he has an eye for faithful reporting of actual people, scenes and occurrences. He is reported to have said in an interview: "I get all influences from life, from the surroundings, a little bus-stop or a street-stop."[52] Likewise Malgudi is a world which is recognizable to a certain extent. Narayan seems to have "a model in his mind's eye."[53] Talking about the filming of *The Guide*, Narayan tells us in his article entitled "Misguided Guide," published in an Asian edition of *Life* magazine, that he told the producers:

> My story takes place in South India, in Malgudi, an imaginary town known to thousands of my readers all over the world. . . . It is South India in costume, tone and contents. Although the whole country is one, in the matter of characteristics there are diversities, and one has to be faithful in delineating them. You have to stick to my geography and sociology. Although it is a world of fiction there are certain inner veracities.[54]

The setting of a novel has an intimate relationship with its theme and treatment. If one divests the novel of its geographical context and sociological specificity, it loses its authentic flavour, and credibility. That is why Narayan tried to advice the film makers of *The Guide*. He says: "I had spent a whole day taking them around Mysore to show the river-side, forest, village, and crowds, granite steps and the crumbling walls of an ancient shrine which combined to make up the Malgudi of my story (it would not be far from fact to observe)."[55]

The world of Malgudi or the Malgudi world thus becomes a replica of the actual world.[56] And Narayan is "primarily concerned with telling stories and presenting Indian characters against the cyclorama of Malgudi, which is for him, only secondly a symbol of India."[57]

Narayan presents a variety of people through all walks of life because he acquired a valuable experience and familiarity with a variety of human types. He also portrays the social-cultural changes that have been taking place in Malgudi. And it is true that what is true of Malgudi is true of all India. Thus Narayan creates an awareness of "a significant part of the national condition"[58] and becomes "both a spokesman of the community in which he lives and of himself"[59] with an ease because he is very much "a product of the society in which he lives.[60] And Narayan's outlook, as O.P. Mathur observes, "broadens out from the family to the community and the nation."[61] And his novels can be said to be a faithful reflection of an India as real as Anand's or Raja Rao's.[62] True to his word he sticks to his "little bit of ivory" and writes only about that place and people – a section of society he knows very well and of which he himself is a part. That is why William Walsh remarks, Narayan's novels "send out long sensitive feelers to the villages where the inhabitants are innocent and unsophisticated in most matters excepting their factions and fights."[63]

India is a religious land and the traditional beliefs and customs still hold a sway over the people. Their enormous faith even changes a sinner into saint. Raju's transformation certainly has the approval of the Gods.[64] The saints and *sadhus* are still believed to be there and the traditional way of life reaffirms itself however much disruptive the outside influences prove to be. Nataraj still holds dear the image of Lord Nataraja, given him by his grandmother, who finds it in a packet of saffron. He and his friends celebrate "Radhakalyan" the temple festival with great pomp and ceremony and Nataraj manages to save the temple elephant Kumar, the traditional Indian symbol for "Gajendran" from Vasu, the modern *rakshasa*, by the timely intervention and help of the Divine Lord Vishnu. Jagan makes a pilgrimage to Badri Hill temple to beget a child. Susila's last outing with Krishnan ends with a visit to the temple, where she looks "divine" indicating what is to come, though at the time Krishnan is hardly aware of the significance. Ravi's mother hopes to cure him by God's Grace and takes him to the temple. Margayya realizes the Grace of Lakshmi, the Goddess of Wealth, only after his visit to the temple. Jagan renounces the world "to watch a Goddess come out of stone." The tiger and the Hermit retire to Mempi Hills to have discourses on *Bhagavad Gita*, the "Song of the Divine." Rivers too are sacred for Indians. Sarayu is actually formed by Lord Srirama's arrow and likewise each river has its own history of its holiness. It is by the river that Gandhi stays. Raju bathes daily in the river at Mangal during his "enforced sainthood." Then there is the Iswara Temple in the North Extension which serves the people of Malgudi as a place of worship, for it is there the people of Malgudi offer *Puja* and worship the God. That is why one feels that "Whatever happens in India, the reader feels happens in Malgudi, and whatever happens in Malgudi he is perusaded might well happen in his own life. Malgudi is an image of India and a metaphor of everywhere else."[65] Perhaps the greatest tribute paid to Narayan may be said to be the American citation of 1982, presented to Narayan on his being made an honorary member of the American Academy of Arts and Letters. The U.S. Ambassador Harry G. Barnes said: "In honouring India's best-known and best-loved novelist in the English Language, Americans were paying homage to a great creative artist who helped view life both with laughter and through tears and in the process had enabled us to recognise that we are all part of the entire continent of humanity."[66] To conclude in the words of Warren French: "No other twentieth century novelist besides William Faulkner has so well succeeded in creating through a succession of novels an imaginary community that microscopically reflects the physical, intellectual and spiritual qualities of a whole culture as has Narayan in his tales of the South Indian Community of Malgudi."[67]

NOTES

1. K.R. Srinivasa Iyengar, *Indian Writing in English* (New Delhi: Sterling, 1985), p. 361.
2. William Walsh, "Sweet Mangoes and Malt Vinegar: The Novels of R.K. Narayan," *Indo-English Literature*, ed. K.K.Sharma (Ghaziabad: Vimal, 1977), p. 123.
3. Eudora Welty, "Place in Fiction," *Critical Approaches to Fiction*, ed. Shiv K. Kumar and Keith McKean (New York: McGraw-Hill, 1968), p. 254.
4. M.K. Naik, "The Spirit of the Place," *Literary Endeavour,* Vol. III, Nos. 3 and 4, Jan.-June 1982, p. 14.
5. R.K. Narayan, in an Interview given to S. Krishna, quoted by Hilda Pontes in *R.K. Narayan*, ed. Nissim Ezekiel (New Delhi: Concept, 1983), p. 21.
6. Graham Greene, "Introdution," *The Financial Expert* (Mysore: Indian Thought Publications, 1984), p. vi.
7. Suresh Kohli, "Views of an Indian Novelist: An Interview with R.K. Narayan," *Indian & Foreign Review*, May 1975, pp. 13-20.
8. Nirmal Mukherji, "Some Aspects of the Literary Development of R.K. Narayan," *Banasthali Patrika*, Vol. 13, 1969, p. 87.
9. Walter Allen, *The English Novel* (London, 1954), p. 305.
10. Meenakshi Mukherjee, *The Twice Born Fiction* (New Delhi: Arnold Heinemann, 1971), p. 25.
11. Ved Mehta, "The Train Had Just Arrived at the Malgudi Station," *John is Easy to Please* (London: Secker and Warburg, 1971), p. 55.
12. *Ibid*.
13. R.K. Narayan, *My Days* (Mysore: Indian Thought Publications, 1975), p. 94.
14. Susan E. Croft, "Interview with R.K. Narayan," *R.K. Narayan: A Critical Spectrum* (Meerut: Shalabh, 1983), p. 30.
15. Nirmal Mukherji, p. 78.
16. *Thomas Hardy's Note Books*, ed. Evelyn Hardy (London, 1955), p. 95.
17. M.K. Naik, p. 7.
18. K.R. Srinivasa Iyengar, p. 360.
19. P.P. Mehta calls Narayan "the father of the regional novel in India. All the novels of Narayan are set in the surroundings of Malgudi. The regional novel finds its full expression in R.K. Narayan," *Indo-Anglian Fiction: An Assessment* (Bareilly: Prakash, 1983), p. 199.

A.V. Krishna Rao also calls Narayan "a regional novelist," *The Indo-Anglian Novel and the Changing Tradition* (Mysore: Rao and Raghavan, 1972), p. 136. And William Walsh observes: "Narayan's Malgudi novels are regional, but not parochial and Malgudi is "a world which has background, a context, an immediate presence and a nervous individual centre [and], impresses the reader with the quality of its completeness," *R.K. Narayan: A Critical Appreciation* (New Delhi: Allied, 1983), p. 7.

20. Uma Parameswaran, *A Study of Representative Indo-English Novelists* (New Delhi: Vikas, 1976), p. 50.
21. Graham Greene, "Introduction," *The Financial Expert*, p. vii.
22. R.K. Narayan, *Swami and Friends* (Mysore: Indian Thought Publications, 1983), p. 3.
23. R.K. Narayan, *The English Teacher* (Mysore: Indian Thought Publications, 1984), p. 29.
24. William Walsh, "Nataraja and the Packet of Saffron: The Indian Novel in English," *Readings in Commonwealth Literature* (Oxford: Clarendon, 1973), p. 54.
25. R.K. Narayan, *The Dark Room* (Mysore: Indian Thought Publications, 1986), pp. 26-27.
26. R.K. Narayan, *Mr. Sampath* (Mysore: Indian Thought Publications, 1985), p. 26.
27. M.K. Naik, p. 11.
28. R.K. Narayan, *The Financial Expert* p. 158.
29. Jayant K. Biswal, *A Critical Study of the Novels of R.K. Narayan* (New Delhi: Nirmal, 1987), p. 19.
30. A.N. Kaul, "R.K. Narayan and The East-West Theme," *Considerations*, ed. Meenakshi Mukherjee (New Delhi: Allied, 1977), p. 51.
31. C.D. Narasimhaiah, *The Swan and The Eagle* (Simla: Indian Institute of Advanced Study, 1969), p. 148.
32. H.M. Williams, *Indo-Anglian Literature*, p. 7.
33. R.K. Narayan, *The Man-Eater of Malgudi* (Delhi: Hind Pocket Books, 1979), p. 231.
34. H.M. Williams, p. 62.
35. A.N. Kaul, p. 55.
36. Jayant K. Biswal, p. 26.
37. R.K. Narayan, *The Vendor of Sweets* (Mysore: Indian Thought Publications, 1981), p. 182.
38. R.K. Narayan, *The Painter of Signs* (England: Penguin, 1985), pp. 13-14.
39. O.P. Mathur, "West Wind Blows through Malgudi," *Perspectives on R.K. Narayan* (Ghaziabad: Vimal, 1981), p. 36.

40. Jayant K. Biswal, p. 28.
41. O.P. Mathur, p. 35.
42. *Ibid.*
43. S.C. Harrex, *The Fire and The Offering* (Calcutta: Writers Workshop, 1977), pp. 36-37.
44. William Walsh, "R.K. Narayan," *A Manifold Voice* (London: Chatto and Windus, 1970), p. 11.
45. R.K. Narayan, Postscript of *Talkative Man* (Mysore: Indian Thought Publications, 1986), p. 1.
46. *Ibid.*
47. H.M. Williams, p. 56.
48. Jayant K. Biswal, p. 30.
49. H.M. Williams, p. 50.
50. K.R. Srinivasa Iyengar, p. 36.
51. Cited by Hilda Pontes, *R.K. Narayan*, ed. Nissim Ezekiel (New Delhi: Concept, 1983), p. 19.
52. Suresh Kohli, Views of an Indian Novelist: An interview with R.K. Narayan, pp. 13-20.
53. R.M. Varma, p. 101.
54. Abha Agarwal, Quoted in "*The Guide*, From Novel to Film," *R.K. Narayan: A Critical Spectrum*, ed. Bhagwat S. Goyal (Meerut: Shalabh, 1983), pp. 125-26.
55. R.K. Narayan, *My Days*, p. 174.
56. C.D. Narasimhaiah observes, "Malgudi (is) the microcosm of traditional Indian society," and "Narayan's novels are essentially stories on Indian life, reflected in Malgudi life." *The Swan and the Eagle*, p. 136. Iyengar remarks, "the inhabitants of Malgudi although they may have their recognizable local trappings – are essentially human, and hence, have their kinship with all humanity. In this sense 'Malgudi' is everywhere," p. 360.
57. H.M. Williams, p. 62.
58. R.M. Varma, p. 103.
59. Suresh Kohli, p. 18.
60. *Ibid.*
61. O.P. Mathur, p. 35.
62. H.M. Williams, p. 49.
63. William Walsh, "Sweet Mangoes and Malt Vinegar," p. 123.
64. *Ibid.*, p. 139.
65. William Walsh, "R.K. Narayan," *A Manifold Voice*, p. 22.
66. *The Times of India*, January 21, 1982, p. 5.
67. Cited by Hilda Pontes in *R.K. Narayan*, ed. Nissim Ezekiel, p. 31.

The Intricately Woven Fabric:

The Family in *Swami and Friends, The Bachelor of Arts, The Dark Room, The English Teacher, The Financial Expert* and *The Vendor of Sweets*

The present chapter aims at examining the family theme in some of the novels of Narayan, early and late. In an interview given to Ved Mehta, Narayan is reported to have said: "To be a good writer anywhere you must have roots—both in religion and family. I have these."[1] Obviously he was generalizing on the basis of his own personal experience as a practising novelist in India. Other novelists here or elsewhere may not endorse his view. But Narayan's statement has the virtue of indicating the particular importance the family and all that it stands for has for him as an individual and as a writer of fiction. One would have wished that he had elaborated on his cryptic statement. In the absence of any explanation from him we have to draw inferences regarding the special importance of the family for him, from his practice as a novelist and from some of the other statements he has made now and then regarding his art.

The family in India even today, in spite of a number of far-reaching changes taking place in it, happens to be a network of a variety of relationships among its members. It includes husband and wife, parents and children, grand-parents and grand-children, a number of close as well as distant relations such as uncles and aunts, grand-uncles and grand-aunts, and a variety of cousins. Thus the family forms in itself a little world, and particularly so if it were to be a "joint family." The different kinds of relationships are kept up even though the members of a given family do not live under the same roof. What is more, one's family is an important means of establishing one's identity. Narayan's novels present in different ways virtually all these relationships. William Walsh has aptly remarked: "Family indeed is the immediate context in which the novelist's sensibility operates, and his novels are remarkable for the subtlety with which the family relationships are treated."[2] Individuals who are deeply involved in their families provide the life-blood for Narayan's novels. He makes use of the family sphere, family situations, and the disintegrating joint family to study human nature and to depict complex inter-personal relationships. It may be said in a way that his novels seem to be concerned with an examination of intimate human relationships which are more familial than social.

The family is a recurrent element in the novels of Narayan without exception irrespective of their dominant themes. It is first of all used as a backdrop or background against which the lives of his characters are presented. Aspects of family life and familial relations form the main subject of such novels as *The Dark Room, The English Teacher,* and *The Vendor of Sweets. Swami and Friends*, Narayan's very first novel illustrates the point. It is mainly about the adventures of a school boy, Swami, in and out of school, and about his growth towards adolescence. Though his world comprises his friends, teachers and cricket he is aware that his identity and security are in his home, where he lives under the constant watch of his disciplinarian father, the affection of his mother, and the protective warmth of his pampering grandmother. After his escapades at the end of the novel he returns to the security of the family fold and feels whole.

There is considerable range and variety in Narayan's handling of the family theme in his novels and short stories too. He shows himself to be aware of the different aspects of the theme, covering the personal, emotional, social, economic, cultural and other ties operating in the family. To mention some of them as they are seen in the novels: the tender feelings and affectionate bonds between parents and children, filial duties and obligations, relations among brothers, cousins, grand-aunts and grand-nephews, the stresses and strains of parent-child relationship, the family at the cross-roads bristling with numerous problems, generation gap, the disintegrating joint-family, the security and stability of the family, the bliss of happy married life as well as its irresistible discord, the problems of development of the self within the family fold, the family as a hindrance to the evolution of the self, and the urge to free oneself from familial bonds, the four stages or *asramas* of the traditional Hindu way of life, etc. The family is always seen as an integral part of the larger world of Malgudi and of society in general. Though occasionally one would catch a note of nostalgia, Narayan nowhere yields to the natural temptation of idealizing the family and its virtues. While portraying the family as a miniature of society, he reveals how the social, economic, psychological, religious and other functions and problems of the family are not dissimilar to those of the society.

As noted already, the themes of Narayan's novels are inter-related and appear in different combinations. For example, renunciation, which is a recurrent theme of his novels, cannot be thought of as being independent of the other themes including the family. In *The Vendor of Sweets*, the protagonist Jagan decides at the end of the novel to detach himself from his familial bonds and withdraw himself into a mango grove, because he is not able to solve the knotty problems created for him by his son Mali. In this novel we find in combination such themes as father-son relationship, inter-generational tensions, inter-ethnic marriages, and bipolar contrast of traditional and non-traditional values.

There are certain close affinities between the first two novels of Narayan, *Swami and Friends* and *The Bachelor of Arts,* which are readily recognizable. Like several other novels of his, they too are protagonistic. They have in common growing up for their main theme. Swami the protagonist of *Swami and Friends* grows from boyhood towards early adolescence and Chandran of *The Bachelor of Arts,* who sometimes looks like a grown-up version of the boy Swami, grows from early youth to adulthood. In either case the protagonist goes through an emotional crisis involving his relations with some people, which makes the growth possible in him. The family provides the immediate context and background for the two heroes. The novelist presents them amidst a network of close familial relationships. They have a strong sense of kinship which binds them to their families. Thus they are not only rooted firmly in their respective families, but are seen growing up and becoming stable within their fold. Further, when they are jolted out of their sheltered existence by certain unexpected crises in their lives, it is their good fortune that they are able to return to the security of the care and affection of their parents who understand them with exemplary sympathy. Thus the family theme in both *Swami and Friends* and *The Bachelor of Arts* has an important though a secondary place.

Swami and Friends is an unpretentious novel which tells the story of the school and home-life of Swaminathan. As the title itself indicates, it is mainly about the boy Swami and his friends. In a series of episodes somewhat loosely linked it narrates engagingly and through the comic perspective – his activities, adventures and misadventures in the company of his friends in and out of school, and on the cricket field. The real interest of the novel, however, is in the intense friendships he forms and tends to lose, in the affections, little harmless rivalries, jealousies and loyalties among the school boys, and in Swami having to come to terms with inevitable changes that come about in this world of growing boys as time passes by. In portraying Swami and his several friends like Mani, Rajam, Sankar, Samuel and Somu, Narayan displays a remarkable insight into the working of a child's mind.

"Swami's world is a world of parents, grandmother, teachers, policemen, friends and enemies, his gang."[3] Although the greater part of his energies are absorbed by his activities outside home among his friends, his home happens to be his secure haven. The novel gives us some meaningful glimpses into his home, his familial background, and his relation to the different members of his family. Thus we get to know about his father and mother, his grandmother, and his little brother, and his attitude to everyone of them. We gather from the novel that they are a compact middle-class family, well-to-do enough to afford a cook at home. Swami's father, W.T. Srinivasan, is a lawyer by profession. Until the arrival of the little brother, which is described impressively in Chapter I of the novel, Swami is the only child in the family loved by his parents, pampered and spoiled by his grandmother. In fact he has hardly any clash or conflict with them, but for an occasional grievance he imagines with them. The true emotional centre of his life lies with his friends and all his emotional upsets are due to them.

As Lakshmi Holmstrom has pointed out, the members of Swami's family "have fixed roles to play."[4] Swami's father is the first of the members that we get to know of in the novel, though indirectly. The occasion is a letter of protest he writes to the Head Master of the school to which Swami goes. The provocation for it comes from certain "Unchristian"[5] remarks made by the Scripture Master. Swami, whose "blood boiled" (6) at those remarks, naturally complains to his father to whom he goes for protection and reassurance. And hence the letter. It shows him as a somewhat pompous but well-meaning and dignified man who feels hurt by the fanatical remarks of the teacher as well as concerned by the teacher's rough handling of his son Swami. We have our first glimpse of him in Chapter III of the novel, as he gets ready to go to the Court. He is very much the master of the house, somewhat authoritarian though by no means autocratic. He is both loved and feared by his son. This is more or less the role that convention assigns to a father in his household.

Swami is deeply attached to his parents and his grandmother, in spite of being annoyed with them now and then. He is genuinely fond of his baby brother, although he is just a little jealous of him, and feels "a sneaking satisfaction" when the baby is "overlooked" and everyone fusses over him during his convalescence. (169) A small incident described in Chapter X of the novel brings out well Swami's loving attachment to his people. In a bid to get enough money to acquire a hoop from the coachman, Swami places before the household gods a couple of pebbles in a cardboard box covering them well with sand and leaves, and hopes in his innocence that as a result of his prayer and promises to the gods, the pebbles would be miraculously transformed into coins. When he finds that the gods have not cared to answer his prayer, he vents his rage on the box by kicking and stamping upon it. But very soon he regrets his action: "He paused and doubted if the Gods would approve of even this. He was afraid that it might offend them. He might get on without money, but it was dangerous to incur the wrath of the Gods; they might make him fail in his examinations, or kill his *father, mother, granny, or the baby*."[6] Swami's mother, by the side of his father, is a somewhat shadowy figure, though affectionate and loving. The father being the most important person at home, Swami can take her for granted.

The grandmother-grandson relationship is one of the most impressive aspects of the family theme in this novel. In Narayans's much later novel *Waiting for the Mahatma,* this aspect is taken up again and developed at some length. The grandmother's attachment to her grandchildren is proverbial in Indian households. Swami's grandmother is particularly attached to him. She makes much of him and even seems to spoil him. After the night meal everyday, he rests his head on her lap, nestles close to her, and feels very snug and safe. It is then that he becomes talkative and tells her ecstatically about his friends and all the happenings of the day at school. And he goes to sleep as he listens to her telling him a story from the epics and *Puranas*. In her he has always a champion of his cause. On a certain occasion when Swami pretends to be ill because he does not want to go to school, she is the first to support him. When he disappears from home she is beside berself with grief and anxiety. It is most touching to see her hobble about the house agitatedly in spite of her age, praying to the God.

When Swami is brought home safe after his adventure in the forest, he is flattered by the special attention given to him by his parents and several visitors calling upon him. His grandmother and mother hover round him ceaselessly, temporarily overlooking the needs of his baby brother. He basks under the sunshine of their loving attention. Before long he is restored to complete health, which is made possible entirely by the love and concern of his parents and grandmother, and the security of his home, which proves his haven.

If *Swami and Friends* depicts the carefree buoyant world of a school boy, the next novel *The Bachelor of Arts* presents a few phases in the life of Chandran an undergraduate student of the Albert Mission College of Malgudi, who eventually becomes a Bachelor of Arts. It is mainly concerned with the emotional ups and downs of his life until he settles down as a married man. In some ways Chandran would appear to be young Swami grown up. He seems to begin where the other leaves off. Like Swami he too has to go through certain deflating experiences before he achieves a measure of emotional maturity and stability. Chandran has to cross "the shadowline between carefree youth and responsible manhood."[7] In this process, his parents also play a significant role. Thus the theme of growing up is taken a stage further in this novel. But the family is still a secondary theme in this novel, the focus being on Chandran's growth. However, it has a more conspicuous and important place than in

Swami and Friends, where it is by and large a backdrop to the young boy's activities.

The novel is closely organized under four parts, and each part presents a certain stage in the growth of the protagonist Chandran as he leaves college as a graduate to face the odds of worldly life before he finally settles down as a happily married and contented man with a loving wife and a lucrative job. Part One is mainly concerned with Chandran's college life and its comedy, and it gently exposes his ambitions, vanities and snobbery. It also shows him at home in the company of his parents and his younger brother Seenu. Parts Two and Four give a more detailed picture of his relationship with the different members of his family, including his uncle, aunt and cousins. It is in these parts of the novel that the family theme becomes an important strand of the narration.

At home Chandran is the darling child of his parents, though he is not the only child or son. Exercising the privilege of an elder brother he bosses over his younger brother Seenu occasionally. Like Swami's, Chandran's too is a compact and close-knit family whose members are bound to each other by the silken bond of love and affection. They are a well-to-do family so that Chandran has hardly any financial worry and has all the freedom he desires. But now and then he plays with the idea of asserting his independence of his father's authority, regarding himself as an emancipated young man, no longer an adolescent. But it is amusing to see him shrink back with a deferential awe towards his father, although he is anything but authoritarian. He lives a sheltered and complacent life, all his movements being between two secure points, his loving home and his college where he is exposed only to the mock-disturbances of the Debating Society and the baseless, wholly imaginary and short-lived fears of his teachers. It is only after he leaves college he is unexpectedly jolted out of this security and complacency when he falls romantically in love with a girl whom he has seen only from a distance, and is disappointed.

Parts Two and Three of the novel are concerned with the consequences of Chandran's falling obsessively in love with a girl called Malathi. This "love-at-firt-sight trauma"[8] marks a decisive turning point in his life. It creates tension in the family and brings him apparently into sharp conflict with both his father and mother and with the long-established customs, conventions, and beliefs of their clan. It is in this context that we are enabled to see the kind of relationship he has with his father and mother. It might seem at this stage that the rest of the novel is going to be about father-son and mother-son confrontation. But it turns out to be something different. It is to be noted that Chandran broaches the topic of his marriage first with his father Venkatachalam Iyer rather than with his mother, although he feels much more free with her. Interestingly he chooses a time when his mother is away from home to raise it with his father, although he has to muster all the courage at his command to approach him. The reason for it is not far to seek. Chandran's father is more like an affectionate, elderly and understanding friend to him than a censorious, authoritarian father demanding and expecting implicit obedience.

Chandran's mother conforms to the conventional image of a mother pious and loving, one to whom her home is the whole world. Her son's happiness is closer to her heart. It is over Chandran's ardent desire to marry the daughter of D.W. Krishna Iyer, who is no more than a Head-Clerk that tension builds up between mother and son. For all his sympathy for his son, Venkatachalam Iyer is not able to override his wife's objections because he is undecided about his own attitude to custom. In spite of their differences of opinion, Chandran's parents love their son so deeply that they cannot bear to see him unhappy and miserable. It is deeply touching to see them risking going against some of the age-old customs and initiate with the help of Ganapathi Sastrigal, negotiations with D.W. Krishna Iyer. But after considerable hope, expectation, and much suspense, Chandran is unfortunately disappointed, because of astrological objections. The disappointment of his parents is no less acute, for the sake of their son. Narayan deliberately plays down the sharpness of it by presenting in a comic light the detailed though vain astrological discussions between Sastrigal and Krishna Iyer.

The health of Chandran, who is heartbroken, breaks down. As soon as he recovers he insists on being sent out of Malgudi to Madras for a change. Having reached Madras he impulsively decides against going to his uncle. He believes that he has left his home for good. He becomes a mendicant *sanyasi.* Part Three of the novel is concerned with this phase of Chandran's life. The inexperienced young man becomes a wandering holy man only as "a revenge on society, circumstances, and perhaps, too, on destiny." (111) After some months of wandering living on the charity of gullible and credulous people who take him for a real *sanyasi*, Chandran realizes that he has been humbugging through life. He thinks of his parents and is filled with great remorse that he has caused them so much agony because of his "silly infatuation" for Malathi: "He had deserted his parents, who had spent on him all their love, care, and savings. He told himself that he had surely done this to spite his parents, who probably had died of anxiety by now. This was all his return for their love and for all that they had done for him."[9] After such introspection he decides to put an end to this life of a deserter and counterfeit and return home. He "takes an important step towards maturity when he realizes the moral futility of deception." (115)

Part Four of the novel is all about Chandran's return home and his rehabilitation. The way the different members of the family receive him on his return reveals their attitude to him as well as their own nature. Both his father and mother are careworn. Anxiously and prayerfully they wait for the return of their son, languishing for eight full months. But his mother understandably is not able to contain herself as she looks at his emaciated person: "You are looking like a corpse. How your bones stick out! What sunken cheeks! What were you at all these days?" (115) His father exhibits remarkable restraint and asks him an apparently harmless question: "Did you travel much? What were the places you visited?" His brother Seenu, who is a cricket enthusiast like Swami, asks him about the cricket bat he had asked him to bring. After the initial embarrassment of reunion after a long absence is over, Chandran's parents not only do not ask him any inconvenient question, but they try to play down the anxiety and suspense they suffered during his absence. There is a blend of pathos and humour in each pointing to the other as the more anxious and worried of the two.

Chandran is deeply moved to find that his room has been kept spick and span in his absence by his mother as if it is a hallowed place. The garden untended, overgrown with grass and weeds, reveals Chandran's father's condition in his absence. When asked about it he gives only an evasive answer. Chandran's uncle and cousin at Madras when he visits them do not feel the same delicacy while talking to him, although their affection for him is not in doubt. It is his uncle who helps him to acquire the agency of *Daily Messenger.*

Without fussing over Chandran, his father by his quiet and undemonstrative concern helps him to regain his calm and sobriety. In a mood of restlessness Chandran thinks that he has wasted a lot of his time irresponsibly, and been still leeching on his father. Without further delay he wants to get employed to be of support to his family. His father however not only assures him quietly that there has been no waste of time at all on his part, but attributes the delay in his schooling to his falling ill with typhoid as a boy. Some discussion with and persuasion by his friend Mohan enables him to decide in favour of marriage. There is mild and humorous irony in his belief that only to please his parents he would marry. Five days hence, Chandran and his mother go to Talapur to see the prospective bride. Before long, he is a married man. That he voluntarily and gladly accepts the bride chosen by his parents, settles down to a conventional life, and finds himself completely devoted to his wife, is a measure of the strength of his family ties. His final return to the family fold is "symbolic of the strength and sustenance of the traditional family."[10]

Both *Swami and Friends* and *The Bachelor of Arts* in different ways reveal the strength and sustaining power of the traditional family, whatever its limitations be. The next two novels of Narayan deal with the world of adult experience which includes among other things the sharp pain of neglect, disappointment, frustration, bereavement and grief as well as exquiste love and happiness. "Taken together, *Swami and Friends* and *The Bachelor of Arts* portray the first stage of the Hindu way of life – the scholar in childhood and early manhood respectively."[11] At the end of *The Bachelor of Arts*, Chandran is seen becoming a householder, marrying the girl chosen by his parents, and thus entering the second stage of the traditional four-fold division. It seems therefore natural that Narayan should choose married life as the theme of his next two novels. *The Dark Room* (1938) and *The English Teacher* (1946) are wholly concerned with different aspects of married life. They may also be called domestic novels. They present the obverse and reverse of the medal of married life. *The Dark Room* tells a tale of discord in married life, and *The English Teacher* presents a story of married love and fulfilment in spite of a heart-rending bereavement. Both novels revolve round husband-wife relationship, although other familial ties and situations are also brought into their fold.

The Dark Room is mainly about the sad and frustrating married life of its protagonist Savitri, the neglected wife of Ramani. It is a somewhat unusual work among Narayan's novels in the sense that it is not in his characteristic vein. It looks like a *problem novel* on a specific social problem. In his *My Days* Narayan himself briefly explains what his frame of mind was, then he spun out the fate of Savitri:

> I was somehow obsessed with a philosophy of woman as opposed to man, her constant oppressor. This must have been an early testament of the "Women's Lib" movement. Man assigned her a secondary place and kept her there with such subtlety and cunning that she herself began to lose all notion of her independence, her individuality, stature, and strength. A wife in an orthodox milieu of Indian society was an ideal victim of such circumstances. My novel dealt with her, with this philosophy broadly in the background.[12]

The title given to the novel too is unusual. It is symbolic, contrary to the novelist's preference for protagonistic titles to his novels.

A story of marital unhappiness and domestic disharmony, *The Dark Room* "examines the marriage relationship in a state of crisis."[13] The story centres on Savitri, the neglected wife of Ramani. When the narrative begins they have already lived fifteen years of married life and have their children. The opening pages of the novel give us a sample of the relation between the husband and wife, what married life has been for Savitri, and what kind of man Ramani is. As she fusses over their son Babu who feels suddenly ill at school-time, Ramani orders the boy out of the bed and, asks him to go to school. Then he commands his wife: "Go and do any work you like in the kitchen, but leave the training of a grown-up boy to me. It is none of a woman's business."[14] His tyrannical and callous nature throughout their married life of fifteen years makes her feel sad and helpless leading her to think that she ought to have asserted herself in the beginning.

Having been brought up in an orthodox and conventional tradition to believe in wifely duty and unquestioned obedience, and in the authority and superiority of the husband, it is doubtful whether Savitri would have really asserted herself at all. As for Ramani, he even refuses to take the children with him and his wife to the film-show because children are a hindrance to their enjoyment of the film. (26)

It is because Savitri has tried to adjust herself to the whimsical ways of Ramani, they have managed to maintain "a more-or-less harmonious relationship . . . a fluctuating surface tranquillity combined with occasional deeper satisfactions."[15] With the passage of time, however, she begins to feel increasingly unhappy, neglected and frustrated. Whenever she feels utterly helpless, as it happens for instance when Ramani beats rather cruelly their son Balu, all that she can do by way of protest is to sulk in the suffocating dark room of their house.

The *Navaratri* display of dolls is a significant episode in the novel. It suggests symbolically Savitri's own condition in her house. Her lot is not very different from that of the *Navaratri* doll, put on display or shut up in a cask according to the whim of the master or mistress. Ramani regards her as an attractive possession to be vain about and make a display of on such occasions as a visit to the cinema. The *Navaratri* display also shows how her home and her family form virtually the entire world for Savitri. Moreover, as Lakshmi Holmstrom points out, "the dolls also link Savitri with her family; this is brought out in her childhood memories as she unpacks the dolls her mother gave her and her direct reflection that she must write to her sister in Bombay now."[16] Though her memories of her parents, brother and sister are strong and nostalgic, there has been little contact or communication among them since her marriage. (117) That is a measure of her involvement in her own family, her husband and children.

The semblance of domestic peace and harmony is shattered when Ramani becomes infatuated with Shanta Bai, an employee in his office. The sudden change in Ramani's hours of returning home raises disturbing doubts in Savitri's mind. Rumours about his affair reach her ears. She is deeply hurt and upset. But her devotion to her husband is such that she blames and despises herself for suspecting him. It is pathetic to see her invent and imagine explanations in justification of his conduct, and to convince herself of his innocence. "She was not going to let her foul mind spoil their life." (65) She wants to reassure herself that Ramani has great consideration for her feelings. She gets only a rebuff from him in answer to her anxious queries, yet she is willing to be satisfied if he promises that he will not go "near her [Shanta Bai]" again. (110) Savitri's moral sensibilities are so shocked by his infidelity that she moves away from his touch, and in a mood of defiance, leaves her home, her husband and children.

In this mood of desperation, Savitri sits on the last step of the river Sarayu, contemplating suicide and all her familial ties come to her mind: her brother, sister and parents, and her children. Even her husband is not away from her mind and ironically she feels less unfavourably disposed towards him. Conventional notions of wifely duty and obedience she had been fed on assert themselves. Rescued from drowning by Mari, a tinker-burglar, she finds employment in the village temple, spends one night in utter solitude in the dark room of the temple, and grows homesick. She is so much emotionally involved in her children that she feels starved for their presence and solace. She has to accept that she is not at all equal to the defiance and fight she had impulsively undertaken. She needs the support of her family and cannot do without it, whether the family needs her support or not. The children are most happy to find their mother back home, and Ramani sighs with relief. For Savitri, however, there is not much joy in homecoming. It is essentially a return to her dark room. Ramani remains substantially the same unfeeling husband, without a trace of change in him. She feels that an essential part of her is dead. The novel closes on this sad and pathetic note.

Real and deeply moving as Savitri's predicament is, Narayan refrains from sentimentalizing it. He remains detached and unprejudiced. His sympathy for Savitri is tempered by an awareness of her shortcomings. She has none of the tough fibre in her to defy her husband successfully and assert herself as wife, mother, and individual. Nor is she equal to renouncing all of her familial attachments. She is too much of a mother to resist the pull of her children.

Written eight years after *The Dark Room,* Narayan's next novel *The English Teacher* (1946) is a companion piece to it in the sense that it too is concerned with married life. But it presents a luminous evocation of harmony in married life. It tells a story of married love which is deep and abiding but without any of the romantic trappings that generally go with a story of love. In a sense *The English Teacher* would appear to be a logical sequence to *The Bachelor of Arts.* The theme of marriage and love continues in this novel from the point at which it is left off in the earlier novel. Chandran appears to have matured into Krishnan, the protagonist of *The English Teacher.* At the close of the novel Chandran, who has been married for two months to Susila who is yet to join him, is so completely engrossed in thoughts of his wife that he cannot bear to be without any letters from her even for a few days. In such absorption in his wife he anticipates Krishnan, whose wife also is called Susila. There is in *The English Teacher* another large theme which is intimately and inseparably related to the theme of married love: and that is, a mature acceptance of both life and death. The title of the American edition of this novel, *Grateful to Life and Death*, draws attention to this theme. The entire novel can be seen as moving towards this philosophical end. However, it is important to note that Krishnan is able to attain this wisdom as well as tranquillity of mind he had been deprived of by his wife's death, chiefly through the active mediation of the spirit of Susila.

The novel presents the story of Krishnan who teaches English in the Albert Mission College of Malgudi. It falls conveniently into two almost equal parts. The first half is mainly concerned with the domestic life of Krishnan, Susila and their all too short domestic bliss of three years, and ends with the unexpected and premature death of Susila. The second half of the novel recreates Krishnan's sense of bereavement, disconsolation and utter loneliness, and his efforts to come to terms with his wife's death, her absence, and ends with his achieving a spiritual communion with her. Thus the novel will be seen to have been built around the husband-wife relationship. In the course of the narrative other familial relationships are brought in at appropriate places insofar as they are relevant to the central concerns of the novel.

When the novel opens, Krishnan is already a mature adult nearing thirty. He is married and has a young wife and baby daughter. As his wife and child are still at her parents' place, he has not yet set up his family, his own establishment, at Malgudi. Therefore he has been living in the College hostel. Life for Krishnan, in the college hostel, where he has lived for a decade, has been comfortable enough. But from the moment it is suggested to him by his father in a letter that he should set up his family, he suddenly develops an aversion for the hostel, which now looks like a "hell on earth."[17] He longs to see his wife and child. Search for a house becomes an obsession with him. And he cannot rest until he has found one in Sarayu Street, although at first he feels rather nervous whether he can manage to look after his little child. (18) The kind of house that Krishnan wants for himself indicates his attitude to family life. First of all it should have a room for each one of them in the family and for a guest or two. It must keep them all together and yet give them enough privacy when they want it. Above all it must be neither too near his college nor too far from it so that he can "enjoy" his "domestic life." (22) His notion of a good house combines some of the needs of a joint family and those of a modern unitary family.

Krishnan's own upbringing was in a joint family. As he muses over his father's letter to him we have a glimpse of his childhood. We also see how deep and strong are his roots in his family. He is filled with nostalgic memories, and recalls his expedition as a boy to Kavadi in a bullock cart in the company of his elder brother, his two sisters and father who would buy the ingredients for making ink enough to last a whole year. His father's letter also reveals the concern his parents feels for him, his wife and child.

The whole of Chapter Two is devoted to an account of Krishnan and Susila's domestic felicity and bliss. K.R. Srinivasa Iyengar observes: "The story of their wedded life is a prose lyric on which Narayan has lavished his best gifts as a writer. . . . Narayan is an adept at giving form and meaning to this glory of wedded love."[18] M.K. Naik commenting on this part of the novel calls it "a delighful prose idyll."[19] Narayan's restrained rendering of the love and happiness of Krishnan and Susila deserves the high praise bestowed upon it by these critics. Particular mention must be made of Narayan's description of Krishnan's waiting in the railway station of Malgudi for the arrival of the train which is to bring his wife and baby daughter, and of their reunion. Seeming to be merely matter of fact, Narayan brings out all the deep feelings and emotions inherent in a situation of reunion of a young couple, and also the deep attachment that has grown between them. Krishnan is all in a flutter and confusion with "great agitation," "suspense," "despair" and "needless anxiety" about the difficulties of helping his wife and child out of the train and of unloading the luggage, all in "just seven minutes." (31) Once his wife and child are safe on the platform, he feels immensely relieved. Krishnan is particularly touched by the very warm and tender welcome given by his mother to her daughter-in-law and grandchild; all his misgivings about his mother and how she would receive her daughter-in-law vanish at once.

The mother-in-law and daughter-in-law theme has only a limited importance and function in this novel. Therefore the novelist rightly does not dwell upon it at any length. The understanding and harmony between Krishnan's mother and his wife, in contrast to the strained relations between his mother and his sister-in-law, makes no mean contribution to his happiness at home. Grand-parent and grand-child relationship is yet another aspect of the family theme in this novel. In its own way it too contributes to Krishnan's tranquillity of mind, especially after the death of his wife. This aspect is given the attention appropriate to it in the latter half of the novel.

Krishnan, Susila, and the child, left to themselves, comprise the young family until an old friend of Krishnan's mother joins them. The rest of the second chapter of the novel is devoted to presenting a picture of their domestic felicity. As husband and wife Krishnan and Susila are a complete contrast to Ramani and Savitri of *The Dark Room.* Theirs is married love, which Savitri does not have the good fortune to know or experience any time. It is deep though rarely showy. At least Krishnan can take the help of Wordsworth's poem "She was a phantom of delight" to suggest indirectly what he thinks of his wife and what she means to him. Susila is particularly undemonstrative. Little and simple gestures reveal her regard for him. For instance, under the pretext of playing with her child, every evening she waits in the garden of their house for Krishnan to return home from college. They are completely absorbed in each other and each tries to share in the other's interests. Every evening they spend together an hour or more in harmless gossip. Thus their relationship is nourished and strengthened by mutual respect and trust.

The undiluted happiness of Krishnan and Susila comes to an unexpected and premature end when she dies of typhoid. They intend to buy a suitable house for themselves and together go searching for one in Lawley Extension, where she contacts the fatal infection. This expedition, reminiscent of Krishnan's earlier house-hunting, brings out once again not only the deep attachment between the two of them, but also reveals how strong and firm their familial ties are.

The remaining half of the novel is "mainly an account of Krishnan's spiritual catharsis of despair and salvation."[20] With remarkable restraint Narayan renders the grief of Krishnan. The device of first-person protagonistic narrative enables him to give the account an immediacy. But he also takes care that it does not lapse into mere sentimentality and melodrama, a danger ever present while narrating situations fraught with pathos. His first problem after his wife's death is to overcome the blankness and emptiness possessing him. Memories of his wife and things associated with her are so dear and precious to Krishnan that he, contrary to the expectations of others, refuses to move to another house. As he himself explains: "Yes, at first I put it down to a general disinclination for change, but gradually I realized the experience of life in that house was too precious and that I wouldn't change it for anything." (111) Further, the house has "subtle links with a happy past." It also brings him "harrowing memories." Recalling both and contemplating them not only gives him "a new peace" but helps him to acquire "a view of life with a place for everything." (112) That is, to continue to live in the very house is a part of his effort to learn acceptance of all that life offers. Krishnan loses all interest in teaching at college. Nothing interests him except his daughter. When he is in this state of apathy, restlessness and listlessness, he makes very unexpectedly a contact with a person interested in psychic experiments. This contact proves momentous and marks a decisive turning point in the life of Krishnan. Through the mediation of this new friend, who actually seeks him out, he is able to communicate and commune with the spirit of his dead wife Susila. Gradually by means of periodical contacts with her husband she is able to save him from disintegration, restore his faith in life, help him by her soothing counsel to develop a measure of detachment towards their daughter, and finally discover his true vocation in life.

Sometimes Susila behaves "more like an animated philosophical treatise than an immortal soul."[21] However, to respond to the novel properly and to understand the continuing bond of love between Krishnan and Susila beyond death, the reader will have to do two things: first, suspend his disbelief in the psychic and the supernatural, and secondly, appreciate the difficulties inherent in the novelist's task. In answer to Krishnan's question, "How will you make me feel your presence?" Susila says: "At first it will be a matter of belief – a belief in the possibility of my presence. Later on as you progress, you will know I'm there by your side." (181) This suggestion applies to the reader too.

It is very significant that Krishnan associates the perfume of jasmine with his wife from first to last. He refers to the perfume of her presence. Susila carries a perfume with her in whatever state she may be, alive or otherwise. Music too is associated with her. She tells Krishnan: "Music is ever with us here, and it transports us to higher planes. . . . And a song or melody can establish a link between our minds." (148) Perhaps the novelist suggests that senses of smell and sound perceive better than the eye, what is subtle and ethereal. Krishnan himself reflects: "of all the senses it is smell which is the subtlest: it takes you back to the core of your experience." (146) Susila's existence after death as a disembodied spirit is to be smelt and heard rather than seen.

The novel closes with a kind of mystical union between Krishnan and Susila. For the first time after he began his psychic experiments, the communication between the husband and wife takes place directly without the need of a medium. The boundaries of their personalities dissolve resulting in a harmony of souls which brings them "immutable joy." Tacitly the spirit of Susila approves of what her husband has done. The conclusion of the novel affirms the transcendental power of their married love.

The Financial Expert and *The Vendor of Sweets* have for their central concern the theme of father-son relationship and a more or less total breakdown of communication between the generations. Narayan explores in them through his characteristic comic imagination, the complications and complexities that inevitably result when fathers who are excessively attached to their sons, pamper and spoil their sons who are insensitive and indifferent. In this regard *The Financial Expert* may be viewed as anticipating *The Vendor of Sweets*. There are certain readily recognizable resemblances between their protagonists. To mention a few, Margayya, the financial expert, and Jagan the vendor of sweets, inordinately love their sons born to them rather late in life. They also love money and accumulate it. Money is one of the chief causes for their sons getting spoiled. There is a failure of communication and understanding between the fathers and sons. But *The Vendor of Sweets* is not a mere repetition of *The Financial Expert*. In either novel the central concern gets blended with other strands and motifs and acquires a different emphasis. The crises that Margayya and Jagan have to face, the choices they make, and the solutions they find for their problems are very different. Together these two novels give us a considerable insight into the theme of father-son relationship, which is an important aspect of the family theme.

One of Narayan's acknowledged masterpieces, *The Financial Expert* is a closely and compactly organized novel. Its focus from first to last is unswervingly on its protagonist Margayya. The novel tells the story of Margayya's financial ventures and the vicissitudes of his fortunes. But that is not all. It also tells the story of his inextricable involvement in his only child and son Balu, born to him long after his marriage. Margayya has two major obsessions in his life, money and then his son. Between these two, money seems the stronger obsession and for a considerable time the ruling passion of his life. In his single-minded and relentless pursuit of wealth, he does not hesitate to employ methods "both holy and impious."[22] In his craze for money he would have struck us as little more than an insensitive Mammonite but for his relationship with his son, wife and brother, and his domestic background in general, all of which are firmly particularized in the novel.[23]

There is something absurd, comic, and yet deeply sad in Margayya's love for his son. It remains unshaken in spite of the ups and downs of his life, the different phases through which their relationship passes, and the grave disappointments that the son causes him. It begins as a middle-aged father's blind lovc for an only child born late in life. It develops into Margayya's feeling proud of his son and entertaining naively, dreams of a prosperous future for the growing boy. Next comes the phase of great anxiety, tension, agitation and exasperation over the education of the boy who refuses to learn anything. This is followed by a short period of apparent indifference towards the son who happens to abscond. Finally comes the phase when the fond father accepts his son for what he is, whether he cares for him or not.

The novel acquaints us with Margayya's fond attachment to his son well before it tells us about his preoccupation with money. He is obsessed with his son long before he becomes obsessed with money. Every evening as soon as he returns home from his so-called offices, the first thing he does is to hoist his son up on his shoulders and fondle him for a while. And then only he attends to other things. This is almost a daily ritual. His wife is equally attached to Balu although she is far less blind and demonstrative. Of course, both make enormous fuss about the boy's burnt finger, although the burn is only a negligible patch.[24] Margayya resents any adverse comment on his little son even though it is made by his wife and on just ground. Such is his partiality that he admonishes her rather than the boy: "Don't get cantankerous about such a small child." (39) The "small child" knows how to exploit his father's fondness for him. He makes demands for toys and peppermints at all hours, flings his food away, and lets out a howl for no reason whatever. (16) Initially Margayya wants to have money for his bare physical needs and also for what it can buy for his son. Later it becomes an obsession with him. "*That son of mine, that Balu I could give him everything*." (Italics mine) Margayya's visionary dream of his son continues:

> His mind gloated over visions of his son. He would grow into an aristocrat. He would study, not in a Corporation School, but in the convent, and hobnob with the sons of the District Collector or the Superintendent of Police or Mangal Seth, the biggest mill-owner in the town. He would promise him a car all for himself when he came to the college. He could go to America and obtain degrees, and then marry perhaps a judge's daughter. His own wife might demand all the dowry she wanted. He would not interfere. . . . He would buy another bungalow in Lawley Road for his son, and then his vision went on to the next generation of aristocrats. (23)

The passages cited above of course reveal Maragayya's deep attachment to his wife and son. What is much more significant is that in the huge castles in the air that he builds there is hardly a thought concerning his own personal comfort. It is mostly about his son that he dreams. It is to his credit that he thinks of his wife and her needs too.

Margayya is so foolishly fond of his son that he regards him as an exceptional child, superior to all other children. During his visit along with the temple priest to the weaver's family, he sees their children obediently restraining themselves from biting their nails when the *puja* is in progress. At once he is reminded of his own son and feels gratified to reflect that Balu in such a situation "would have insisted upon doing what he pleased – and not only bitten his own nails but other people's as well. He would have upset all this holy water and camphor flame." To Margayya this unruliness seems "a most enchanting self-assertiveness on the part of the child," which makes him superior to all these children. He feels like going home at once and "spoil his son." (25) Then again, his fondness for Balu is such that it makes him imagine impossible dangers to him. When the temple priest tells him with some emphasis that wealth "comes only to those who pray for it single-mindedly," Margayya is seized with the fear that the priest, who is perhaps a sorcerer, may ask him to cut off his son's head to obtain wealth. In his frenzy he imagines Balu "being drugged and taken into the shack" of the temple. (29) That night he sleeps badly, harassed by recurring nightmarish dreams about his son. (30)

Margayya's excessive attachment to Balu is understandable because not only is he his only child but one born late in his life, in answer to a prayer and a vow to the Lord of Tirupati. (131) He allows such reckless freedom to his little son that he does not leave him in peace or allow him to attend to his work. Strangely not only he does not mind it but is even proud of it. But this very freedom given to the boy leads finally to the undoing of both. The "red book" episode is one of several instances in the novel which shows how Margayya's life and his changing fortunes are all involved in his son. This episode marks a decisive turning point in his life. On a certain morning when he is busy looking into the little red book, which contains a record of all his trade secrets and complicated transactions of money-lending, the boy Balu impulsively snatches it away and flings it into the street gutter irretrievably. Margayya can only rave in sheer helplessness and impotent anger. The loss of the book creates endless complications for him as he can hardly transact any business under the banyan tree, and sets him "groping for the next step in making money." In spite of all the complications created by the boy and his own travails to find ways of making money, Margayya's fondness for him continues unabated as before. In no time he forgets the episode and forgives the son. He looks at him benignly and muses: "This boy must grow up like a prince. The Goddess willing, he'll certainly." (42)

That Balu is rarely out of Margayya's mind and that he thinks of him without any reference to money, is revealed rather unexpectedly on many an occasion in the novel. Two may be cited as examples. Once the self-styled sociologist Dr. Pal, whose acquaintance Margayya accidentally makes during his search for red lotus prescribed by the priest for the *puja*, asks him challengingly if there is a moment in his life when he does not think of either money or sex. Margayya replies that he thinks of plenty of things other than these two, and cites as an example: "About my son and what he is doing." (68) Another instance of Margayya's remembering his son in an unexpected moment occurs when he goes to the printer Madan Lal to negotiate the printing and publishing of *Domestic Harmony.* Madan Lal offers Margayya many tempting sweets to eat. At that moment, although he himself is hungry, some of his first thoughts are about his son: "He ate the *jilebis,* and wondered if it would be proper to carry a bit home for little Balu. He was racked with a feeling that he was stealing some delicacy which ought to have gone to his child." (78)

With the publication of *Domestic Harmony* Margayya's prosperity begins. He has to go a considerable way before he becomes the much admired and envied financial wizard. His financial ambitions are still under control. On the home front one of the first things he does is to think of his son's schooling. A great irony of his life is that this very commendable desire creates a major crisis in his domestic life. He begins in right earnest to turn into a reality his dreams about his son.

Prosperity brings Margayya power and status in society. In spite of his being a very busy man the education of his son remains uppermost in his mind. He involves himself completely in it. And that becomes the major cause for the conflict between father and son. Not only does he want his son "to grow up into an educated man, graduating out of a college and probably going for higher studies to Europe or America," but he feels immensely confident of shaping his son's future "as if it were just so much of clay in his hand." (87) At school, however, Balu proves himself to be good for nothing. At first Margayya, who loves his son blindly, thinks that the school is thoroughly in the wrong. Next as a prudent step, he gets elected as the school secretary, though it is "unprofitable honorary work."

The attempts that anxious Margayya makes to educate his pampered and recalcitrant son are at once comic and pathetic. He converts the small room in their old-fashioned house into a study room for Baḷu. Then he hangs a framed picture of Saraswathi, the Goddess of Learning and Enlightenment, on the wall and instructs the boy to pray ceremoniously to Her every morning. And then he asks him untiringly whether he has made his prostrations. To these and other queries he gets only perfunctory and at times impertinent replies from the boy. Margayya feels unhappy and angry and does not know how to bring his son round. He blames it on his wife although there is no basis for his charge. (14) In his anxiety to educate his son he even once in a while tries to teach him at home, making themselves miserable in the process. (104) Next to money, naturally Balu becomes "the greatest burden" on his mind. The moment he is left alone from money matters, he starts thinking of him. When the results are out the truth about Balu's performance is known. He wrings his hands in despair and clenches his teeth and declares in wrath: "You are no son of mine. I cannot tolerate a son who brings such disgrace on the family." He is stupefied when Balu answers back in a gruff voice: "Don't talk nonsense, father." (113) Accustomed to the conventional notion of unquestioned obedience of paternal authority and expecting it from his son, Margayya is taken aback by the boy talking back to him and asserting his independence. He is offended by the aggressive manner of the boy who talks back to him with the same emphasis as he did. Having doted on Balu since his childhood justifying his lapses and allowed him to have his own way, now Margayya finds it difficult to accept the fact that the boy has grown up and would like to have his own way even now. He fails to understand his son's mind and therefore cannot communicate with him meaningfully. In his helplessness he turns his wrath upon his wife who has been watching in stony-faced silence both the father and son: "It's all your doing. You have been too lenient. You have spoilt him beyond redemption. You with your—." (114)

Having pampered Balu from his childhood by pandering to every whim of his, Margayya deprives him of opportunities to learn how important as well as necessary it is to strive for a thing. He also fails to realize the paramount importance of communicating with his growing son, and thus over the years he loses altogether the way to communicate with him. His affluence only builds a barrier between the two. It only helps Balu to grow to be one of the idle rich.

After the row over Balu's failure in the examination, Margayya regrets that he should have lost his temper with his son and is only too eager to make it up with him. When he broaches the topic with Balu, he gets a reply both defiant and definite: "I will not read again. . . . Father, if you hate me and want to make me miserable, you will bother me with examination and studies." (116) Balu even snatches away from his hands the S.S.L.C. register, tears it to pieces, and runs away from home. The father-son tension leads to the son's absconding.

Strangely Margayya's prosperity improves much further after Balu's disappearance. It is during this phase that he becomes absorbed wholly in accumulating money and comes very close to being dehumanized. He appears so much accustomed to the absence of Balu that he ceases to think of it as "a primary cause" for unhappiness. (119) His affluence buoys him up and enables him to bear the loss of his son. He does not find any time "to brood over Balu."

Before long an unexpected situation arises which not only gives Margayya a rude jolt but tests severely his love for his son and his humanity. As he walks home he finds his wife wailing and soon he comes to know that his wife has received a postcard conveying the sadness of his son's death. Margayya now sits grieving and his grief for his son is certainly genuine, but it is corrupted by his obsessive love of money, which has a dehumanizing influence upon him. His wife, always a contrast to him, is the very picture of maternal grief.

During the search for Balu at Madras, Margayya, for all his grief, appears to be more worried about his business at Malgudi than his son and his whereabouts. However, the moment he hears his voice and sees him in the cinema house, he feels as if he has "swallowed a live cinder." When he sees the boy in dirty clothes, uncut hair and sunken cheeks, he cannot hold himself back. He rushes forward with tearful eyes, crying indistinctly: "Is this spectacle my son? What has come over you?" (141) Balu, who has to surrender himself, is not at all happy to return home and does not seem to feel for his father or mother. He is afraid that he would be forced to resume his studies. Margayya, who is filled with love and feels indescribable pity for his son, assures him: "You need not go near the books: you can do just as you please . . . you eat, rest, and grow fat – that is all you are expected to do, and take as much money as you like." (142-43) Reunion with his son restores Margayya's former indulgent love for him. What is more, while he accumulates money with far greater vigour than before, it becomes a shade less important than his son.

The peace and harmony restored in Margayya's household after the son's return is short-lived. Balu's hours of returning home in the evening cause continuous and great anxiety to his fond parents who treat him with the greatest consideration. Margayya goes into a panic if Balu absents himself too long from home. In his son's presence he does his best to be "docile and agreeable," and avoids "any suggestion of intimidation and effrontery" in his talk with him. (147) He does not know what to do with the boy who lives an absolutely idle life. To marry him appears the best solution. After the marriage he insists that Balu should set up a family independently and overrules all his wife's objections to it.

In addition to this commendable desire to promote the happiness of his son and daughter-in-law by giving them freedom, there is yet another prudent consideration which is very characteristic of Margayya. He hopes to forestall possible attempts by his son to assert his independence and demand a share in the property. Therefore he gives him a house and a settlement. Balu is only too eager to go away. His more sensible wife Brinda takes proper and respectful leave of her mother-in-law before leaving for her house at Lawley Extension. It is bitterly ironical that these legitimate expectations of Margayya are completely defeated thanks to Pal who becomes a constant visitor to Balu's establishment.

Margayya finds it imperative to wean Balu away from Pal's harmful influence. He involves Pal in his new deposit scheme which he hopes, would have a double advantage: it would keep his son safe and more money would flow into his bank, thus satisfying his two obsessions. But a shocking surprise awaits him when he feels most secure and complacent. Unusually Balu shows up at his office on an evening, and the sight of his son as always makes him happy. But he exasperates the father by creating a scene. This encounter between the father and the son is narrated dramatically by the novelist. After the preliminary conversation on Balu's family is over, he rather hesitantly asks his father for more money, which is readily granted. Margayya never grudges giving his son as much money as he wants. Next he demands, to the bewilderment of his father, his share of the "ancestral property." (167) In spite of Margayya's explanation, he persists in his demand and blocks his way. Margayya slaps him on the face and he bursts into tears. He too is moved to tears. Speaking directly from the depth of his heart, he tells Balu: "Here I am, your father, ready to do anything for you: only ask what you want. . . . All that I have is yours, my boy. Everything that I have will come to you: who else is there? To whom can I pass these on after my time?" (168-69)

After the clash with his son Margayya becomes restless. He feels that perhaps he has been too severe with the boy, and wants to investigate more sympathetically what his troubles are. His reflections on his way to Balu's house late that night are full of paternal affection and concern. He is particularly attached to his daughter-in-law and feels very proud of her. He gathers from her the mischief Pal has been playing with his son. He is torn between caution and impossible rage, but on second thoughts counsels himself caution. With a great deal of tenderness he assures his daughter-in-law that he will set everything right. But the moment he sees his son and Pal, all his caution and discretion is swept aside by the indignant father in him, and he assaults Pal. The very next day Pal engineers a run on his bank and his financial empire collapses. He risks his riches and happiness for the sake of his upstart son, who never cares to understand his father. What is remarkable is that Margayya is able to face this grave crisis and survive it. It is the strength of his familial ties – his deep love for his son and grandson, for his wife and daughter-in-law, and his strange attachment to his brother that saves him from utter collapse.

This is suggested by a superb touch given by the novelist with which the novel closes. Crestfallen Balu has to return to his father with his wife and child. He stands uncertainly in the passage of the house while his wife Brinda appropriately goes to her mother-in-law in the kitchen. Margayya is filled with deep pity for his son who is unwilling to go to the banyan tree in front of the bank. He tells him: "Very well then, if you are not going, I am going on with it, as soon as I am able to leave this bed—*Now get the youngster here. I will play with him. Life has been too dull without him in the house*." (178, Italics, mine) The comments of Rajeev Taranath are worth noting here: "Margayya as a human entity is preserved all through his changing fortunes as a financial expert, by his unchanging, slightly awkward tenderness towards his wife, son and later, the daughter-in-law and grandson. His affection for the family is the constant which keeps the other constant of him as an average person, alive."[25]

In *The Vendor of Sweets* we have once again the story of a father and son who fail to understand each other and to establish communication between themselves. Narayan, the novelist, explores this aspect of the family theme in this novel with greater concentration and penetration than in *The Financial Expert*.

The Vendor of Sweets tells the tragi-comic story of the deep but absurd affection of Jagan, a sixty-year old widower and a prosperous vendor of sweets, for his only child and son Mali, who is an upstart and a prodigal and who does not quite require his father's affection. The poignancy of the story is in the complete failure of understanding and communication between the father and the son because of an impenetrable barrier which has grown between them from the time Jagan's wife died years ago when Mali was still a boy. With time the gulf between them has only widened to the great embarrassment of Jagan. The father-son tension and the gap between the generations are viewed from the comic perspective by the novelist. The comedy and the pathos both spring mainly from the contradictions in the character of Jagan—he is in fact a bundle of contradictions—and the situations he creates for himself chiefly because of them. He professes high-minded Gandhian principles, wears *khadi* only, spins on the *charkha* regularly, lives an austerely simple life, and is devoted to the *Gita* and its ideals. At the same time he is also attached to his son, who is the apple of his eye, and to money. He makes handsome profits and accumulates money by evading tax. He takes delight in tucking away in the loft of his house bundles of crisp currency saved thus.[26] His love for Mali, born to him long after his marriage, is infinitely greater.

The first two chapters of the novel make clear, among other things, Jagan's love of money and his love for his son, which far outweighs the former. At no time Jagan's mind is divided between his money and his son, as it happens in the case of Margayya, the financial expert. As Jagan walks back home from his shop at the end of the day, he feels a "thrill" at the prospect of catching a glimpse of his son Mali near the statue of Sir Frederick Lawley. When he actually spots his son among the young men who are hotly discussing film stars, cricket, and fashions in dress and deportment, he is filled with joy. He feels "very proud of his son's height, weight and growth" and wonders what God has in store for him. But peculiarly, he avoids drawing Mali's attention, because he does not want to "embarrass" him. (24) Here is a hint of the gap between the father and the son, and between the generations, which becomes more and more pronounced as the novel develops. Silence reigns in the house where only two of them, Jagan and Mali, live. In spite of Jagan's passionate involvement in his son, and his eager readiness to satisfy any of his desires and demands, there is hardly any conversation or communication between them. Mali either spends most of his time outside the house or shuts himself in his room. When spoken to by Jagan, he gives replies in "half syllables and clipped sentences." (30) There is hardly any meaningful relationship between them. Jagan's almost maternal preoccupation with Mali's nourishment and his brooding over his diet night and day, especially since the time of Ambika's illness and her subsequent death, comic as it might seem, would appear to be the only opening for him to communicate with his son and express his love for him.

Communication between the father and the son has not been normal or satisfactory at any time. Jagan is not able to know why there is "always an invisible barrier between them." (42) Mali is dismayed and puzzled when his father, instead of telling him what the doctor told him about Ambika's condition, breaks into a loud wail. Jagan, who cannot forget the "coarse, raw pain he had felt at the sight of Mali" on the fateful day of his wife's death, believes that "from that day, the barrier had come into being. The boy had ceased to speak to him normally." (43-45)

The communication gap becomes more pronounced as Mali reaches his late adolescence. Like Margayya's son Balu, he too develops an aversion for studies. Matters reach a head when he announces to his father rather brusquely and aggressively that he does not want to study. But Jagan, who has become a "cowardly father" and is afraid to mention school or college to his son, asks him inconsequential questions instead of asking him to "run off" to his college. (30) He shies away from discussing with his son his problems. Rather than ask Mali straightaway why he refuses to study, he seeks the help of his ubiquitous cousin—who, incidentally, does not seem to have a family of his own—to find out what the matter is. When it is reported by the cousin that Mali wants to become a writer, and that perhaps someday he would become a great writer, Jagan feels greatly relieved.

Jagan's reaction to Mali's plans to go to America ostensibly to learn the art of writing, is quite characteristic of him. A clear pattern may be discerned in Jagan's reaction to his son, to whom as an indulgent father he gives unfettered freedom. When he is disturbed by his son's ways, he shrinks away from his parental responsibility of correcting or guiding or admonishing him, as the occasion may require. Instead, he gets agitated to start with, and then identifies himself with his son's ways and imagines or invents a rational justification for it. Now he is surely shocked by Mali's plans to go abroad and has momentary panic at the thought of his son removing himself geographically so far. Once Mali reaches America, Jagan feels very proud of it and tells everyone he comes across about his son.

The somewhat sudden return of the prodigal son creates for Jagan several problems of which acceptance of Grace as his daughter-in-law is the least difficult. It is true that when Mali introduces her to Jagan as married to him, he feels completely confused. Several questions spring to his mind. But he lacks the courage as before to ask his son these questions.

But Jagan's relations with his now Americanized son remain what they were before. Their living arrangements in their ancestral house, Jagan living in the rear part and Mali and Grace in the front (now modernized for Mali's convenience), underline the separation between them, and their alienation from each other.

Mali seeks financial support of his father for his proposed scheme of manufacturing story-writing machines. But Jagan distrusts Mali's scheme totally and refuses to finance his fantastic scheme. To resist the subtle moves of Mali and Grace to make him part with his money, he resorts to "a sort of non-violent non-co-operation" by "ignoring the whole business." (92) A silent tension grows. But he cannot dodge them for long. On a morning as he sets out for his shop he is trapped by Grace. Mali summons Jagan to his presence and demands a definite answer. Instead of advancing the money for the dubious enterprise, Jagan offers to give his son his business: "If you feel you can take up the business and run it, do so; it is yours if you want it." (95) But Mali sneers at this offer and says that he has "better plans than to be a vendor of sweets." (96) This contemptuous reference to his business of a lifetime which provided the money for this spendthrift son hurts Jagan very deeply. With quiet dignity he leaves the place. He feels so sad and confused that impulsively he reduces drastically the price of all the sweets in his shop, because there seems little point in making money which has only deprived him of happiness.

Jagan realizes now that the time has come for him to do some serious thinking regarding himself and his relation to his son. As he tells the cousin: "Tonight and tomorrow I will have to do a lot of reckoning with concentration. I have left things to drift too long." (99)

At this psychological moment he comes into contact with the sculptor Chinna Dorai. From this time onwards begins the process of Jagan's cultivating a measure of detachment from his son and the problems created by him. But he has to go some more way and receive a few more shattering blows before he can attain it. He is anxious about losing his daughter-in-law. But she makes the startling revelation that she and Mali are not married at all. It rudely shocks Jagan's moral sensibilities and his notion of married life. To live together for a man and woman without getting married is to live in sin. Jagan is not able to swallow and digest the facts revealed. Grace's conduct amounts to a betrayal of faith and trust. He feels that his son and she have "tainted his ancient home." (141)

In the presence of the puzzle created by Mali who displays a new facet at every encounter, Jagan's euphoria about his being on the verge of a new birth gets diluted.

One more shock regarding Mali awaits Jagan, as a sort of parting shot, before he makes his final retreat to the mango grove. The cousin, who meets him on the road, tells him of the scrape Mali has got into by violating the prohibition laws. This is too much for Jagan to bear. Tears blur his vision. He feels faint and giddy. With some effort he recovers his composure and attains clarity of mind. He is able to think of his son with some detachment. He refuses to return home and be caught up again in Mali's affairs, and leaves it to the cousin to arrange for legal help to his son. He instructs him to run the sweet shop efficiently till the time Mali can take it over. But his attitude to his son and to himself is now clear from what he tells the cousin – his readiness to help Grace to return to her country if she so desires. It is clear that Jagan is still attached to his son and Grace, although he has been able to overcome his obsessive and blind love for Mali. Therefore he is able to go away from him without much regret. It is also clear from the context that the step of withdrawal becomes necessary for him because it is impossible for him to solve the puzzle created by Mali and to set right the relations between themselves.

NOTES

1. Ved Mehta, "The Train Had Just Arrived at Malgudi Station," *John is Easy to Please* (London: Secker and Warburg, 1971), p. 148.
2. William Walsh, "Nataraja and the Packet of Saffron," *Readings in Commonwealth Literature,* ed. William Walsh (Oxford: Clarendon, 1973), p. 54.
3. Haydn Moore Williams, *Studies in Modern Indian Fiction in English*

(Calcutta: Writers Workshop, 1978), vol. I, p. 65.

4. Lakshmi Holmstrom, "Women Characters in R.K. Narayan's Novels," *Perspectives on R.K. Narayan*, ed. Atma Ram (Ghaziabad: Vimal, 1981), p. 58.
5. R.K. Narayan, *Swami and Friends* (Mysore: Indian Thought Publications, 1983), p. 7.
6. S.C. Harrex, *The Fire and the Offering: The English Language Novel of India 1935-1970* (Calcutta: Writers Workshop, 1978), vol. II, p. 58. Italics mine.
7. *Ibid*. p. 57.
8. R.K. Narayan, *The Bachelor of Arts* (Mysore: Indian Thought Publications, 1985), p. 108.
9. S.C. Harrex, p. 66.
10. A.V. Krishna Rao, *Indo-Anglian Novel and the Changing Tradition,* (Mysore: Rao and Raghavan, 1972), p. 72.
11. S.C. Harrex, p. 68.
12. R.K. Narayan, *My Days* (Mysore: Indian Thought Publications, 1979), p. 119.
13. Harrex, p. 69.
14. R.K. Narayan, *The Dark Room* (Mysore: Indian Thought Publications, 1986), p. 5.
15. Harrex, p. 69.
16. Lakshmi Holmstrom, *The Novels of R.K. Narayan* (Calcutta: Writers Workshop, 1973), p. 44.
17. R.K. Narayan, *The English Teacher* (Mysore: Indian Thought Publications, 1984), p. 19.
18. K.R. Srinivasa Iyengar, *Indian Writing in English* (New Delhi: Sterling, 1985), p. 367.
19. M.K. Naik, *The Ironic Vision: A Study of the Fiction of R.K. Narayan* (New Delhi: Sterling, 1983), p. 23.
20. S.C. Harrex, p. 76.
21. *Ibid*., p. 81.
22. Shirley Chew, "A Proper Detachment: The Novels of R.K. Narayan," *Readings in Commonwealth Literature,* p. 67.
23. *Ibid*., p. 9.
24. R.K. Narayan, *The Financial Expert* (Mysore: Indian Thought Publications, 1984), p. 9.
25. Rajeev Taranath, "The Average as The Positive," *Critical Essays on Indian Writing in English*, ed. M.K. Naik (New Delhi: Macmillan, 1977), p. 317.
26. R.K. Narayan, *The Vendor of Sweets* (Mysore: Indian Thought Publications, 1981), p. 20.

Society is All but Rude to This Delicious Solitude

The Family in *The Guide, The Man-Eater of Malgudi* and *The Painter of Signs*

In the preceding chapter attention was focussed on R.K. Narayan's imaginative exploration of certain types of familial relations, the psychological as well as human problems created by them, and the insight into human nature and character provided by them. The protagonists of these novels discover meaning within the framework of the family and familial conventions. Those few, like Chandran of *The Bachelor of Arts* and Savitri of *The Dark Room*, who consciously or otherwise go against them, finally choose to return to the family fold and its security. Even Jagan the vendor of sweets, who deliberately withdraws from his son Mali, does not reject the family and its ties. As he is not able to solve the problems created by his son, much less establish any meaningful communication with him, he decides to retire into the grove to help the sculptor Chinna Dorai to make the image of the Goddess of Radiance. Jagan's displeasure with his son is largely due to the fact that he has callously flouted the age-old familial sanctities. In withdrawing from his family, Jagan only enters the stage of *vanaprastha*, which is enjoined by the scriptures and tradition of his society. In the three novels to be considered in this chapter, namely *The Guide, The Man-Eater of Malgudi,* and *The Painter of Signs,* the novelist directs his attention to study in terms of fiction certain types of people who find themselves as misfits in the family and go out of its fold either by choice or by necessity. Some of them find the family too narrow and constricting a sphere for the growth of their personalities and the fulfilment of their lives. A few others in the absence of the salutary discipline of familial ties and obligations become a menace to themselves and to the community of people amidst whom they live. Thus these three novels of Narayan look at the family theme from a different angle and prove in the exploration of this theme complementary to the novels considered in the earlier chapter. However in these novels the family is a secondary but by no means unimportant theme. As always with Narayan's novels, it is interwoven with the main theme of each novel, and the protagonist is invariably seen and presented amid a network of family relationships.

The Guide (1958) is perhaps the most discussed of Narayan's novels, and also his most complex and "most sophisticated" in its form and narrative technique.[1] It is "based on a superb comic idea: the incredible progress of a rogue into a saintly redeemer."[2] Its centre of interest is its protagonist Raju, a one-time tourist guide, lover of a married woman, impresario, impostor, jail-bird, fake priest and *sadhu*, who is finally transformed into a martyr under the impact of the absolute trust and unqualified faith of an unsophisticated rural community in him and in his saintliness. Raju who finds himself playing the role of a holy man, a *swami* actually does not renounce or abandon his family to become a *sanyasi,* because he has none having been isolated from it long ago, since the time of his liaison with the dancer Rosie. However, the novel gives us a detailed and vivid account of his family background, his parentage, his upbringing, his secure and happy life as a boy with his parents first, and later on with his widowed mother and his relations with his maternal uncle. The purpose of this account is to indicate what familial ties, sanctities and attitudes does Raju disregard or flout in his infatuation for a married woman. When the role of a holy man is thrust on him by Velan, the rustic who ironically comes to him with a domestic problem arising in a joint family set up, he enjoys playing the part least suspecting that before long he would be driven into an inescapable corner and made to face a challenging situation when he has to choose by an effort of will an unprecedented course of action entirely on the strength of his inner resources. This crisis brings out some of his unsuspected potentialities, which perhaps would not have been brought to light had he continued to live within the confines of the family, its attitudes and conventions.

In *The Guide* Narayan adopts a "dual narrative structure"[3] and presents the story from a "dual point of view."[4] There are two parallel narratives alternating in the novel, one told in the third person by an impersonal omniscient narrator in the historical present, and the other by the protagonist Raju himself as a first person retrospective and confessional narrative to Velan, who becomes instrumental in bringing about his transformation. The two modes of narration are braided together so that Raju is always kept in focus. He is seen as he wishes to be seen and also as others see him. This narrative strategy enables the reader to have a fuller view of Raju and all those who are involved with him.

When the novel opens, Raju is just then released from jail. He has "nowhere" to go and wants "to be away from people who may recognize [him]."[5] As his confessional narration to Velan reveals, his own misdeeds have rendered him homeless, and therefore he has to seek asylum in the temple of Mangala. Therefore, he exiles himself from his people and his family, certainly not to seek self-definition or self-development, but to hide himself from all those known to him. Ironically to such a man as this, Velan brings a domestic problem for a solution, and gives him an account of his own family which is a rural, close-knit joint family with its responsibilities as well as strong ties, which cannot be easily shaken off. Velan, as the head of the family, feels responsible for the welfare of his step-sister, who is the youngest daughter of his father's third wife. He does everything that is expected of him as the eldest brother as a matter of course. An implied contrast between Velan's family and Raju's is suggested since, in the text of the novel Velan's account of his family and the problem created by his step-sister is followed by Raju's narrative account of his father and mother, his own happy life from his childhood to youth as the only child of his parents, with hardly a care.

Raju's meeting with the archaeologist Marco and his wife Rosie, and his subsequent emotional entanglement with her, marks a turning point in his life as well as that of Rosie. The first of the far-reaching consequences is the wrecking of the married life of Marco and Rosie. Then, his involvement with a married woman with whom he starts living deeply hurts the sentiments and sensibilities of his widowed mother to whose well-meant warnings he pays no heed. That is followed by his open defiance of his maternal uncle with whom he clashes because of Rosie. This belligerent uncle, who is Raju's mother's elder brother, is bound to his three sisters by strong familial bonds and affection. He is "a sort of general adviser and director of all [their] family matters" and is invariably consulted by all the members of the family. (147) Now he drops like a bolt from the blue, to solve his sister's domestic problem. He accuses Raju of not respecting family traditions. Raju's mother makes her position regarding Rosie very clear to her son: "She is another man's wife. She must go back to him – If she is not going, I have to leave the house." (153) As good as her word, she leaves with her brother, more sad than angry. Her parting advice to her son is: "Don't fail to light the lamps in the God's niche. Be careful with your health." (155) But for a brief meeting in the court on the last day of his trial she does not meet him again. With her going away to the village with her brother, Raju's most important familial link and bond is broken once and for all. During the days of his affluence as Rosie's impresario, his moving into a different and stylish house from his own old-fashioned house built by his father, symbolizes the almost complete snapping of all his familial ties. His mother's desire to return to their old house and live there all by herself troubles him: "To have Mother live in the house, I should have to pay a rent to the Sait. Who would look after her? I was so busy. . . . After all her brother is dear to her, and he will look after her. *Why* should she come here and live all alone." (166) In this fashion he rationalizes and quietens his conscience. Thus Raju sets at naught all the conventions of the family. Intoxicated by success, fame, and wealth as Rosie's impresario, Raju drifts into a life of ethical ambiguity, and finally he gets caught on a charge of forgery and is jailed for a couple of years. After his release from the jail, there is not any indication that he regrets his past life. What is more, he thinks of neither Rosie nor his mother, nor of what was once his home. He wants to avoid all those who know him or can recognize him. There seems to be no one who wants to meet him. The last person to meet him while in jail is his former secretary Mani. His isolation from all personal and familial connections is complete. His immediate problem is to find a place where he can find creature comforts. It is at this juncture that Velan meets him by chance in the ancient shrine at Mangala and mistakes him for a holy man. Thus Raju drifts into one more role, that of a *sadhu,* a saint, in his life of playing roles which more often than not come to him rather than he seeks them. As always he accepts this role too purely for selfish reasons. It assures him of free supply of food, and along with it, it brings him exalted status and reverence from the village community. Once in the role of *swami* he performs it with as much relish and perfection as he played earlier the roles of tourist guide, impresario, connoisseur of Bharata Natyam, and convict in jail. Before long he becomes a public figure with no scope whatsoever for any private life.

Exercising his ready wit, gift for improvisation, and histrionic talents Raju remarkably succeeds in playing the role of a saint. Such is the intoxication of his success that he even persuades himself that he has become an authentic saint: "He began to feel it was but right they should touch his feet; as a matter of fact, it seemed possible that he himself might bow low, take the dust of his own feet, and press it to his eyes. He began to think that his personality radiated glory." (94) This is a measure of his bloated ego. When he is called upon by his devotees to perform a penance through fasting and thus bringing rains to the parched land, he is forced to realize that he has "created a giant with his puny self." (96) But he has no escape from the position he has worked himself into, though he does try in the early days of fasting to run away from it all. "What keeps him back," as Meenakshi Mukherjee points out, "is not practical considerations or fear of being caught, but very surprisingly, the faith of the peopl."[6] As the narrator tells us, Raju "felt moved by the recollection of the big crowd of women and children touching his feet. He felt moved by their gratitude." (97)

It is the unquestioning and collective faith of the people of Mangala that transforms Raju, makes him worthy of their devotion, and drives him "until he identifies himself as an instrument of their will"[7]:

> "If by avoiding food I should help the trees bloom, and the grass grow, why not do it thoroughly?" For the first time in his life he was making an earnest effort, for the first time he was learning the thrill of full application, outside money and love; for the first time he was doing a thing in which he was not personally interested. (213)

In this moment of illumination Raju succeeds in going beyond his limited egotistical self. The illumination itself, however, comes to him after some introspection on his part, and his earnest effort to lay bare the truth about himself to Velan. He begins by telling him: "I am prepared to fast for the sake of your people and do anything if I can help this country—but it is to be done only by a saint. I am no saint. . . . I'm just an ordinary human being like anyone else." (98-99)

Although his intention in unfolding the story of his life is to escape fasting, it marks the beginning of a change in him for the better. It indicates that he has begun to free himself from the shackles of pretension and duplicity. By the time he has finished telling the story of his life, he is a changed man. In the process of faithful confession to Velan, Raju grows in self-awareness and goes beyond his solitariness and isolation. Therefore he is able to continue the fast till he collapses. It is not quite relevant to ask whether his fasting really brings the rains down and ends the drought. More important is what happens to him and how he redeems himself.

From the point of view of the family theme Rosie is a more complex study of a misfit in the family than Raju. She also happens to be perhaps the most complex woman character created by Narayan so far. She seeks more consciously and deliberately than Raju a definition of herself and discovery of her own individuality outside the family sphere. But even she is in a sense driven to it partly by her husband and partly by her accidental involvement with Raju. Had she found in her husband a more understanding and sympathetic man, she might not have broken the bonds of family life and of husband-wife relationship.

From the moment Rosie and her husband Marco arrive in Malgudi, it is sufficiently clear that they are a maladjusted couple, their interests clash. His reaction to her desire to see a dancing king cobra is: "If it interests you, you can make your own arrangements. Don't expect me to go with you. I can't stand the sight of a snake—your interests are morbid." (58) She is bored by his interest in archaeology, which for her is no more than an interest in "cold, old stone walls" and wall-gazing. (73) It is Raju's observation that anything that interests her seems to irritate him. By Rosie's own admission to Raju: "When we are alone and start talking, we argue and quarrel over everything. We don't agree on most matters, and then he leaves me alone and comes back and we are all right, that's all." (74) But there is more to their married life than these clashing interests. As she explains to Raju, she belongs to "a family traditionally dedicated to the temples as dancers" who are viewed as "public women" and considered neither "respectable" nor "civilized". (75) Her mother plans a different kind of life for her and gives her a good education. Marco's willingness to marry her is welcomed by her people. After much discussion it is decided that she should prefer marriage to a career as dancer: "All the women in my family were impressed, excited that a man like him was coming to marry one of our class, and it was decided that if it was necessary to give up our traditional art, it was worth the sacrifice. He had a big house, a motor-car, he was a man of high social-standing." (75-76) Much more than wealth and status, Rosie and her people visualize for her a life of social acceptability as well as respectability as a married woman. An additional point in favour of Marco is: "He had a house outside Madras, he was living in it all alone, no family at all; he lived with his books and papers." (76) Significantly nothing more is said about Marco's familial background. It is not clear why Marco ever wanted to marry at all. He appears to be so happy to be a solitary, lost in his world of books and papers and cavefrescoes that a wife would be an encumbrance. He is not cut out for the role of a husband. He needs a caretaker rather than a wife. There is a point in Raju's fanciful, though uncharitable, thought that Marco would have been a happy man had he Joseph the caretaker for his wife. (113)

Lakshmi Holmstrom has pointed out that when Rosie "attempts to move outside her caste and into respectable society . . . [her] position becomes ambiguous. Two things pull against her role as wife; her need for passion and her need to dance."[8] Marriage with Marco creates two kinds of conflicts for her: conflict between husband and wife because of temperamental incompatibility, and conflict between the housewife and the devoted artist in her. Again, as Lakshmi Holmstrom puts it, Rosie's "attempt to contain all her needs within marriage ends hopelessly."[9] As a man Marco is prosaic and insensible though not unfeeling where his wife is concerned. But he neglects her in more than one way and fails to communicate with her at any level. He leaves her to herself while he is busy researching in ancient ruins. He does not seem to think much of her intelligence. When she offers to try to sing the "musical notations" he has discovered, he curtly tells her: "I doubt if you can. It's more difficult than you imagine." (112) Thus he inflicts on her an unbearable loneliness. Though he does not regard his wife as his possession or property as Ramani of *The Dark Room* does regard his wife Savitri, he is indifferent to her legitimate need for some of the common pleasures of life: "She liked to loaf in the market, eat in a crowded hotel, wander about, see a cinema—these common pleasures seemed to have been beyond her reach." (78) One of the strong reasons for her being drawn to Raju is that he understands and appreciates this side of her personality. When he takes her all over Malgudi, she behaves "like a baby—excited, thrilled, appreciative of everything." (77)

Much more frustrating to Rosie is Marco's attitude to her dance, which is her "primary obsession." (107) Even as a child she danced in the temple of her village. Although an ignoramus regarding dance, Raju speaks in praise of it and offers to give anything to see her dance chiefly to endear himself to her and retain her affection. Whenever he mentions dance her eyes brighten up with a new fervour. In contrast, Marco feels "stung" whenever the word dance is mentioned. He dismisses it contemptuously as "street acrobatics." (130) He therefore has extracted a promise from Rosie that she will not mention it, let alone practice or perform it. Sacrificing dance is the price she is asked to pay for the respectability of married life. (131) In spite of such opposition, Rosie dreams of dance day and night. She wants to dance and dance professionally, and thinks of every detail connected with it. Even during the early days of his acquaintance with her, Raju understands her mind correctly: "Her art and her husband could not find a place in her thoughts at the same time; one drove the other out." (108) Encouraged by Raju's enthusiasm for her dance she entertains hopes of a career as dancer with his active help. She even wishfully becomes optimistic about her husband's consent.

Rosie's attitude to her husband, particularly after becoming intimate with Raju, becomes uncertain and confused. She begins to feel guilty of being unfaithful to him, and therefore shows excessive consideration for him. Having been emancipated from the class of temple dancers, who have to live outside married life, she has accepted the traditional notions of husband-wife relationship. Troubled in conscience now she cries:

> Is this right what I am doing? After all, he has been so good to me, given me comfort and freedom. What husband in the world would let his wife go and live in a hotel room by herself, a hundred miles away? . . . As a good man, he may not mind, but is it not a wife's duty to guard and help her husband? (106)

But, as Raju rightly says, "she would have to spend only a few hours with him to come downhill raging against him, saying the worst possible things." (106) However, she is temperamentally so made that she cannot do anything in secrecy for long. Nor can she openly defy her husband and break away from him. She is anxious to save her marriage with him. She feels that she has committed an enormous sin. Like a prisoner at the bar she stands before him and says: "I have come to apologize sincerely. I want to say I will do whatever you ask me to do. I committed a blunder." (133) Although he ignores her completely, she follows him day after day, like a dog waiting on his grace. In spite of the humiliation, somehow she begins "to like him very much" and it seems enough if he can forgive her and take her back. But Marco makes his position unmistakably clear: "you are not my wife." (134) He abandons her on the railway station of Malgudi and goes away. While his deficiencies as man and husband are obvious, perhaps in fairness to him it could be said that the shock is too great and the hurt too deep to reconcile himself to the situation created by Rosie.

When Rosie comes to live with Raju, her position becomes even more ambiguous.[10] Under his roof she feels apparently secure and at home. Encouraged by him she practises dance regularly with great devotion, "least bothered about her past," and looks forward tremendously to the future. She is completely devoted to Raju's mother and assists her in several household chores as any daughter or daughter-in-law would do. The old-lady, who is generally kind and sympathetic towards her, understands within a short time everything. She objects to Rosie's stay on the ground that she is a "dancing girl" and "a tainted woman." Her solution to Rosie's problems is that of a conventional woman: "Why can't she go to her husband and fall at his feet? You know, living with a husband is no joke, as these modern girls imagine. No husband worth the name was ever conquered by powder and lipstick alone." (137) She cannot imagine any other kind of life for a woman once she is married. Not content with telling her son her view of the situation, she rather naively and elusively, alludes to the problems of husband and wife whenever she speaks to Rosie, and concludes her homilies and parables with saying that it is "always the wife, by her doggedness, perseverance, and patience" that brings the erring husband round. (137)

Raju's uncle, who descends on him, drives home with brutal emphasis the ambiguity of her present position:

> Are you of our family? . . . You are not of our family. Are you of our clan? . . . No. Are you of our caste? No. Our class? No. Do we know you? No. Do you belong to this house? No. . . . After all, you are a dancing girl. We do not admit them in our families. . . . You should not be seducing young fools, deserting your husband. (150)

With Raju's mother going away with her brother, he and Rosie are left to themselves. She keeps the house for him and all day long she dances and sings. Raju thinks, unaware of the irony of it, that they are now "a married couple to all appearances." (145) In Rosie's case, there is a significant shift in her scale of values. As Raju himself points out: "She was a devoted artist, her passion for physical love was falling into place, and had ceased to be a primary obsession with her." (145) She steadily works towards becoming a professional dancer and succeeds in it. By the time she emerges as an artist under the new name "Nalini," the many disturbing aspects of her past life, the embarrassments of her caste, her husband Marco, and the difficulties of her married life, are apparently forgotten.

By the time Rosie is established as a popular and great artist, there is a shift in her attitude to her art and career, which begins to divide and separate her from Raju. Her devotion to dance becomes so total that her own fame and the inevitable commercialism that accompanies her performances, professional success and rivalries and the like actually vex her. She cherishes the garland of jasmines rather than the fabulous cheque she gets at the end of a performance. She feels immensely happy in the company of musicians, actors and other fellow artists rather than the eminent men of society. These artists "have the blessing of Goddess Saraswathi on them, they are good people. I like to talk to them." (169) During their itinerary if they are guests in a house, she generally likes "to sit around with the womenfolk and chat endlessly with them." (172)

In the euphoria of worldly success Raju practically overlooks the fact that Marco exists, and assumes that Rosie does not like to be reminded of him. But the arrival of Marco's book by post, which he tries to hide from her view, and her excited reaction to the review of the book in *The Illustrated Weekly of Bombay,* and her eager desire to see it prove how utterly mistaken he is. Further, Raju is shocked to notice that she has cut out the photo of her husband and placed it on her dressing mirror. She demands an explanation from Raju for hiding the book. Her explanation for this interest in her husband and his book is: "Anything happening to him is bound to interest me. I'm pleased he has made a name now, although I don't know what it is all about. . . . After all, after all, he is my husband." When Raju taunts her about the way Marco treated her, her reply is: "I deserved nothing less. Any other husband would have throttled me then and there." (179) Now she feels disposed to think that she "may be mistaken" in her judgment of Marco who was "kind" to her. (180) Lakshmi Holmstrom has made the perceptive observation about Rosie that "Paradoxically" the more she is outside the ordinary social rules, the more traditional her values become.[11]

When Raju is caught on a charge of forgery Rosie feels such a sense of shame that she thinks that she cannot face the public again. In answer to his question, what will she do then, she replies: "Perhaps I'll go back to him." If Marco does not admit her over the threshold, then "it is far better to end (her) life on his doorstep." (197) Perhaps it is Raju's utter lack of ordinary character and betrayal of trust that induces these thoughts in her. For all her reluctance to dance, she goes through all her engagements and earns enough money to meet the legal expenses. She demonstrates that she is in full control of her life and affairs, and that she can lead an independent life of her own. Raju has to recognize, in spite of his jaundiced vision, that there is an extraordinary strength and single-mindedness in the call of her art: "She would never stop dancing. She would not be able to stop. She would go from strength to strength. . . . Neither Marco nor I had any place in her life, which had its own sustaining vitality and which she herself had underestimated all along." (199)

Raju feels gratified to be told by Mani that after the case, Rosie and Marco went in different directions. That is as it should be. In fact a reunion of the husband and the wife would have been inconsistent with their natures, whatever might have been Rosie's thoughts regarding her husband in moments of gloom. It is an irony of her life that she has to give up a life of respectability as a married woman, which she and her people so earnestly sought, to remain a dancer. She would have very much liked to remain within the family fold and its conventions as she found them, and still realize her aspirations as an artist. But she steps out of them more out of necessity than by any deliberate choice. Abandoned by her husband for her folly, she has to go to Raju for refuge. Once launched on her career as a dancer she discovers her individuality as well as her potentialities as an artist. Dance becomes for her a cause, a devotion. In her dedicated pursuit of it she goes beyond a life of mere passion as well as a life of mere respectability, to a life of fulfilment. She discovers that there is in her a quiet determination to go about it alone, without the support of a husband or a lover. In her own way she too, like Raju, transcends her former self in her dedication to art.

Published some four years after *The Guide* (1958), *The Man-Eater of Malgudi* (1962) by virtue of its like reminds one of Jim Corbett's famous jungle novel *The Man-Eater of Kumaon.* But Narayan's novel is no jungle story, although the forests around Malgudi and the wild life in them figure in it. The novel is chiefly about the conflict between the peace-loving people of Malgudi and a man called Vasu, who is a taxidermist by profession and who becomes a formidable menace to them. Vasu is the dreaded "man-eater" of the novel. To give point to this conflict, it is particularized as an unequal tussle between the printer Nataraj, a quiet but timid man who may be taken as representing the Malgudi community, and the wild taxidermist Vasu, who is an intruder into Malgudi. The climax of the conflict is reached when Vasu dies at his own hands. The central theme of the novel, then, is the destructiveness as well as self-destructiveness of evil. Narayan, while telling this dramatic story, works into it the analogical parallel of the *Puranic* Bhasmasura myth. It is obvious that the family theme can only be of secondary importance in the novel. The title chosen for the novel indicates, among other things, the implications of the family theme in this novel. Just as the man-eating tiger makes an outcast of itself from its tribe and the jungle by developing an unnatural taste and fondness for human blood, Vasu by his deliberate defiance of every bond, norm, convention and belief of the family and society becomes a dreaded outcast and invites destruction to himself.

The Man-Eater of Malgudi tells a straightforward story, rich in little comic episodes, from the point of view of printer Nataraj who is also the protagonist-narrator. A distinction of this novel is that Narayan studies evil in human nature through the comic mode. His narrative strategy is to blend the factual and the fabulous, sustaining at the same time an illusion of reality consistently. Haydn Moore Williams has rightly said that this novel "derives its power from Narayan's skilful presentation of the relationship between Vasu and Nataraj, the wild man and the quiet one."[12] From the point of view of the family theme, perhaps these two characters could be taken as representing two opposed attitudes to the family, Nataraj the traditional and conventional, and Vasu its radical opposite.

The opening chapter of the novel gives a detailed account of Nataraj's family and its background. He is shaped and stamped by his family and ancestry, and is steeped in the life of Malgudi unlike Vasu who is rootless. At present he lives in his ancestral house with his small and compact family of three, himself, his wife and little son Babu, all living a contented and happy life. However from the time of his birth till his youth, his life was lived in a large joint family of five brothers, their wives, and children numbering fifteen. As long as his paternal grandmother was alive she kept the brothers together "acting as a cohesive element among members of the family." She was assisted by one who was called the "Grand-Auntie" in the smooth running of the family administration. With the grandmother's death "the unity of the family was also gone."[13] The disintegration of the family is described in a tragi-comic spirit in terms of the protracted quarrels over the division of property: "Everything that could be divided into five was cut up into equal parts and given one to each. Such things as could not be split were given to those who clamoured the loudest." (12)

An interesting feature of the family was that while the elders quarrelled among themselves "all the children continued to play in the open courtyard, unmindful of the attitude of the elders to each other." (13) By the time Nataraj's narration begins what was once upon a time a crowded house with "numerous children, womenfolk, cousins, relations and guests milling in and out all the year round" (14) has become almost empty but for the small family of Nataraj. There is no indication that there is any kind of contact kept up among the different scattered members of the family. There is a passing reference to another large family the head of which is an old man whom Nataraj meets every morning. This family is at once a comparison and a contrast to Nataraj's joint family. Its several members are all scattered over the country, although the old man manages to retain contact with them and hold them together in some fashion. (12)

The impressionable years Nataraj has spent in the joint family have shaped his outlook. His tendency to be accommodative seems to have been the result of living in a joint family. Basically he is a gentle, normal, devoted husband and father. He has willingly practised monogamous chastity all his life. The attraction he feels for the temple dancer and prostitute Rangi, later in the story, is only a momentary observation caused by tension and overwork in his press. Somewhat indolent and easy going in his own profession as printer, he prefers listening to the idle drive of journalist Sen and the insipid verses of the monosyllabic poet, to clearing the backlog of work in the press. More altruistic than he really need be, he delights in running errands for others. He is a peace-loving man and a gentle pacifist, who is averse to all forms of violence. It is only natural that he should feel utterly shocked at the slaughter of creatures that Vasu indulges in. His aversion to violence and killing and respect for all forms of life are due to the kind of upbringing he has had in a traditional home. He himself tells us:

> I had been brought up in a house where we were taught never to kill. When we swatted flies, we had to do it without the knowledge of our elders. I remember particularly one of my grand-uncles . . . who gave me a coin every morning to buy sugar for the ants. . . . He used to declare, with approval from all the others, "You must never scare away the crows and sparrows that come to share our food; they have as much right as we to the corn that grows in the fields." (67)

Nataraj is "jerked out of the pleasant idle routine of his daily life by Vasu."[14]

For an analysis of the family theme in this novel a study of Vasu's character is of particular importance because he is not just a misfit in the family like Raju and Rosie of *The Guide* and Daisy of *The Painter of Signs* but he is the very negation of it. Perhaps there is not another character like Vasu in the entire world of Narayan's fiction in the sense that he is wholly villainous, and in comparison with other characters he appears extraordinary rather than ordinary. He is everything that Nataraj is not. Nataraj's first glimpse of him – "a tanned face, large powerful eyes under thick eyebrows, a large forehead and a shock of unkempt hair, like a black halo" (117) – is an indication of his demoniacal nature which becomes apparent by and by. Half way through the novel he is explicitly compared with a *rakshasa*. The way he comes into the press practically tearing aside the curtain violating "the sacred traditions" of the press (17) is symbolic of his attitude to all human societies including the family.

Vasu's egotism, his rude and overbearing manners and pugnacity, his cynical disregard of all authority, his ruthlessness and indiscriminate slaughtering of animals and birds, all set him apart as utterly antisocial. But his education – "I took my Master's degree in History, Economics, and Literature" (21) – his several terms of imprisonment because of his participation in the civil disobedience movement followed by his apprenticeship to a *pahelwan* in Nagpur and his subsequent role as an athlete and acrobat, his stay in Junagadh to learn taxidermy, and what he calls his philosophy of life that man must prove his "superiority to nature" (20) – all these emphasize that he is not only an outsider to the Malgudi community but that he does not have roots anywhere in this country and its tradition. His isolation and alienation is also underlined by his occasional use of the American style of speech. Two more hints are also given to indicate further his deficiencies. First, he does not care for children and would scare them away. When Nataraj's son Babu happens to come to the press, he virtually orders him away. (23) Second, he "never" reads poetry because he has "no time" for it, (24) although he claims to have studied literature for his degree.

As seen already, it is the general practice of Narayan to present his important characters against the background of their families and familial relationships. He makes it a point to describe, however briefly, their parentage, upbringing and kinships. But Vasu seems to be the only exception to this practice of the novelist. There is no mention at all, even in passing, of Vasu's familial background. In view of the kind of man that he becomes, the omission of any mention of his family appears to be both significant and deliberate. Vasu himself does not refer anywhere to his domestic antecedents, while he is quite eloquent about his adventures, exploits and achievements in different fields. Could it be surmised, then, that the novelist intends to suggest indirectly that Vasu has been an exile and an outcast from the family even from his early days, all because of his diabolical nature?

It is not just the sacred traditions of Nataraj's press and its parlour that Vasu violates. He respects no authority, no code or convention. He becomes a law unto himself and makes himself the measure of all things. He becomes a psychological menace to the peace-loving people of Malgudi who are a traditional and conventional community. He drives them to an impotent rage and indignation by his reckless and indiscriminate slaughter of animals, including domestic pets. He scandalizes their sensibilities by flouting all their conventions and holds to naught their cherished values and beliefs. His determined though unsuccessful bid to kill the temple elephant Kumar during the temple procession marks the climax of his diabolical career of continuous negation of all life. That he should kill himself in the process is the inevitable consequence of his nature and machinations. It is as it were the Brobdingnagian collapses by the sheer weight of his own body.

What Vasu thinks of man-woman relationship and marriage, which are so very important to familial life, is another facet of his negative approach to life. He airs his views in this regard freely. When Nataraj is busy printing the invitation cards of the adjournment lawyer's daughter's marriage, which is to take place shortly, Vasu virtually snatches him away from the press for a long drive into the jungle. When Nataraj protests that he should be back at the press to print the cards, Vasu comments cynically: "If the man is willing and the woman is willing—there is a marriage. What has a printer to do with it?" (40) That Vasu is not thinking of either the traditionally approved *gandharva* type of marriage, to which there is a passing reference in *The Painter of Signs*, or to the more common love marriage of today, but that he views all types of marriage with dismissive contempt becomes obvious when he tells the angry but helpless Nataraj: "Only fools marry, and they deserve all the trouble they get. I really do not know why people marry at all. If you like a woman, have her by all means. You don't have to own a coffee estate because you like to have a cup of coffee now and then." (41) His equating women with coffee and drink is not a mere instance of his self-congratulatory "wit." He proves as good as his word and has no inhibitions in this regard. Nataraj is taken aback at the number and variety of women that he brings to his room for his pleasure.

In the context of Vasu's perverted views on marriage and man-woman relationship and his equally perverted behaviour, *Radha Kalyan* the long poem of the monosyllabic poet and the spring festival in the temple at which it is dedicated to God, both acquire a special significance. It goes without saying that Narayan the novelist pokes harmless fun at the monosyllabic poet as well as those who patronize him. That is only incidental. However, his irony is not directed against the theme of the poem, which is the marriage of the divine pair Radha and Krishna. The ritualistic celebration of the wedding of this divine pair is the heart of the temple festival in which the entire Malgudi community participates, Vasu alone being a solitary exception. Krishna-Radha theme hallowed by tradition and the temple festival in their honour not only sanctify man-woman relationship but also make a sacrament of marriage. That is how the Malgudi community would view them. Their significance is not affected even though many mortals do fall much short of the ideals they imply. No family, no society which cherished these ideals can afford to accommodate such a man as Vasu, nor can he with his bloated ego, with no ties of any kind, with no sense of responsibility or obligation to anyone ever remain within the confines.

In *The Dark Room,* which was written in the late thirties, Narayan, as seen already, tells the story of Savitri, a married woman living with her husband and children, trying to assert her individuality and freedom in vain. She abandons her attempt and returns home because she cannot live without her children, nor can she ignore the established conventions altogether. In *The Painter of Signs* (1976), written after almost four decades, Narayan tells the story of a young man called Raman and a young woman called Daisy who choose not to be bound by the accepted familial and social conventions. The young woman in particular, who is the more dominating character between them, asserts her independence as a woman, demonstrates that she has a will and mind of her own, and chooses a course of life for herself which takes her out of the confines of the traditional family, its relationships and conventions. This she does at some risk to her personal happiness.

The Painter of Signs appears a somewhat unusual work among the novels of Narayan in the sense that there is considerable and uninhibited talk about sex, judged by Narayan's practice as a novelist. Raman the protagonist, a painter of signs by profession, is frequently troubled by "sex thoughts" and is anxious to "get away" from them.[15] And the other chief character, the young woman, who is given the non-denominational name of Daisy, is a relentless crusader for family planning. The time of the story, the novel tells us, is the year 1972, when the little town of Malgudi is no longer what it was, at least apparently. In addition to "a hydroelectric project somewhere on the Mempi Hills," increased and crowded traffic along the Market Road, (13) there is also a Family Planning Centre in Malgudi (27) to indicate the changing times and changing society. But the real focus of interest is on the relationship of the two protagonists of the novel, Raman and Daisy, who come from different domestic backgrounds and have different kinds of upbringing. They feel drawn to each other in spite of sharply differing temperaments and attitudes. But before their love can find its fulfilment in marriage, they part, particularly because of the voluntary choice made by the young woman, who rejects married life and all that it entails in favour of life as a crusader for a cause, namely family planning. Allied to the Raman-Daisy relationship is the aunt-nephew relationship, which needs to be considered first. It provides the familial background of Raman.

Raman lives in his ancestral home with his widowed and childless aunt who has been looking after him, almost pampering him, ever since he was orphaned as a child. Long ago his parents along with him and his aunt were on a journey, and were involved in a train accident. While his aunt and he survived, his parents died. (123) Since then he has been ungrudgingly and faithfully looked after by his aunt who had been married to a head-constable and widowed without any children of her own. One of the most heartening things about the family theme in this novel is the aunt-nephew relationship, the devoted and affectionate care with which the aunt looks after her nephew as though he is her own son, expecting nothing in return. This reminds us strongly of the grandmother-grandson relationship in another novel of Narayan, *Waiting for the Mahatma*. Such relationships are a legacy of the joint family system. In either instance, the novelist presents the relationship very delicately.

Raman's aunt is very old, pious, old-fashioned and conventional in her beliefs and attitudes. She has remained so in spite of the changing times and changing society. Yet she has given her nephew all the freedom of movement and thought, although he feels irritated by some of her queries regarding his movements, which are asked only out of a genuine concern for him and his welfare. He is so much used to her that he almost tends to take her for granted and feels irritated by some of her queries and beliefs. He prides himself in being a "rationalist," and wants to establish if he could "the Age of Reason." (8) A major irony of his life is that he has to discover and come to terms with the sheer irrationality of human affections, emotional involvements and bondages. His affection for his aunt is never in doubt. But engrossed in his own activities and preoccupations, he is "extremely considerate to her at times and extremely rude at other times." But the aunt on her part accepts both treatments "with equal composure." (31) As he himself knows, she has given "for years, unwavering attention to his needs," has "rarely asked him for anything in return" and made "no demands whatever." (25) The only request she makes to him is to help her to go to Benares. But much has to happen before she decides upon this pilgrimage.

Understandably Raman is a little put off by some of his aunt's eccentricities, although they are harmless. For instance she is never tired of repeating to him the story of her grandfather—"the Poona Grandee"—

who soon after his marriage deserted his young wife and ran away with his concubine to Poona where he lived in grand style, until years later his wife, walking all the way with pilgrims going North, cornered him there, managed to make him desert his concubine, and go back with her to their original home at Kumbakonam to live "a happy life," bringing forth "several sons and daughters." But that is not the end of the story. When the old man's wife died when he was seventy-five years old, he married again a girl of seventeen. (32) Raman's aunt repeats this story even to Daisy when she calls at his place. She does not seem to find anything objectionable or wrong in it. On the contrary, she seems to admire the courage, perseverance and heroism of her grandmother in bringing round her errant husband. Herself one of several children in a large family, born at a time when people were not afraid of having children, (19) she honestly believes like the people of her generation that it is God who gives children. (46) When Raman's imagination becomes "overactive" and he feels "depressed, panicky, and bewildered," because of what he believes to be his own disgraceful behaviour towards Daisy during their tour of the rural areas, he wishes very much that "he had [his aunt's] stability of mind":

> His aunt kept up her routine life from five in the morning till ten O'Clock at night, when she laid her head on a wooden plank for a pillow, and slept on the bare floor, finding the coolness of the cement surface agreeable. . . . She lived like clock-work, performing her duties at home without a question or doubt of any sort. She had been the same as long as he could remember. (85)

It is only after Raman gets involved with Daisy that his aunt begins to lose her peace of mind. Rumours about them reach her ears. Her background, upbringing and attitudes being what they are, she cannot approve of Raman's decision to marry Daisy. Her decision to leave for Benares on pilgrimage, perhaps never to return, is largely due to the unconventional marriage he has decided to make. It is not easy for Raman either to let her go. But once having made up her mind, she does not go back upon it. Her state of mind is revealed in the following remark to Raman: "You must live your life, that is all, although if I had known that you were ready to marry, I had a dozen horoscopes offered." (120) Without a hue and cry she resigns herself to it. Till the last minute of her departure she is busy instructing her nephew about household matters. During Daisy's very first visit to his house, in the early days of their acquaintance, Raman happens to tell her half-apologetically that he has not interfered with his aunt's old-fashioned way of running the house. (146) But now as he listens to his aunt's instructions regarding rice, oil, pickles, etc., he realizes how much his daily comfort in life has been dependent on her way of running the house. As the narrator puts it:

> Raman was getting an inkling of the enormous industry at home that had gone on unseen in minute detail, to keep him nourished day after day for thirty years. Aunt had no other occupation but gathering fodder for him night and day and keeping them in proper condition. He was aghast at the amount of work involved.—She had lived on one meal a day for years, as he knew. He marvelled at the simplicity of her life and her minimal wants. . .
>
> She seems to have existed only for [his] sake. Except the evening visit to the temple, her world was purely and totally dedicated to his well-being. (128-29)

The aunt-nephew relationship in this novel presents a familial tie fostered by the traditional joint family system. The relationship between Raman and Daisy presents a different aspect of the family theme, which is characteristic of changing times and changing attitudes towards certain familial relationships. Raman meets Daisy for the first time in his capacity as a professional painter of signs. He is at once attracted by her and his thoughts hover around her person. For all his profession of a rational and modern outlook, he wishes to know if someone can tell him who is "her husband or father or brother," or where does she come from. (28) He would have liked to know who is "her protector, what [has] happened to him, that this slender creature should be left to tackle the population problem of this nation single-handed." It is obvious that he views Daisy as any conventional young man would have. Before long, he is obsessed with thoughts of her, which disturb him even while he is asleep. Given to introspection as he is, he realizes that this is contrary to his earlier choice to remain a bachelor and to his wish to establish that the "man-woman relationship [is] not inevitable and that there [are] more important things to do in life than marrying." (38) Now this edifice of self-discipline appears to crumble down. He thinks that he can still resist her attraction. Ironically, he becomes more and more involved with her emotionally. He is only too glad to join Daisy in her tour of the village as the painter of family planning messages.

From the beginning Daisy strikes as one who has a certain spirit of independence. Perhaps her voice, which is "a little masculine" (28) is intended to suggest that she is not the shy, docile kind of conventional expectations. When Raman calls at her place under the pretext of seeking some clarification about the board to be painted, he finds her anything but self- conscious, while he is all nervousness. She seems to know "her mind and its limits," (31) and fully self-possessed. During the tour of the villages other traits of her personality are revealed to him. The first thing he understands is that she is "a zealot on the population question" and she seems "to carry a furnace of conviction" within her. Raman is astonished by her adaptability, her austere routine, and complete freedom from all taboos regarding food, accepting hospitality "even in the lowliest of huts." (48) He is bewildered by the intensity of her devotion to the cause of population control: "I like to serve the people in what seems to me the best way." (48) Strangely, Raman finds a question crossing his mind: "Why will she not be my wife?" (49) which indicates that he has moved considerably away from his earlier position.

During the tour of villages, Daisy quietly, firmly, and with conviction speaks to her audience comprising men, women, and children on whose presence she insists, explaining all aspects of family planning without feeling "shy or hesitant." At this point Raman discovers a trait in her which is rather unusual and unnatural in a woman: "she was not really a lover of children and viewed them perhaps as symbols of defeat for her cause. She never patted a child or tried any baby talk." (49) While taking leave of the teacher and his family in one of the villages they visit, she looks critically at their children and tells their mother that children must be taught early in life not to suck their thumbs, to stand erect and not to slouch. (64) All this indicates a certain deficiency in her personality.

How unconventional Daisy can be is proved once again when she calls on him on an evening apparently to remind him of the travelling and other allowances due to him. This visit is made after a considerable time since their return from their tour, during which their relations appear to have become somewhat strained. This visit proves momentous in that the two come closer to each other in spite of Daisy's earlier stand-offishness. Not only does she patiently listens to Raman's incoherent account of his love for her, his hopes and aspirations, she tells him something about her own life and her own self. Although she says that she chooses to tell him about herself to satisfy his curiosity and "to pay off the debt of having listened to [his] own life," it is quite clear that she too is drawn to him and is getting emotionally attached to him. Her account of her life amounts to a confession so that Raman may know her for what she is "rather than have foolish notions" about her. (100)

At this point of the narrative the domestic background and upbringing of Daisy is given by the novelist to indicate the factors shaping her mind, spirit, and attitudes. Daisy does not give a clear, sequential account of her life or be specific about the place of her birth and upbringing. But it is made quite clear that she seems to have been an unusual child, quite consistent with her choice of an unconventional life later on, outside the limits of the family. She was born in a village into a very large joint family consisting of numerous "brothers, sisters, uncles, sisters-in-law, grand-aunts, and cousins." Of this population fifteen were children. The household was like "a hostel." She sometimes wished to be "alone," but there was no "privacy." The noise made by the youngsters as well as elders was maddening, and "there was no time or place to consider what one should do or think." "It was a madhouse." Everything in the family repelled the child Daisy, although her parents were very kind, her uncles affectionate, and the others "extremely friendly." But she could not like "so much common living." (101)

Even at school Daisy seems to have been an unusual and precocious child, because she found her studies "dull and lifeless." In her own words: "I was always obsessed with the thought that I ought to be doing something better, something more useful than this routine life; that I was in a meaningless organization from which there seemed to be no escape." (101) To live like the other children became increasingly difficult for her: "All individuality was lost in this mass existence." (122) When she came of age she had to go through the humiliating experience of being viewed and examined by a prospective bridegroom and his people, regarded as a highly respected family. When the entire family was very hopeful of the outcome, she shocked everyone by her unconventional and defiant behaviour, and the whole proposal collapsed. She was regarded as disgracing the family and damaging its reputation. (104) There was, however, no compromise for her where her sense of her individuality and self-respect were concerned. The feeling that she was in a wrong world and that she was a stranger in the midst of her people in the family grew upon her. The next phase in Daisy's apparently unconventional life was to run away from home and make her way to Madras, hitch-hiking and travelling without tickets, at great risk to her personal safety as a woman. At Madras finally she "studied with the help of a missionary organization, refused baptism and changed her name to Daisy. She was trained by a missionary in social work, and to live in all sorts of slum areas helping and educating the slum-dwellers. (121) Her involvement in the family planning programme and her total dedication to it were the natural consequence of this training.

As an individualist jealously guarding her own beliefs and convictions, Daisy can appreciate Raman's aunt's desire to go to Benares to live the rest of her life there: "Let her seek her life's pattern as she likes." (122) It implies that she would like to seek and live according to a pattern of her choice. Having become intimate with Raman, for whom she does really care, she has to make up her mind about marrying him and settling down to a family life. That is the ardent hope of Raman who makes a number of alterations in his ancestral home to suit the needs of Daisy. She seems inclined towards marrying him. Raman explains to her the five kinds of marriage he had read about. Both come to the conclusion that the *gandharva* type is "the most suitable one for them." For, according to this type: "When two souls met in harmony the marriage was consummated perfectly, and no further rite or ceremony was called for." (124) Daisy, who has "no faith in any ancient custom," accepts this form. But while she agrees to marry him, she makes it clear that she will not change her name after the marriage. Further, she also lays down two conditions before accepting his proposal.

It is at this point when Daisy states her position categorically that Raman sees an analogy between themselves and Santhanu and Ganga of the *Mahabharata* story. Raman is so much wrapped up in his love for Daisy that he submits to her decision and will. (125) He makes himself ready to be subservient to every one of her wishes, although she remains for him "a great puzzle at every turn." Sometimes he wonders whether he is not making a fool of himself by marrying her. (132) When she visits him on an afternoon and spends a few hours under his roof, he believes that their marriage is really consummated and "the bride has come home." (136)

The day and the time for Daisy to move into his house is fixed. When Raman goes to her office to fetch her he has a rude jolt and shock. She puts it to him in clear and decisive terms that marrying and living with him is impossible for her. In spite of his pathetic and desperate appeal to her, she tells him feelingly: "Let us face the fact. Married life is not for me. I have thought it over. It frightens me. I am not cut out for the life you imagine. I can't live except alone. It won't work." (139)

Faced with a difficult choice between married life and an impersonal ideal which demands sacrifice of personal happiness, Daisy chooses consciously and deliberately the latter. For her marriage, motherhood and children, all appear to be shackles to her freedom of action. Therefore she chooses to reject the family, its norms and conventions which would have inhibited against her individual identity and her fulfilment. Perhaps there is not another character among Narayan's creations who rejects the family in this sense. The contrast in this regard with Rosie of *The Guide* is obvious. Both, however, happen to be misfits in the framework of the traditional family. Rosie wishes to but cannot retain familial ties. But Daisy does not want familial ties of any kind from the beginning. She chooses to pursue a lone course, fully aware of the hazards in such a life but confident of facing them, and fulfilling her own destiny.

NOTES

1. H.M. Williams, *Studies in Modern Indian Fiction in English* (Calcutta: Writers Workshop, 1973), vol. I, p. 89.
2. S.C. Harrex, *The Fire and the Offering: The English Language Novel of India 1935-1970* (Calcutta: Writers Workshop, 1978), vol. II, p. 113.
3. *Ibid.*, p. 116.
4. *Ibid.*, p. 117.
5. R.K. Narayan, *The Guide* (Mysore: Indian Thought Publications, 1972), p. 8.
6. Meenakshi Mukherjee, *The Twice Born Fiction* (New Delhi: Arnold-Heinemann, 1974), p. 124.
7. *Loc. cit.*
8. Lakshmi Holmstrom, "Women Characters in R.K. Narayan's Novels," *Perspectives on R.K. Narayan*, ed. Atma Ram (Ghaziabad: Vimal, 1981), p. 67.
9. *Ibid.*, p. 68.
10. *Loc. cit.*
11. *Loc. cit.*
12. Haydn Moore Williams, vol. I, p. 79.
13. R.K. Narayan, *The Man-Eater of Malgudi* (Mysore: Indian Thought Publications, 1968), p. 13.
14. Haydn Moore Williams, p. 75.
15. R.K. Narayan, *The Painter of Signs* (England: Penguin, 1985), p. 15.

No Man is an Island Entire of Itself: Everyone is a Part of the Main

"Narayan presents everything from the viewpoint of the individual and society."[1] Narayan's protagonists are deep-rooted in their social reality. And they strive for some ambition grappling with their fate. Having their own ambitions and hopes they struggle hard to work out their destiny, sometimes in the process, even going outside the norms of society. In this conflict of society and individual, always at the end the society or community triumphs and makes the individual aware that he is a part and parcel of a delicately and intricately woven social fabric and that he or she cannot exist in isolation.

The protagonist usually sets out on a quest for something or the other. Sometimes it is money, at other times it is self-identity or love and marriage, yet other times it is a meaningful relationship with his family members and many more. That is why Narayan's novels are "Novels of Character"[2] which seem to comment that man in the crowded world is all alone, and he is what circumstances make of him.[3]

Swami the protagonist of *Swami and Friends* confirms this view. Swami is a young school-going child. His world is made up of his friends, teachers, parents and cricket. In his own world of innocence he has problems that are very serious to him. That of being called a "Tail," being unable to participate actively in the cricket match, and of having fallen out of grace with Rajam as a consequence, and becoming broken-hearted thus – all these problems are very real for Swami. As an individual, he tries to extricate himself from such situations.

His world comprises Somu, Samuel, Mani, and Rajam. He meets Rajam, the Police Superintendent's son who is to become his best friend at school. Rajam, first thwarted but later accepted by Swami's circle of friends, even becomes the leader of the group. Soon afterwards Swami faces problems at school and flits from school to school. In the course of events he becomes a cricket player and together with Rajam he forms M.C.C. Cricket Club. "Swami reminds one of Mark Twain's Tom Sawyer or any schoolboy, East or West: the eternal hostility of school-masters, the vagaries of parents, the rivalry of cricket, the pain of growing up."[4]

Swami safely cocooned by his family and entrenched in the school life at once finds life unbearable and tries to escape from the society. He loses his way, fails to take part in the match that is to be held, falls out of favour with Rajam and is finally found. Swami's running away from home is his way of rebelling against the society for inflicting pain and misery on him. He does not realize that it is the way of the world, that is what reality is with all troubles and joys, pains and pleasures. He thinks he can escape from the sordid reality of the society and all that it imposes on him as an individual. Here is an individual poised against society all alone. But towards the end he realizes that if he has to make any meaning out of life, then he has to stay in the fold of society and be a social being as well as an individual. He realizes that he cannot exist in the society all by himself and mould his life according to his own free will. If he has to have peace within and without, he has to conform himself to the norms of society and has to accept it as it is the real, substantial earthy world. In the process, he grows up attaining maturity. Rajam, Swami's friend leaves for another place, for Rajam's father is transferred and Swami bids him farewell.

Chandran of *The Bachelor of Arts* is the grown up Swami. The novel shows "individual freedom coming to terms with external constrictions."[5] Chandran's failure and frustration in love-affair, the consequent mental upset and loss of balance, giving up of his social obligations and responsibilities (other than to himself) leading to his renunciation of society, assumption of the role of a fake *sadhu*, the sudden realization of the deceptiveness of it all, his return home, back to the enveloping folds of society, his accepting the agentship of *The Daily Messenger* thereby shouldering the responsibility for his own self as an active social being, and further his recognition of the traditional norms and values in the form of an arranged marriage reveal that he accepts society and all that it stands for even going to the extent of appraising the very same values he has scorned earlier.

The novel is easily divisible into four parts. The first part picturizes Chandran's life at college. Chandran, soon to become the Bachelor of Arts is a student of Albert Mission College and is "essentially a free spirit hedged round by rules and restrictions both in the college and at home."[6]

Chandran as a college-going youth is immersed in his world of professors, friends, books, examinations, secretarial activities and cinemas. At college Chandran has to organize the inaugural meeting as the secretary. But due to the restriction on him as a student he has to tread carefully with his professors, even though some of them he may not admire owing to their alienness. Further, he has to prepare for his examinations within a certain time limit, which becomes a Herculean task for him. At home also there are limitations as to how he can behave. That is why the idea of his father's disapproval worries him greatly when he wants to go to a night-show with his friend, Mohan—the poet. With all these restrictions imposed on him as a student and son, he is happy with his existence in society, until he falls in love with a girl he has seen on the banks of the river Sarayu. He does not have any direct contact with her but enjoys an optical communion with her and does not even try to meet her or speak to her directly, hindered as he is by the strict social code. The society in which he lives permits only custom-bound arranged marriages and it does not permit young people to talk to each other and move freely. He fears that she may not be of the same caste. He wants to marry the girl, and lets his parents know his intention. There goes on an endless debate on "custom and reason" between Chandran and his mother who says that "as long as she lived she would insist on respecting old customs."[7]

Chandran understandably in a rebellious mood raves: "To the dust-pot with your silly customs." (70) That later on he comes to accept these very customs and conventions without the slightest protest is of course quite another matter. The marriage proceedings take place and the parents find out that the horoscopes do not match, and refuse the marriage. Chandran who has till now adhered to the social code, by trying to get his marriage arranged by his parents, now, frustrated in love becomes desperate and dejected. Chandran's plight is the same as that of Krishna's in the short story, *The White Flower*. He sees the girl at the street tap, falls in love with her, but could not progress beyond "eloquent glances." Helped by a mutual friend the families try to arrange the marriage but the horoscopes mismatch. There is a wife-killing planet in Krishna's horoscope and the girl's father refuses to agree to the match. But unlike Krishna, Chandran leaves Malgudi and for the first time ventures into the outside world. At the railway station he gets out and instead of going to his uncle's, where he is supposed to go, he goes to a hotel and finds himself in company with Kailas—a drunkard and a womaniser. Chandran, born and brought up in a traditional home which gives enormous importance to moral values, is horrified at Kailas and all that he represents. He realizes that his place is not with Kailas and this is not the way for him and flees from Kailas. But having decided not to go back he feels a dilemma as to where his further course lies and after much speculation decides to renounce the world.

Thus he finds an easy way out of his troubles. He goes to Kapaleeswar temple and asks the barber to shave his head and in reply to the barber's question says "my heart is dead." Although Chandran does not realize it, becoming a *sanyasi* itself indicates a kind of death. Ironically it is the barber, Raghavan, who realizes that "Chandran hardly knows enough about life to give it up."[8] Hence his surprise "Master at your age."

Chandran becomes a *sanyasi* and halts at a village in his wanderings. There, coming upon the innocent villagers who believe in him and take him to be a real *sanyasi,* he feels ashamed. This is the incident which is to later become the central theme of *The Guide.*

Chandran realizes that he is different from the "*usual sanyasi.*" His renunciation is almost a revenge on society. He returns home, back to Malgudi, reality, understanding that he can't shelve his responsibility any more and that he has to take up his own place in society as a social being, takes up the agency of *The Daily Messenger*, does well, and drops his "vague desire" of going to England, and settles down. He agrees to marry according to his parents' wishes, accepting as his friend Mohan says, that "there ought to be a proper synthesis of life," (154) goes and sees the girl, falls in love with her immediately and realizes that what he has felt for Malathi is nothing but an illusory infatuation. Soon he is married. Syd C. Harrex sums up the situation and the conclusion of the novel aptly in the following words:

> It is a completely conventional and orthodox marriage with the bride returning to her parents' home until it is time for her to come to live with her husband. They exchange ecstatic letters. And the novel ends with Chandran completely in love, but left suspended in emotional mid-air as he pedals off into the distance to see his wife from whom he hasn't heard for six days; six days which seems to him an eternity.[9]

Now Chandran has no conflict with the society. And his soul, once "a playground of powerful antagonistic forces, both social and metaphysical,"[10] is at peace having been freed from "distracting illusions and hysterics."

Thus the novel depicts individual freedom simmering into revolt by voluntarily coming to terms with the traditional norms.[11] The theme of Chandran's growth towards maturity is further taken up in the next novel, for Krishnan of *The English Teacher* is no one but the married Chandran. As the novel opens, Krishnan is a happily married man with a baby daughter, still very much in love with his wife and blissfully happy. Their life is "a poem of love in marriage."[12]

The novel, "enough achievement for a life time,"[13] falls into two parts. The first part describes Krishnan's life as a college lecturer, his dissatisfaction with his profession, his idyllic life with his wife Susila and his daughter Leela, and the sudden death of Susila which deprives him of everything in life. The second part of the novel depicts Krishnan's grief and despair, his desperate attempt to communicate with Susila, his coming to terms with reality, his being reconciled, meeting Leela's headmaster, realization of the futility of his teaching at Albert Mission College, his resigning the job at the college and taking up the school teacher's job to a life of meaningful existence, finally his achieving, independently, spiritual union and oneness with Susila.

Gradually he reconciles himself to his wife's absence. He tends his little daughter Leela and finds some solace in it. But the burning pain in his heart remains. After a while Susila contacts him through a medium and with her help he is able to understand that death is not the end of all existence. His love proves to be transcendental. Thus *The English Teacher* is an intimately personal account of man's quest for a positive philosophy of life and his attainment of spiritual maturity[14] which is characteristically Indian. Because Krishnan has already enacted the roles of *brahmacharya* (student) and *grihasthya* (householder) and is ripe for *vanaprastha* (renunciation) which is the third stage of life according to traditional Hindu society, Krishnan's development follows a recognizable *vedantic* path to selfhood.[15] Written before *The English Teacher, The Dark Room* depicts the plight of a traditional Indian house-wife a long suffering woman, symbol of middle-class values.

Though the novel deals with the (same theme as that of the *The English Teacher*) husband-wife relationship, it is totally different in its treatment. The novel depicts the sufferings of a traditional Hindu wife in a male-dominated society, and her brief attempt at rebellion. Savitri, thinking that she is tainted by her husband's behaviour, walks out on her tyrannical and womanising husband, when he orders her to keep shut, even after she finds out about his extra-marital affairs and his unfaithfulness, secure in the knowledge of his social position and place in the centuries-old male-dominated society and social structure. Savitri, after leaving home, finds out to her mortification that she cannot keep up her show of freedom and independence. The very values that she nurtures make her weak and she realizes that her defiance against her husband and her rebellion against society is much too feeble and that she has no alternative but to go home. Her maternal instincts make her surrender to her husband and family and bow down to the society. But Savitri who comes back is not the same who ventured out. She realizes that a part of her is dead symbolizing her emotional death. She ultimately realizes that she doesn't possess or own anything and has no right to call anything her own, that her own free will and individuality doesn't exist in her husband's house of authority.

The title of the novel is symbolic in the sense that it reminds one of

Savitri. The dark room is the place where Savitri retreats to when something happens to annoy her. The dark room, as K.R.Srinivasa Iyengar has pointed out, "used to be as indispensable a part in an Indian house as the kitchen, and was a place for safe deposits, both a sanctuary and a retreat."[16] But in the case of Savitri it only underlines and symbolizes her helpless lot.

When Savitri retires to the dark room one does not know what happens to Savitri. No clue is given by the novelist as to what happens in her mind. What one is aware of is what happens in the whole family and entire household as a result of Savitri's withdrawal from her duties. For, even then she still remains its centre. "The cook revels in his temporary freedom; Ramani demonstrates his "calm indifference by whistling loudly within hearing of the dark room, the children though distressed and frightened at first, know how to deal with the situation."[17] Thus Savitri's withdrawal is a disturbance but not a serious threat. "The dark room is within the house, surrounded by the family; it implies a limited privacy, a limited protest."[18] which is significant in terms of what is to happen in future.

Savitri comes to know of his liaison with Shanta Bai, the office assistant, through Gangu. But unable to believe such a thing she tries frantically to attract her husband and fails in her pathetic efforts. She is all ready to compromise, to forgive and forget provided Ramani gives a promise not to go near the woman again. She gives an ultimatum: "You are not having me and her at the same time, understand? I shall go out of this house this minute"[19] to which the only reply she gets being that she can please herself. Enraged beyond limits and unable to tolerate his presence as well as his touch, she leaves the house.

Savitri leaves her home with the notion that, "no one who could not live by herself has a right to live." (120) But there is a conflict within her between the traditional values of ideal womanhood where it is a sin even to talk back to one's husband and disobey him thus, and her new-found individuality. On her way to drown herself into the river she is surprised at her own show of independence: "Am I the same old Savitri or am I someone else? Perhaps this is just a dream. And I must be some one else posing as Savitri because I couldn't have had the courage to talk back to my husband. I have never done it in my life." (115-16)

Saved by Mari the tinker-burglar, she seeks independent existence and rejects all charity. Mari and Ponni along with Savitri go looking for jobs but the search proves to be hopeless. Savitri finds herself untrained for any career. At last in the village temple Sukkur she finds work. The priest offers her a job of menial task. She has to sweep and clean the temple premises for a measure of rice and a pinch of salt.

Once again Savitri finds she has to live in a dark room, the shanty in the temple. She does not last more than a day in the shanty. Her love for her children makes her restless and unhappy and she knows that "it is not possible for her physically and emotionally to be away from children and she returns home."[20]

Her rebellion is short lived. "It is keeping with both her character and cultural heritage."[21] It is a critique on the impact of traditional values and attitudes of life. In coming back to the husband she scorned, she realizes that she is coming to terms with reality—the reality here being society and accepts that.

But this does not mean that she is unaware of her individual entity. She knows that having surrendered to the age-old social structure she has to bear the indignities (Like Ramani's association with Shanta Bai) it heaps on her. She knows that she herself proved to be her own enemy.

Ibsen's Nora asserts her own fundamental right as a human being and an individual when faced with a similar situation. Nora feels she has already fulfilled her duties as a wife and a mother which ceased to be, the moment Helmer suspected her, and now her duty is towards herself. Narayan's Savitri, "an unforgettable picture of the long-suffering Hindu wife," lacks such courage and conviction needed to lead an independent existence. Because Narayan himself admits: "I was concerned with showing the utter dependence of woman on man in our society."[22]

Savitri's failure thus makes one see the depth of an Indian woman's despair as a wife and mother—an eternal victim. That is why "unlike Ibsen's heroine, Narayan doesn't bang the door but has it banged on her and that in the end."[23]

There are thematic interconnections between *The Dark Room* and the short story *Shelter*. In the short story Narayan once again takes up the theme of suffering Indian housewife and her rebellion aginst her husband. An estranged couple part under similar circumstances of *The Dark Room* and meet each other again under a banyan tree quite accidentally while running for shelter during a rainstorm.

The anonymous lady of the story is made of much sterner stuff than Savitri. She refuses to be her husband's toy, to be picked up and thrown away at his whim and fancy. Having ordered her, like Ramani, to get out of his home, he pleads for her to come back now. However, determined as ever, she refuses his offer of temptation. The irony implicit in it is that the very shelter that has been denied her is being offered now. Hence the title *Shelter*. Unlike Savitri's husband, he fails to have a hold on her. She darts out in the rain, back to her life as a social worker to her new-found world of freedom and liberty, where she is recognized as a human being.

Like Savitri, Sampath also tries to rebel but returns just the same to the society. Sampath, the printer of Malgudi is a pompous and flashy person. He reminds one of Nataraj in *The Man-Eater of Malgudi* in some of his ways. An egregious person, he always manipulates people and is able to persuade them to his own way of thinking. He lives on his own terms and doesn't recognize any moral or ethical rules of society. Srinivas, the journalist-editor of the weekly journal of *The Banner*, is amazed and astonished by Sampath in his first meeting itself. To quote an instance, when Srinivas is looking for lodgings, "They come to a costly furnished room upstairs – a very special room as a board hung outside it says "For Ladies & Families only." Srinivas halts before it, finding another excuse: "we are neither ladies nor families. How can we go in?" "These rules are not for us,"[24] the other says. Thus for Sampath no rules do exist.

Sampath prizes his individuality more than anything else. His cherished notion of independent spirit gives rise to the conflict with the outside world. Sampath has to face the cold harsh reality after all his experiences.

It is as it were Sampath plays various roles but is not confined to any one of them. First of all, he is a printer, and it is only as a printer he comes to meet Srinivas, the editor of the weekly, *The Banner*. He declares: "When a customer enters our premises he is, in our view, a guest of the Truth Printing Works. Well, you think *The Banner* is yours. It isn't. I view it as my own." (21) He takes Srinivas completely in hand and dominates him. Srinivas is caught in his spell and when *The Banner* comes to a halt due to the "alleged" strike of Sampath's staff, he involves Srinivas in his movie venture and takes Srinivas along with him to look at the studio, and without the knowledge of Srinivas involves him in the film production.

Sampath piloted him into it so deftly that before he knew where he was he found himself involved in its problems, and what is more, began to feel it his duty "to solve them" (89) which speaks volumes for Sampath's expert manipulation of and influence over people.

Sampath decides to produce an epic film based on the legend of "The Burning of Kama," under the banner of "Sunrise Pictures." He employs Ravi, an artist in the studio, with the recommendation of Srinivas and soon declares that he has found the suitable person to act the role of Goddess Parvathi and introduces his new formal cast as "Shanti, his cousin" who is going to act Parvathi. As Srinivas observes, he seems to get on very well with her and professes to be in love with Shanti regardless of the fact that he is married and has children.

He doesn't have any scruples to mortgage his wife's jewellery to get the cash for his precious film. He says, "we have accumulated a variety of silver things you know." (145) He even goes to the extent of threatening his wife to set up another household.

When Srinivas tells him that he has no right to cause any pain or unhappiness either to his wife or to his children, he makes a mockery of marriage. Soon after, he finds himself in a fix due to the refusal of the actor owing to the non-payment of adequate fee. And it is now that he plays yet another role in life – that of an actor. "I will do Shiva myself. I've been an actor once." (184) Sampath's versatility takes Srinivas's breath away and he looks on Sampath with amazement.

But the shooting of the film is interrupted by Ravi, who, being madly in love with Shanti, tries to snatch her from the arms of Sampath, playing Shiva, and in the process creates chaos and confusion and goes mad. Amidst all this confusion Sampath escapes to Mempi Hills rest-house with Shanti. But after a few weeks he returns to Malgudi and looks up Srinivas and says "I'm still a monogamist. Don't worry." He realizes his real role in life. "I am a printer, when all is said and done." (215, 217) And decides to become invisible for sometime and to start life afresh. He declines the invitation Srinivas extends to him. "I'm going to the railway station. I'll manage there." (219)

Thus Sampath turns out to be an individual with the capacity to play different roles like the printer, film producer and an actor. His is a multi-faceted personality. "With his furious energy, greed, ambition, amorousness and inordinate vanity,"[25] he refuses to be confined to any role and delimits himself. He does not fit into the frame of family and he scorns at all social institutions and violates the sanctity of marriage, and does not recognize any social code. As a matter of fact, he remains a selfish individual to the end though he realizes his isolation from and rebellion against society and returns to its welcoming fold.

Waiting for the Mahatma portrays a young man's struggle to achieve what he wants out of life. In one way, the novel can be said to be a repetition of the earlier theme – romantic love of a boy for a girl, which appears for the first time in *The Bachelor of Arts* through Chandran. But unlike *The Bachelor of Arts, Waiting for the Mahatma* is a prolonged love-story acted against the Gandhian Movement. Like Chandran, Sriram, the protagonist of the novel, falls in love at first sight, with a girl called Bharati, when she comes to collect funds for the Indian Freedom Movement. Soon after Sriram finds her with Gandhi on the dais where he is addressing people and comes to know that Bharati is a disciple of Gandhi. He too decides to follow Gandhi in order to be near Bharati. He meets her and finds out that she is a woman with an ideal, wanting to achieve some meaningfulness out of life. She is vivacious and full of life and it is her vitality which makes Sriram fall in love instantly. In fact he wanted to ask: "How old are you? What caste are you? Where is your horoscope?

Are you free to marry me?"[26] It is noticeable that he has fallen in love against the normal social code. The society to which he belongs allows only arranged marriages. Yet, he still retains enough consciousness to find out the girl's caste and creed. "The Malgudi Portia"[27] makes him aware of beauty, Gandhi and truth. Sriram makes up his mind to become the follower of Gandhi. Bharati tells him that he will have to face Gandhi if he wants to work with them. He does so and is asked to get the permission of his grandmother. He leaves a note for his granny, thinking that she might not understand. He realizes for himself that if one were to live in this camp one has to follow the orders that emanate from the great soul. He comes to understand what people are doing for their own country, discharging their social responsibilities. The process of self-development does not come easily to him. He goes through a process of self-tempering, a rather hard task, for he often finds on checking his own thoughts, that they are still as undesirable as ever. By sheer persistence he learns to spin and feels excited in wearing clothes made by his yarn.

With growing self-confidence Sriram starts spreading Gandhian messages against the foreign rule, in the various villages, but soon he finds life impossible and becomes disheartened by peoples' attitude.

Sriram waits for Gandhi's permission to marry Bharati but does not receive one except for the message asking him to go to jail. But he keeps himself out of jail only to get into the company of Jagdish a terrorist. Sriram enjoys his activities as a terrorist for a while but soon feels that he is losing all sense of direction. Thus his deviation from the accepted norms of society proves to be futile. Sriram learns his lesson—that "terrorism dissociates the revolutionary from the society."[28] He comes to know of Bharati's imprisonment and goes to meet her, but Bharati refuses to meet him.

Meanwhile he is arrested for his terrorist activities and is put in jail. There he feels that he is losing his identity as well as the patriotic aim and even goes to the extent of blaming Bharati for it and wishes that she had not been such an "uncompromising zealot." He thinks of escaping from the jail but gives up the notion in fear that it may make him unworthy of Bharati. He even rejects the proposal of release on "an undertaking to report his movements to police." With the dawn of Independence he is released from jail. He meets Bharati after a long separation and finally wins her hand with Gandhi's blessing.

Raman's love for Daisy in *The Painter of Signs* is a variation of Sriram's love for Bharati. But whereas Sriram and Bharati strive for the same ideal of national freedom, both Raman and Daisy are dedicated to diametrically opposite causes.

Raman proclaims to be a rationalist and wants to be scientific. I want a rational explanation for everything, he says. "Otherwise my mind refused to accept any statement." He was bursting with self-declarations. "I am a rationalist and I don't do anything unless I see some logic in it."[29]

Raman is in the habit of "communicating on two planes – audibly and inaudibly at the same time." Thus he always carries a double dialogue within himself recognizing his own end of the freedom in society. However much he may dislike certain values and goings on in the society, he cannot voice them all which will mean going against the social code. Therefore, "he separates his world into the public and private and is content to allow himself the freedom in the latter which many others demand in the former."[30]

Raman seems to represent neutrality and non-commitment of his society. He prefers to take the easy way out of any crisis – certainly not the way a rationalist shall behave. Further he claims to hate money and sex, the twin evils of modern society, but he is obsessed by the thoughts of both. "Money and sex, he reflected, obsessive thoughts, too much anywhere – literature, magazines, drama, or cinema deal with nothing but sex all the time, but the female figure, watersoaked is enchanting." (15) Being a typical product of his society, he does nothing to expose the evils of the society. He thinks it is none of his business.

For Raman, a signboard stands for some sort of respectability and nobility of intentions. He considers it a means of communication with people and society. But still he cannot use them to expose the evils of society which is contradictory and to tell us of the state of Malgudi. For, Malgudi too changes with the passage of time. And Daisy is a representative of the modernity in Malgudi. It is due to the impact of modernity that there exist double values and contradictions.

Quite frequently Raman becomes aware of the futility of his job and all he does compared with the burning social problems and social evils like population growth and black-marketing. That is why he feels, "I am not doing the right thing in carrying on with this sign-board painting. I took it up because I loved calligraphy; loved letters, their shape and stance and shade. But no one cares for it, no one notices these values." (27) But he does little to change the situation.

Soon he has occasion to change his opinion about his profession, because he comes across Daisy when he is commissioned to paint a signboard for the local Family Planning Centre.

After much trial and tribulation he is able to win the love of Daisy and asks her to marry him. He even goes to the extent of defying his aunt who is against the marriage and who has brought him up and looked after him for thirty years. His aunt symbolizes the society and its norms and she is all against his marriage with Daisy. For, the society in which she exists neither permits nor allows inter-caste marriages. To her mind the idea of Raman's marriage with a girl without any caste or creed is abhorrent. But Raman defies custom and convention and decides to marry Daisy against all odds. In spite of this he has his own reservations against their marriage. And Daisy too is assailed with doubts. She finally decides marriage is not for her and leaves Raman. Raman, disillusioned, decides that if anything his experience helped him to achieve self-realization and independence, and "mounting his cycle he turns toward the Boardless, that solid, real world of sublime souls who minded their own business." (143) Raman also appears in the short story *Hungry Child*, which is a sequel to *The Painter of Signs*. Narayan depicts Raman's state of loneliness a few years after Daisy's departure. Raman, opens "his eyes every morning to a blank day in his bachelor home."[31] He comes across a lost child in Expo 77-78, and escapes into a reverie imagining the little boy to be of Daisy and desires to bring him up as a token of his love for her, but soon the boy spots his parents in the crowd and runs back to them shattering Raman's hopes. He retreats unfulfilled and defeated K.V.S. Murti remarks: "Narayan seems to suggest the ideal that man is to accept failure with sportsman spirit and find identity in his conviction and commitment to 'serve humanity.' Otherwise life becomes miserable."[32]

Margayya of *The Financial Expert* also tries to go against the society but returns, just the same, to the fold of society as Raman does. The novel is a get rich quick fable and the story revolves round Margayya, the ambitious financial expert.

Margayya has his offices under the banyan tree and helps the ignorant villagers to get unlimited loans from the Co-operative Bank defeating the very purpose of the bank.

After the humiliatng encounter with the Secretary of the bank, Margayya feels that the world treats him with contempt because he has no money and becomes obsessed with thoughts of money. Thus he starts battling against the society which insults him because he has no money and wants to acquire an individual status. Meanwhile his son Balu throws away his account book into the Malgudi gutter thereby bringing his business to a halt.

Obsessed with thoughts of money-making, he thinks that "Money alone is important in this world. Everything else will come to us naturally if we have money in our purse."[33] Undecided about further course, he goes on speculating as to which profession he has to take up. He considers selling snuff at first, then of tooth powder, and thinks seriously on taking it up, but finally rejects the idea as unsuitable.

Margayya's love of money passes through different stages before it becomes an incurable obsession with him, At first Margayya wants to acquire wealth so that he can provide well for his family, especially his son Balu whom he dotes on. That is why it is ironic that he should become the cause of his son's degeneration and downfall. But for now he wants money for the sake of his family, his individual needs and existence and to uplift his social status. That he can do everything for his own people, he is convinced of.

Equipped with Dr. Pal's manuscript he goes to Madanlal, a printer from the North and on partnership basis publishes the book retitling it as "Domestic Harmony." The venture proves to be a success and Margayya gains riches as he desires. But even this is not in a right manner. For, knowing the harmful influence the book would have on people, Margayya still publishes it, which in itself means going against the ethical code of the society.

From this point onwards Margayya never looks back. He achieves the social status he craved for. But in doing so he becomes money-minded and loses his perspective.

Narayan's portrayal of Margayya as a banker and then as a publisher is based on a real life model, who became a success. "Many years after finishing *The Financial Expert*, I set eyes on the original . . . he sold prayer books, and calendar pictures depicting the gods, but to the favoured ones he produced from under cover a different category of books, nude picture albums, and the *Kamasutra* in simple language. His banking operation seemed to have crashed and he had turned into a shady book-seller, very much like Margayya of the novel, who invested his last cash in a smutty manuscript."[34]

Having acquired a certain social status he dislikes being called the publisher of "Domestic Harmony," sells his rights to his partner, comes out with a lumpsum and with the help of Dr. Pal sets up his office in Market Road as a money-lender. Margayya's attitude to money becomes clear at this stage of his career. He becomes an expert on money matters and has his own theories to advocate. His obsession with money leads to the neglect of his family responsibilities and obligations.

He announces his spectacular money-making scheme, which attracts hundreds of people, at an astronomical rate of interest. Money flows in and Margayya becomes a financial wizard. In this game of deceit played upon the society Margayya does not seem to realize that "Pursuit of money for money's sake is fraught with grave dangers both for the society and the individual."[35]

And he does not hesitate to rob innocent people of their money. Money becomes his one thought. It affects him both mentally and physically as well and restricts his existence because his house is filled up with bundles of currency and there is hardly any space to move.

Narayan modelled this aspect of Margayya on a real life incident. He explains:

> When I was halfway through the book a financial phenomenon occurred in our province. . . . He promised, fantastic, dazzling scales of interest and dividends on the money entrusted to his care, and he became the only subject of conversation until he crashed and landed in jail. About this time the Margayya of my novel was maturing as a financial expert, and I found the new material just what I needed to blend into the story. So Margayya is actually a combination of two personalities.[36]

Balu demands his share of the ancestral property and Margayya enraged gives him half-a-rupee, half of exactly what he has got from his father. Breaking into tears Balu leaves the place. Troubled very much Margayya goes to visit his son and finds out from his daughter-in-law that Dr. Pal is responsible for Balu's fallen ways and encountering Pal he beats him up. Pal wreaking vengeance spreads the rumour that it is unsafe to leave the money with Margayya. People flock together for their deposits and Margayya's financial empire crumbles overnight and he files an insolvency petition and ends up as a petty money-lender again.

Margayya appears as Jagan in *The Vendor of Sweets* for it is a variation of the same theme – father-son relationship. It is also a man's quest towards self-realization. "It is the life of the individual soul, minutely detailed"[37] – which is central to Narayan's world.

Jagan, is a curious mixture of hypocrisy and sincerity. He is a bundle of contradictions. He professes Gandhism but is a rich man and makes profits and hoards money; propagates the *Nishkamakarma* – detached action, and is very deeply involved with his son Mali; he advises everyone to conquer taste and is himself a sweet vendor. But there are various urges in his character that "are often contradictory, [but] find their own way of fulfilment; and conflicting though they may be between themselves, they exist in apparently wonderful harmony."[38]

And in spite of his profession to be a follower of Gandhi, the *Gita* and the *Upanishads*, he is as much involved in worldly affairs as any other man.

As a follower of Gandhi his whole life is conditioned by Gandhian philosophy. He wears *khaddar*, spins everyday to keep up a vow he had made to Gandhi, who came to Malgudi twenty years ago,[39] wears sandals made of leather of an animal which has died of old age, takes twenty drops of honey in hot water, and has given up the use of sugar and thus preaches a life of simplicity which the cousin finds unable to digest on account of Jagan's hoarding of money.

Thus Jagan, in all his activity is caught in the larger conflict in his individual way. His life oscillates between the ideas of the scriptures and the imperfections he must live.[40] His idea of "Free cash, a sort of immaculate conception, self-generated, arising out of itself and entitled to survive without reference to any tax," is against the very ideals *Gita* seems to preach (non-attachment), which Jagan seems to profess reading aloud from a red-bound copy of the *Gita* which he uses even while in his shop combining his spiritual and worldly affairs. One sees nothing wrong in Jagan's professing the teachings of *Gita.* Hence it is a part and parcel of traditional Malgudi society – a society which sees some religious significance even in the most secular event, and which recognizes no bounds between day-to-day life and religion.[41] But his use of the book is hypocritical, hence his actions contradict what the book professes.

Mali returns from America with Grace, an American-Korean girl whom he introduces as his wife. Jagan's first reaction to what Mali says is typically traditional and Indian and very much in keeping with the society he lives. "Married? When were you married? You didn't tell me. Don't you have to tell your father? Who is she? Any way she looks like a Chinese. Don't you know that one can't marry a Chinese now-a-days? They have invaded our borders." (64) Though himself a rebel in his younger days, he expects his son to obey and oblige him. However he accepts Grace as his daughter-in-law, without realizing that more trouble awaits him. Soon Mali starts talking about a story-writing machine which he is asked to finance. Jagan, however, refuses to finance the project but offers him the management of the shop which Mali scorns. Jagan, deeply hurt retorts that it is the very same business that provided for his American trip.

Thinking that money is the root cause of his troubles he reduces the prices in his shop and preaches the *Gita* to his staff and others who come to join him. It is when he is involved in this crisis that he meets Chinna Dorai, the hair-dyer-sculptor. And through him finds a solution "which is truly in keeping with the 'Spirit' of the teachings of Gandhi and the *Gita*." This also is the starting point for an inner change in him since he stops deceiving society.

To his dismay Jagan learns from Mali that Grace is not his daughter-in-law but only his son's mistress. Shocked to know that his cherished notions of marriage and morals crumbled, he realizes that the time has come for him to end that part of his life (as a householder), and begin a new one. Reliving his past in his mind's eye – his own life as a son, a brother and father – he realizes that at some stage in one's life one must uproot oneself from the accustomed surroundings and disappear so that others may continue in peace. He wishes to live the rest of his life on a different plane. Thus Jagan as one in the society reaffirms and reasserts the continued relevance and permanence of the traditional values of society, by returning to its fold.

A society demands a certain code of conduct from man as a social being. He is an integral part of the intricately woven fabric of life. And as such he has to adhere to the rules and regulations imposed by it. Man is not a loner by instinct and as such has to find his identity in society, as part of the whole. "Man as a concrete individual can be identified only by the sort of role that he plays in the social productivity."[42] If, however, he seeks the meaning of his identity in isolation from his socio-economic obligations, he will only be wandering in a world of glorious illusions. If each man is considered to be an island unto himself, the entire social fabric loses its cohesion and becomes a torn fragment. It is with this realization that Narayan's protagonist returns to the fold of society.

NOTES

1. K.V.S. Murti, *Kohinoor in the Crown: Critical Studies in Indian-English Literature* (New Delhi: Sterling, 1987), p. 125.
2. H.C. Raizada, *The Lotus & The Rose: Indian Fiction in English, 1850-1947* (Aligarh: Aligarh Muslim University, 1974), p. 65.
3. Atma Ram, "Preface," *Perspectives on R.K. Narayan* (Ghaziabad: Vimal, 1981), p. xxvi.
4. H.M. Williams, "Precarious innocence in the novels of R.K. Narayan," *Perspectives on R.K. Narayan*, p. 3.
5. O.P. Mathur, "The West Wind Blows through Malgudi," *Perspectives on R.K. Narayan*, p. 28.
6. *Ibid.*
7. R.K. Narayan, *The Bachelor of Arts* (Mysore: Indian Thought Publications, 1985), p. 70.
8. Shirley Chew, "A Proper Detachment: The Novels of R.K. Narayan," *Readings in Commonwealth Literature* (Oxford: Clarendon, 1973), p. 60.
9. Syd C. Harrex, *The Fire and the Offering: The English Language Novel in India* (Calcutta: Writers Workshop, 1978), vol. II, p. 68.
10. O.P. Mathur, p. 28.
11. *Ibid.*
12. K.R.S rinivasa Iyengar, *Indian Writing in English* (New Delhi, Ster-

ling, 1985), p. 366.
13. R.K. Narayan, *My Dateless Diary* (Delhi: Orient Paperbacks, 1969), p. 171.
14. Syd C. Harrex, p. 89.
15. *Ibid.*, p. 77.
16. K.R. Srinivasa Iyengar, p. 371.
17. Lakshmi Holmstrom, "Women Characters in R.K. Narayan's Novels," *Perspectives on R.K. Narayan*, p. 64.
18. *Ibid.*, pp. 64-65.
19. R.K. Narayan, *The Dark Room* (Mysore: Indian Thought Publications, 1986), p. 111.
20. Meena Shirwadkar, *Image of Woman in the Indo-Anglian Novel* (New Delhi: Sterling, 1979), p. 54.
21. Hari Mohan Prasad, "Shades in the Prism—An Analysis of *The Dark Room*," *Perspectives on R.K. Narayan*, p. 88.
22. Cited by Meena Shirwadkar, p. 133.
23. A.N. Kaul, "R.K. Narayan and the East-West Theme," *Considerations*, ed. Meenakshi Mukherjee (New Delhi: Allied, 1977), p. 48.
24. R.K. Narayan, *Mr. Sampath* (Mysore: Indian Thought Publications, 1985), p. 67.
25. H.M. Williams, p. 9.
26. R.K. Narayan, *Waiting for the Mahatma* (Mysore: Indian Thought Publications, 1984), p. 13.
27. K.R. Srinivasa Iyengar, p. 373.
28. O.P. Bhatnagar, "Love, Non-Violence and Freedom in *Waiting for the Mahatma*," *Literary Endeavour*, vol. III, nos. 3 and 4, Jan.-June 1982, p. 63.
29. R.K. Narayan, *The Painter of Signs* (London: Penguin, 1985), p. 8.
30. William Walsh, *R.K. Narayan: A Critical Appreciation* (New Delhi: Allied, 1983), p. 157.
31. R.K. Narayan, "A Hungry Child," *Malgudi Days* (New Delhi: Allied, 1983), p. 229.
32. K.V.S. Murti, p. 144.
33. R.K. Narayan, *The Financial Expert* (Mysore: Indian Thought Publications, 1984), p. 17.
34. Quoted by Atma Ram in *Perspectives on R.K. Narayan*, pp. xvii-xviii.
35. Suresh Nath, "*The Financial Expert*; An Appraisal," *Perspectives on R.K. Narayan*, p. 113.
36. Cited by Atma Ram in *Perspectives*, pp. xvi-xvii.
37. Bruce F. Macdonald, "Humanity and Aesthetic Order in *The Vendor of Sweets*," *Perspectives on R.K. Narayan*, p. 154.
38. Jayant K. Biswal, p. 65.

39. R.K. Narayan, *The Vendor of Sweets* (Mysore: Indian Thought Publications, 1981), p. 15.
40. Bruce F. Macdonald, p. 115.
41. Raji Narasimhan, "The Inward Glance of Narayan," *R.K. Narayan – A Critical Spectrum* (Meerut: Shalabh, 1983), p. 72.
42. Bhagwat S. Goyal, "Thematic Patterns in the Early Novels of R.K. Narayan," *R.K. Narayan: A Critical Spectrum*, p. 20.

In My End is My Beginning:

The Theme of Renunciation in *The Bachelor of Arts, The Dark Room, The English Teacher, The Guide, Waiting for the Mahatma, The Vendor of Sweets, A Tiger for Malgudi* and *The World of Nagaraj*

There is hardly a society or religion, ancient or modern, which does not honour or cherish the memory of one who has given up his all for the sake of others or to strive for a noble goal. But perhaps it is only in India that renunciation has been given a specially exalted place in the Hindu view of life and accommodated in the system of values developed in this country. Respect for this ideal has percolated to all levels of the society cutting across all social distinctions of class and caste. It has been so deeply embedded in the Indian consciousness for centuries that it has been continuously an operative force in everyday life, both private and public. Such is the veneration, the man of renunciation – ascetic or *sanyasi* – enjoys in our society, that he finds an important place even in the realm of active politics, which is notorious for its restless struggle for temporal power. It is very characteristic of the Indian temper that Mahatma Gandhi should be the Father of the Nation. That is why Meenakshi Mukherjee says: "Renunciation has always been an Indian ideal, be it renunciation of worldly goods and possessions or the renunciation of selfish motives, passions and emotional bondage."[1]

Asramadharma, which is an important part of the traditional Hindu view of life, takes a comprehensive view of human nature and human needs. It offers a pattern of organizing one's life which aims at being physically, psychologically and spiritually satisfactory. As said already in the previous chapters, Hindu tradition envisages four *asramas* or stages in one's life of which *sanyasa*, the stage of renunciation is the fourth and final. The other three stages are *brahmacharya* (the stage of the young celibate student), *garhasthya* (the stage of the householder) and *vanaprasthya* (the stage of the forest-dweller or hermit), in the order of succession. Each stage meets the needs of the individual belonging to it. Therefore, they are not set up in opposition to one another. One is expected to move on, graduating as it were, from one stage to another after he has fulfilled the obligations of the stage he has been in. Explaining the rationale behind the four *asramas*, Radhakrishnan says: "Every state is necessary and insofar as it is necessary it is good. . . . We should pass from stage to stage gradually."[2]

The Bachelor of Arts is one of the early novels of R.K. Narayan. It has for its theme the growth of a young man towards emotional maturity and stability, which involves his going through an emotional crisis. Chandran is rudely awakened when he falls in love at first sight. Part Two of the novel deals with this experience of his life, which lies behind his subsequent attempt at becoming a *sanyasi*.

Part Three of the novel depicts Chandran's disappointment in love and the resulting bitterness and frustration. His donning the robes of a *sanyasi* and becoming a mendicant wanderer for a few months is all part of this experience. And it is here that the theme of renunciation is brought in quite explicitly. But the *sanyasi* motif is already introduced into the novel in Part One though with seeming casualness, through an amusing episode. Chandran's mother is disturbed by the fact that every morning all the flowers from her garden intended for worship are being stolen by someone. It becomes obligatory for his father to do something about it. Chandran too, in spite of his determination to devote himself to his studies, volunteers to join his father and his brother in the adventure of catching the flower thief. The novelist describes the episode in mock-heroic tones. On the first day they are outwitted by the culprit, the next day when they catch hold of him, they are shocked and surprised to find that he is no ordinary thief but a *sanyasi*, an ascetic. The mother, noticing the ochre-coloured robes lets him leave unharmed.

This episode brings out the veneration as well as awe in which a saffron robed is generally held in Indian society. The spontaneous response of Chandran's parents to the flower thief as soon as his identity is discovered is an indication of this conventional attitude to the holy man. This episode also reveals the changing attitude of the educated younger generation towards such men. Chandran's cynical attitude is fairly representative of that of his generation. It is one of the ironies of his life that this very young man, under the stress of an emotional crisis, impulsively takes to the robes of a *sanyasi* and wanders as a mendicant for some months. This fact indicates the hold that the *sanyasi* ideal has on the minds of the people of this country, in spite of changing generations.

Alighting at Madras, Chandran avoids going to his uncle's place where he is expected to stay. Instead he chooses to go to a hotel, as he has no clear idea as to what his future course is. At the hotel he makes the acquaintance of one Kailas, a dissolute person, who appoints himself as his companion and guide in the strange city. Chandran, terrified when Kailas takes him to a prostitute's house, manages to escape and flee. Several streets away he sits down exhausted on a pavement and broods over his recent experiences. It is at this stage that he decides to become a *sanyasi.* The novelist analyzes, clearly though briefly, the condition of Chandran's mind when he makes this resolve, to enable us to understand what makes him think of a life of renunciation. He does not understand the significance and purpose of the life of a *sanyasi.* For him it is an alternative to committing suicide. It amounts to an escape from all reason and responsibility. Effectively, in resorting to it he shirks from the problems of his life and finding solutions for them. It is the bitterness of disappointment and helpless anger at powers beyond his control that drives him to this hasty step of going away from his loved ones, in the name of renunciation. It serves for a time to gratify his desire to take revenge on all those people, institutions and beliefs which are responsible for his frustration in love. It is somewhat ironical that one who had scoffed at the flower-gathering *sanyasi* should himself take to the garb of one. His renunciation seems to be a revenge on society, and circumstances.

Chapter twelve of the novel gives a detailed, objective and dispassionate account of Chandran's wanderings as an ascetic, the kind of life he leads, the reaction of the people he comes across, and his eventual return to his home and people. It also incidentally draws attention to the esteem, respect and reverence that a man of renunciation, an ascetic, commands in Indian society, so that all and sundry are tempted to don ochre-robes. Having wandered for about eight months, Chandran reaches on a hot afternoon, a small village called Koppal where he rests for more than a day. His stay in the remote village marks a turning point in his career as an ascetic. For, he comes to the realization that during all these days of his wandering as a mendicant, he has been "a cad, a fraud, and a confidence trickster"[3] because of his disguise as a *sanyasi.* Having realized it, he decides to discard his counterfeit robes and return home to a normal life.

The situation that Chandran finds himself in is similar to that of Raju the protagonist of the much later novel of Narayan *The Guide*. Raju too finds himself in a remote village where he is mistaken for a holy man by a credulous rustic who unwittingly imposes that role on him. In the case of Chandran, the villagers do not impart any holiness to him, as his ochre dress carries with it ideals of holiness as well as renunciation. As he himself realizes before long, they in their naivety and credulousness take his external appearance for the truth about him, and make themselves liable to be cheated.

Chandran's reaction to the villagers' request that he should stay with them for some more days is that of any average man in his situation. He is "touched" by it, and feels a little flattered, as no one had valued his presence so highly till now, though he was treated with consideration everywhere. The novelist shrewdly points out that Chandran is impressed by their worshipful attention, and sits in the correct pose of a man in meditation, "cross-legged and with his eyes shut." (110) Here he almost anticipates Raju of *The Guide*. Fortunately for him, this self-indulgent mood does not last long, and when he opens his eyes at nightfall, the several gifts left by the villagers send a spear through his heart and make him unhappy. He realizes that they are gifts for a counterfeit exchange. His conscience pricks him, for he has practised a fraud on the gullible and credulous villagers. He feels abashed. As an indication of this realization, he moves away from the gifts, and even blows out the lantern as not deserving the light. This significant gesture marks another turning point in his life. He learns that self-deception of the kind he has indulged in is no answer to the problems of his life. He takes an important step towards maturity when he realizes the futility of deception. That very moment he wisely decides to leave the village and also shed once and for all the mask of *sanyasi.* It may be noted in passing that Chandran discards the *sanyasi's* garb for the very reason that Raju the guide prefers to continue it.

It is ironical that Chandran's counterfeit garb of ochre helps him to go away from Koppal and reach a place from which he can send a telegraphic message to his parents about his return. When he throws away finally his ochre robes and has a refreshing bath he feels "resurrected. (114) With his return home from temporary, immature and illconceived *sanyasa,* Part Three of the novel ends. The curtain is drawn once and for all on his career as a wandering *sanyasi,* and there is no mention of it again by anyone including Chandran himself except when he recounts to his friend Mohan his experiences during his absence from home.

Part Four of the novel tells the rest of Chandran's story. He returns home sober and steady, free from some of the illusions he entertained about himself and life. In due course he is settled happily as a married man. It is his wife Susila, chosen by his parents in the conventional way to be his bride, and not at all renunciation, that absorbs all his attention.

The urge to renounce was only a passing phase in Chandran's life. It was a gesture of helplessness and desperation, motivated, not by a desire for non-attachment but paradoxically by excessive attachment. Therefore, it had to be a short-lived one. However, his experiences as a *sanyasi* are not in vain. They help him to grow emotionally mature and stable. *The Dark Room* which comes chronologically after *The Bachelor of Arts* presents another instance of premature and therefore vain attempts at renunciation. Savitri, the protagonist, is driven by the pressure of her domestic circumstances to think of renouncing her family, husband and children. It takes the form of her attempt to go away from them. She too fails like Chandran, though for different reasons. Between *The Bachelor of Arts* and *The Dark Room* the theme of renunciation has far greater importance in the former novel, although in either novel it is only a secondary theme.

The Dark Room is Narayan's "First exploration of married life"[4] and tells the story of discord in married life of Savitri and Ramani, which remains unresolved. The brief conversation between Savitri and Ramani over their son Babu's headache, on the opening page of the novel, gives a reliable example of the husband-wife relationship and the humiliation Savitri has been subjected to. The *Navaratri* dolls festival symbolizes Savitri's predicament, her status at home, her plight and helplessness. In times of great weariness and misery all that she can do is to seek her solace in the dark room of her house. All the same her conventional upbringing being what it is, she respects, fears, admires, and loves her husband and is grateful to him for whatever condescending attention he shows her. She is deeply attached to her three children, who in fact are the chief source of her happiness. Her life is thus ordered and arranged around her family, which virtually forms her world. Acceptance of one's lot rather than protest or revolt has been ingrained in her and she has been taught to find her happiness in it, although it might be irksome to her.

Thus a sort of surface tranquillity is maintained in Savitri's life until it is disturbed by Ramani's affairs with his office assistant Shanta Bai. It takes time before Savitri can bring herself to tell her husband firmly, "This sort of thing has to stop, understand?"[5] Soon it becomes an hysterical outburst, all her pent up emotions trying to find release. It is very nearly midnight when she walks out of the house, and makes her way to the river Sarayu, her mind numb. Conflicting and confusing thoughts and feelings about her husband, his mistress, and herself, her parents, brother and sister, and above all her children and their future, although she is supposed to have left them for good, crowd her mind. Her attempt to commit suicide by drowning herself in the river is foiled by Mari, a tinker-burglar, who rescues her. Ignorant as well as inexperienced in the ways of the world she accepts the ascetic kind of life and even feels happy that this step opens for her a new life. It is at this stage that her thoughts tend towards renunciation of all family ties, bonds, and attachments:

> What more fitting life, she thought, could one choose than serving a God in his shrine? A half measure of rice was more than what she deserved, she felt . . . she would dedicate her life to the service of god, numb her senses and memory, forget the world, and spend the

rest of her years thus and die. No husband, home or children. (170)

In spite of these pious and noble thoughts, she just cannot take her mind away from her children – Babu, Sumati and Kamala and worries about their future. Even though she reminds herself that this yearning for the children is "a foolish, dragging attachment" and that "one ought to do one's duty and then drift away" (112) her mind hovers about them. Her first and spontaneous prayer is for her children. But, determined apparently to continue in her life of ascetic denial and to conquer all fear, she prefers to sleep all by herself in the temple.

The single night Savitri spends in the darkness of the temple is enough to make her realize that she has been attempting something – revolt against convention and society and freedom from all attachments – which is impossible for her. Apart from everything there terrifying her and driving it home to her that she cannot exist without support, she grows homesick. A nostalgia for children, home and accustomed comforts seize her. No wonder that she decides to return home accepting her defeat and inability to fight.

While in *The Bachelor of Arts* and *The Dark Room*, one aspect of renunciation is presented in terms of fiction, in *The English Teacher* which succeeds them chronologically, another facet of renunciation is presented. In *The Bachelor of Arts* and *The Dark Room* it is premature and ineffective renunciation which is dealt with. But in *The English Teacher*, the theme of renunciation is not explicitly stated with reference to Krishnan, the protagonist. Instead it is insinuated into the novel through his character in the second half of the novel. In *The English Teacher*, husband-wife relationship is presented on two planes – "domestic and spiritual."[6] The story falls conveniently into two almost equal parts. The first part, which may be said to end with chapter three, is chiefly concerned with the domestic life of Krishnan and Susila, their all too short bliss of married life of three years which ends with the untimely and unexpected death of Susila from typhoid. The second part comprising the remaining five chapters of the novel, depicts Krishnan's bereavement, his experience of disconsolation and loneliness, his struggle to overcome his grief and to come to terms with his wife's death, and his spiritual development as a consequence of his psychic contact with the spirit of his wife. Thus certain events which occur in Krishnan's life make him accept life with its joys and sorrows alike. As Venkatachari puts it, "It is not resignation that connotes passivity, but acceptance that characterises the attitude which the Narayan hero comes to adopt in the face of experience."[7]

Krishnan's undiluted happiness in family life proves short-lived and comes to an unexpected, and abrupt close with Susila's death by typhoid. Having experienced the bliss of married life just for a few years, he is rudely jolted out of it by her death. During their trip to the Lawley Extension on a certain day to inspect a house, she contacts the fatal illness and after a few weeks of untold suffering she dies.

With Susila's death the first part of the narrative ends. The rest of the novel, comprising the second part traces Krishnan's grief, his dejection, his sense of utter loneliness and desolation, his vain efforts to come to terms with the absence of his wife, and finally his recovery, psychological and spiritual, thanks to his fortunate psychic contact with the disembodied spirit of his wife. She helps him in his spiritual development, and in discovering his vocation. It is during this phase of Krishnan's experience that the theme of renunciation enters the novel and becomes operative.

The days that follow Susila's death become blank and empty for Krishnan. His daughter Leela becomes his sole and only source of relief and consolation. Of course, the child sustains him and saves him from utter collapse. He, in his turn, becomes excessively and obsessively attached to her. And thus he hopes to escape from his oppressive grief. He refuses to marry again or to send his child with her grand-parents, and instead plays both father and mother to her. He rather stubbornly refuses to accept his mother's help and derives a "peculiar satisfaction" in the resolve to "live it out alone, face the problems alone, never drag in another to do the job"[8] for him. How much his sensibilities become blunted under the impact of his bereavement is revealed by the following passage:

> Condolences, words of courage, lamentations, or assurances, were all the same. I had become a sort of professional receptacle of condolence and sympathy, and I had received them in such quantity these months that they had ceased to move me or mean anything. Death and its associates, after the initial shock, produce callousness. (109)

In his present state of mind all hopes and expectations appear illusory. Though the shock of Susila's death gradually wears out, he is still possessed by a weariness, "a terrible fatigue and inertia" (118) which makes him indifferent to his work at the college. Nothing seems to interest him except his daughter.

Into these days of darkness comes rather unexpectedly a ray of hope in the form of a letter from a total stranger whom he has neither seen nor heard of. In this letter he conveys to Krishnan the message he has received from the spirit of Susila. At first Krishnan is baffled to read the message. But slowly he understands it and is seized with elation. Soon he gets in touch with the person who conveyed the message to him. Thus he makes a profound contact in life, which marks a decisive turning point in his life because it enables Krishnan to come into psychic contact, and communication with the spirit of Susila, who gradually wears him away from his crippling and destructive grief and leads him towards his spiritual development. She helps to set his house in order and restore his faith in life. This process of self-development takes place over a period of time and involves much anxiety, suspense and disappointment before he meets with success. It is under the salutary influence of her spirit that he develops a healthy attitude to both life and death, and acquires peace of mind and a sense of freedom from excessive attachments. His self-development which results from this contact, does not come about easily or at once. However, it must be admitted that over a period of time Krishnan develops, with her active help and ministry, a philosophic calm, a balanced and positive attitude of mind which enables him to look at both life and death without regret and in a spirit of gratitude.

As an indication of his changing attitude to himself and his life, Krishnan spends a great deal of his time watching the children of his daughter's school either at play or at listening to the stories narrated to them by their headmaster. It has the immediate effect of mitigating his oppressive sense of loneliness. And his momentous decision to give up his lectureship in the college and devote himself to the education of children is made possible partly because of Krishnan's friendship with the headmaster of the school for children to which Leela is sent. What is relevant to the present discussion is the fact that the headmaster deliberately chooses to renounce a life of material comfort and prosperity to live a life of simplicity, if not poverty, much against the wishes and expectation of his wife. Subsequently he gives up his family and familial ties too. The kind of renunciation he intentionally practises serves to clarify by contrast that which Krishnan happens to adopt in his life.

The headmaster is an extraordinary character in the world of Malgudi. A mendicant hermit-astrologer's detailed prediction of the course of his life including the precise time of his death, clinched the issue, and he left family and home, voluntarily giving up his claims to his share of his paternal property, to the disappointment and chagrin of his wife. At great risk to his domestic happiness and harmony he sets up the school for children. Since then the school and the fascinating and joyous world of children have been everything to him. Krishnan is astonished to find him talk casually of his own death which according to the prediction is to take place within a few hours "as if he were moving to the next street." (184)

All said, the headmaster, human as he is, is not an entirely non-attached man. Inspite of his claims he makes about his indifference to his predicted death, he is indeed disturbed by the prospect, as he himself gladly confesses to Krishnan: "You have no idea how it has been weighing me down all these years, in spite of what I might have felt and said; it was like having cancer and knowing fully when you would be finished." (190) He is indeed glad that he is not after all dead. Perhaps it is again very human that he should feel very happy about his wife's lamentations over his supposed death. One cannot avoid the suspicion that he finds in the school an escape from his impossible wife and children. His supposed death only strengthens his desire to renounce his family. To the crowd assembled near his house he says: "I tell you, friends, no more of this wife and family for me. You may treat me as dead or as one who has taken *Sanyasa Ashrama*." (192) His devotion to an impersonal and noble ideal makes him turn away resolutely from his family, which has been a hindrance to him. Had his wife been more understanding and helpful, he would certainly not have thought of renunciation. Once he renounces his wife and children, he does not retrace his steps.

Krishnan evolves at the end into a man who is mentally, morally and spiritually mature. He chooses voluntarily to live a quiet and simple life of untenacious but purposeful action, characteristic of a man of renunciation. It is also true that he would be the first to repudiate the use of such a sanctified term as renunciation with reference to what he does. Never does he think of renouncing the world or family in the spirit of a *sanyasi*. He continues to retain his familial attachments and obligations. What he needs most, seeks and finds in considerable measure, is an ungrudging attitude of acceptance of both pain and pleasure, freedom from excessive attachment, and serenity of mind. To call him a *sthitaprajna* is too much, but he moves and grows in that direction. In comparison with this achievement, whatever sacrifice or renunciation is involved in his leaving the college appears to be secondary. He resolved on this step because it becomes an intolerable interference with the harmony in life he has been seeking. He makes his exit without any fuss or dramatics. While the whole of his conversation with Principal Brown at the time of his resignation is relevant to explain the tenor of his thinking, his brief reply to the several speeches at the farewell party expresses succinctly how he estimates himself and views his exit from the college. His speech is full of humility and wisdom. (211)

By the end of the novel, Krishnan is able to look upon life and death with considerable equanimity and be able to say spontaneously that he is "Grateful to Life and Death." The concluding sentence of the novel sums up the inner growth and development of Krishnan.

In *The Guide*, Narayan explores, through his comic imagination another aspect of renunciation. He looks at the theme from a different and somewhat unusual angle. Raju, the protagonist of the novel, is a person of doubtful honesty and reputation. Thoughts of renunciation are alien to him. He does not have a family of his own to think of renouncing it. He prefers to live from moment to moment, with little forethought, hardly ever considering the possible consequences of his actions and choices. Such a person finds himself thrust into the role of a *sanyasi* by certain wholly unexpected circumstances. Raju has to live, in the words of Narayan, a life of "enforced Sainthood."[9] The novel studies the consequences of it and tells the story of the apparently "incredible progress of a rogue into a saintly redeemer."[10]

In Narayan's *The Bachelor of Arts*, as seen already, there is only an incidental, brief and indirect exposure of the false ascetic. In *The Guide*, Raju, who is the chief focus of attention, happens to be a fake *sanyasi*, at least for the greater part of the novel. But there is little of satirical exposure of the counterfeit holy man in the novel. For, Narayan's approach to this theme is not satirical at all, and satire proper has only a small place in the total corpus of his fiction. In the present novel he looks at the phenomenon of the false ascetic from two angles: the ascetic as a private individual living his own life, and the ascetic as a public figure who influences the community of people which entertains him, and in turn gets influenced by it.

Like most of Narayan's protagonists, Raju too is one of the ordinary and average. By the time he shows up at the ancient riverside shrine in the obscure village Mangala, at which point in fact the novel begins, he has had already, as his subsequent narrative reveals, an eventful past which includes his playing several parts and roles in the drama of his life.

The novel reveals that it is the natural and understandable desire of Raju, who has just been released from jail, to hide himself from all those who have known him, and to live at least for sometime in anonymity, that brings him to the village Mangala. When Velan happens to meet him sitting on a stone slab in the old temple, Raju has been there all alone for a whole day. It is welcome disturbance to him who has been accustomed to plenty of company. Neither he nor Velan ever knows that this chance meeting is going to prove momentous in their lives. For, it is this meeting that tricks Raju into the role of a Swami. From the very moment of their meeting Velan gazes at Raju "reverentially."[11] When Raju asks him to sit, he chooses a seat two steps below the slab on which the other sits as a mark of respect. Velan studies Raju's face with such "intense respect" that the other strokes "his chin thoughtfully to make sure that an apostolic beard [has] not suddenly grown there." (6) Thus even before Velan explains to Raju his particular problem and seeks his help and guidance, he unwittingly assigns him the mask he has to wear and the role he has to play thereafter.

Raju feels disconcerted by the devotion with which the villager looks at his face and tries to fumble, "I am not so great as you imagine." (8) But before he can get these words out of his mouth, Velan tells him of his pressing domestic problem which has eluded solution till then. Ironically Raju's old habit of affording guidance to others when he was a tourist guide, asserts itself just at the moment he wants to be frank and honest. This situation is revealing because, though he is not the kind to tell the truth straightaway, it shows that Raju is not a deliberate and calculating liar who without any qualms of conscience indulges in falsehood only to make personal gains. By sheer force of habit he asks Velan to tell him what his problem is. The narrator aptly remarks: "It was in his nature to get involved in other people's interests and activities." (8) Raju is a vibrant and adaptable personality which relishes the opportunity for displaying his theatrical talents. His commonsense is enough to make him guess the nature of Velan's domestic problem. When Velan bows humbly to touch his feet for having offered to speak to his recalcitrant step-sister, Raju of course recoils sincerely at the attempt, but permits himself to utter an impressive platitude: "God alone is entitled to such a prostration. He will destroy us if we attempt to usurp His rights."[15]

Ever since Raju is believed to have worked a miraculous change in Velan's obstinate step-sister, his circle of devotees gradually widens. The special and respectful attention the villagers show him makes him "feel uncomfortable," and he even wonders "if he could devise some means of escape from their company." (28) This is an important revelation as it shows that for all his vanity and egocentricity, Raju has not yet become wholly insensitive. It would take some more time for him to feel completely at home in the role of *sanyasi* he is to play.

In fact it becomes an established practice of Velan and his fellow-villagers to bring food for Raju everyday. And he is grateful to them for this supply and prays he is not an unadulterated impostor and fraud and that he is at least honest to himself regarding his intentions and motives. Deliberate deceit is far from his mind. He has to stay on in Mangala and keep up the role into which he has been unwittingly tricked for his survival. Lakshmi Holmstrom has aptly remarked: "Raju accepts the role of *sanyasi* for the reason that Chandran in *The Bachelor of Arts* rejects it: it provides him with an adequate living for which he doles out counterfeit form of spiritual guidance."[12] Once the decision is taken, Raju starts playing the role of holy man in right earnest.

Established seemingly securely as Swami, Raju loses all count of time. He is now so sure of himself that he plays his role with superb gusto, self-assurance and success: "His beard now caressed his chest, his hair covered his back, and around his neck he wore a necklace of prayer beads. His eyes shone with softness and compassion, the light of wisdom emanated from them." (79)

There seems to be no end to the gifts he receives from the villagers who have to bring them to their Swami. He lives in this apparent security and peace until the seasonal rains begin to fail causing considerable damage to the crops and cattle. However, Raju remains unconcerned. He tells himself: "The village people do not know how to remain peaceful. They are becoming more and more agitated. At this rate, I think I'll look for a new place." (84) His reaction to this development shows him most self-centred, unfeeling, callous as well as complacent, and brings him very close to losing all our sympathy for him. The details of the fight and the prospect of another fight soon, as reported to him by Velan's semimoron of a brother bothers him and he worries that his identity might be disclosed. It is this fear that rouses Raju suddenly into activity and makes him think of doing something to avert such a possibility. First he asks the dull-witted young man to tell the villagers that he does not want them to fight. Then in his eagerness he declares rather impulsively: "Tell your brother, immediately, wherever he may be, that unless they are good I'll never eat. . . . I'll not eat till they are good." (87) He has no thought of its possible consequences.

It fits into the pattern of Raju's life that the final episode of his life, namely his fasting, also originates in an "insignificant casual manner."[13] Velan's brother, who is utterly confused by the manner in which Raju handles him, reports to the village assembly an entirely different version of the Swami's message. He blabbers under threatening interrogation: "The Swami, the Swami doesn't want food any more. Don't take any food to him . . . because . . . it doesn't rain." (88-89) As could be expected, the villagers have absolutely no doubt that should their Swami fast it would certainly rain. Their simple and blind faith in the superior wisdom and powers of their Swami is buttressed by the tradition of folklore they have inherited and the stories and legends they have heard. In Raju they now see such a redeemer, whose presence in their midst makes Mangala a blessed place. "He is like Mahatma. . . . If he fasts there will be rain. Out of his love for us he is undertaking it." (90) Thus the confused and distorted report of Raju's message ironically has the effect of making them forget at once their troubles, bickerings, and fights. And all of them as one man go to him to express their gratitude: "Let us all go and pay our respects to Swami, our Saviour." (91)

In the best words that they can muster the villagers speak with feeling and devotion and express their gratitude to Raju for the penance he has undertaken to save them, just when Raju is thinking of the food they would bring him, especially the ingredients for making *bonda.* Though puzzled by their praise and exasperated when they line up to touch his feet he feels that it is but right that they should touch his feet. This indeed marks the height of his self-deception, his egotistical folly, and the peak of his hubris. Therefore a fall is inevitable.

Even when he decides to confess to Velan all about his notorious past, the urge to escape the ordeal of fasting is as strong as the desire to reveal the truth about himself. From this point onwards the motives behind Raju's confession have begun to break the barriers of pretension and duplicity. The process of his transformation has begun.

Raju prefaces his narration to Velan with these words: "I am not a saint, Velan, I'm 'just an ordinary human being like anyone else. Listen to my story. You will know it yourself." (99) He tells the story at one stretch, from his birth to his emergence from the gates of the prison. He does not omit a single detail, nor does he exaggerate or over-emphasize anywhere his lapses or his sinfulness. In this process, he does make an attempt to see himself for what he is insofar as it is possible for him, compressing into these hours of confession, introspection, self-analysis and self-criticism which he ought to have carried out at least since he came to Mangala. To Velan, Raju is, as Lakshmi Holmstrom points out, "already outside the orbit of normal moral standards which are applicable to ordinary man."[14] It is as if listening to Raju's story has only increased his respect for him and redoubled his already strong faith in him.

Raju is now completely cornered and has no choice but to fast. Velan who, at first, unwittingly imposed the role of a holy man on him, now again unknowingly and in all reverence binds him to his supposed vow of fasting and insists on his fulfilling himself. It will be found ultimately that it is he and his fellow villagers that work a miracle, namely the transformaltion of Raju.

Thus begins the final phase of Raju's life. The first few days of the fast he manages well enough as he is able to snatch some morsels of food secretly. From the fourth day onwards he has no food left. He is tormented by hunger as well as disturbing thoughts. In his impotent anger, he even wishes that Velan might be caught by the crocodile while crossing the river.

In spite of such morbid and fantastic thoughts Raju is deeply touched by the enormous trouble Velan is taking day and night to make his penance a success. Velan's devotion to him and his implicit faith in him brings a sudden transformation in him and Raju derives a peculiar enjoyment from fasting. At the back of his mind is the thought: "This enjoyment is something Velan cannot take away from me." (214) The novelist hints in this context that Raju has not fully risen above his ego. After all the ego is not so easily conquered.

The fast makes Raju the centre of public attraction and attention. This happens when he has begun to lose interest in his showmanship and become indifferent to the ever-increasing crowds.

Declining the repeated appeals from the Government to end his fast, Raju continues it despite his precarious physical condition. On the eleventh day, helped by Velan and another, he reaches the river bed. As he mutters his prayer with closed eyes, the sun rises illuminating the surroundings. Raju opens his eyes, looks about and tells Velan: "Velan, its raining in the hills. I can feel it coming up under my feet, up my legs." (227) With these words he sags down, and in all probability dies.[15]

Whether Raju's penance really brings down rains or not is an irrelevant question. Narayan intentionally leaves it ambiguous. It is quite possible that Raju's feeling that it is raining in the hills is not anything more than a deceptive impression caused by his fasting. But the really important question is, what happens to Raju when he is called upon to fast by a community of rustics who have unquestioned faith in him. The sheer force of their simple trust in him helps to bring out his latent potentialities for rising above himself for others' sake and for selfless action, apart from his own wish to rise to the occasion. The entire narrative strategy of the novel is directed towards this end.

If in *The Guide* Narayan tells us the story of "enforced sainthood," in *Waiting for the Mahatma* he portrays the "ideal of sainthood," and presents another aspect of renunciation – taking the risk of introducing Mahatma Gandhi as a character. Though the Mahatma's humanity and compassion are stressed, he is seen as the living embodiment of the very essence of renunciation. Living in the midst of people whose joys and sorrows he shares, he also cultivates at the same time an inner calm.

The Mahatma belongs to the class of the extraordinary while the average and ordinary people are Narayan's forte. And it is in *Waiting for the Mahatma* we do come across someone who has actually succeeded in achieving the ideal of renunciation. The Mahatma himself emerges as a saint who sympathizes and remonstrates with ordinary men true to the definition of *Jivan mukta.* This is the state in which a saint has ceased to have any desires. He may be engaged in doing all kinds of actions but he remains altogether unaffected by them internally.

Narayan has portrayed Gandhi in this novel as he has seen him in his own life – as a perfect saint. Gandhi accepts a cruel death to redeem the suffering of others. Gandhi is not the central character in the story but his influence on major characters like Sriram and Bharati is all-embracing.

Narayan's treatment of Gandhi is conventional and though idealized, is realistic. Nothing is added to the accepted portrait of Gandhi. He is seen to be a living symbol of traditional Indian asceticism. A real *sanyasi* who lives and thinks for the others, for the good of the society and community, the ultimate of the final stage of Hindu way of life – *sanyasasrama.*

The ideal of asceticism is the life-force of Gandhiji. He is the living embodiment of the ideal of renunciation. He devotes his entire life for the well-being of his country and his people. Being dedicated to the cause, he tours the villages on foot and talks to the villagers about spinning, non-violence and religion. He trudges his way through mud and slush, but always earnestly and with immense happiness. During the Hindu-Muslim riots in Calcutta and East Bengal, he walks through the swamps, floods and fields with determination. He makes way through the angry, aggressive crowds threatening to murder him. He approaches them and imparts a message of love and non-violence which makes them fall at his feet. He is the "Mahatma."

The novel gives us a clear picture of Gandhian philosophy and ideals which are in perfect harmony with his personality and character. When he first arrives in Malgudi, the Mahatma describes the saintly philosophy of his life – "we have a system of our own to follow; that's *Ram Dhun*; spinning on the *Charkha* and the practice of absolute truth and Non-Violence."[16] Gandhi explains to the people his creed of non-violence and how it can be practised in daily life: "It is a perfectly simple procedure provided you have faith in it. If you watch yourself you will avoid all actions, big or small, and all thoughts, however obscure, which may cause pain to one another. If you are watchful it comes to you naturally. When someone has wronged you or has done something which appears to you to be evil, just pray for the destruction of that evil. Cultivate an extra affection for the person and you will find that you are able to bring about a change in him." (18) It is not the ordinary human being speaking thus; it is the ever kind and affectionate "Mahatma."

Regarding violence, which is painful to him, the Mahatma says: "Before you aspire to drive the British from this country, you must drive every vestige of violence from your system. Remember that it is not going to be a fight with sticks and knives or guns but only with love. Until you are sure you have an overpowering love at heart for your enemy, don't think of driving him out. You must gradually forget the term "Enemy." (51-52) This is the attitude of an ascetic – one who regards humanity as a whole; a true saint or *sanyasi*. Such a one does not have enemies in the real sense of the word, as he looks upon the world with detachment.

Gandhi, however, has this to say to Sriram, before he leaves Malgudi: "Spin and read *Bhagavad Gita,* and utter *Ram Nam* continuously, and then you will know what to do in life." (64) He takes an active interest in Sriram's activities and guides him through his letter, "your work should be a matter of inner faith. It cannot depend upon what you see or understand. Your conscience should be your guide in every action. Consult it and you won't do wrong." (86)

His humanism is above the narrow distinctions of caste, creed or religion as Bharati tells us, "Bapuji forbade us to refer to anyone in terms of religion as Muslims, Hindu, or Sikhs, but just a human being." And it is this essential quality that makes for the great popularity he enjoyed, which is something unique. No other political or religious leader in any part of the world has ever made place for himself in the hearts of the people around him.

Narayan portrays Gandhi as the very essence of renunciation. He retains the spiritual serenity of a saint throughout the novel. Narayan presents him as a real ascetic, a true *sanyasi* – as a perfect holyman and *guru*. He is held in such high reverence by the people and possesses such magnetism that even the angry, excited and violent mobs fail to do him any harm having backed down before him. Even the criminals utter his name with great piety. To cite an instance, Sriram has a row with one of the fellow-prisoners and says,

> "If I had been out I'd have made you prostrate yourself before Mahatmaji and confess your crimes."
>
> At the mention of the Mahatma, the other brought his palms together and said, "Don't drag his name in here; that great saint." (134)

Waiting for the Mahatma, comments Haydn Moore Williams, the Australian critic, "With its fundamentally serious, heroic theme – the freedom struggle and its outcome – is Narayan's tribute to Mahatma Gandhi, both eulogy and elegy."[17]

The Vendor of Sweets is a novel of Narayan's ripe maturity revealing, like many a mature novel of his, his deep insight into the complexities of human nature and human behaviour. It is while exploring the embarrassments, confusions and complexities of the relationship between the middle-aged protagonist Jagan and his only child and son Mali that the theme of renunciation is brought to fore.

Unable to solve the riddle created by Mali, Jagan voluntarily withdraws himself from all contact with his son and retires into a grove outside Malgudi to live the life of a recluse in a determined bid to free himself from the delusion of attachment. This aspect of the ideal of renunciation is not touched upon in any of the novels of Narayan preceding *The Vendor of Sweets.*

What is interesting and specially relevant to the study of the theme of renunciation in this novel is Jagan's apparent devotion to the *Bhagavad Gita,* the great philosophical classic which teaches the ideals of non-attachment and disinterested action. A copy of the *Gita* is his constant companion from which he reads aloud the Lord's sayings every day for his own edification, and on occasion for the benefit of his staff in the sweet shop. He honestly believes that he understands its teachings and refers to them complacently every now and then, whether relevant to the occasion or not. Jagan's deep attachment to his shop and his love of money, both unaccounted and accounted, conflicts with the *Gita* ideals of non-attachment and non-possession, though he is hardly aware of it. Above all, he cherishes an embarrassing and absurd affection for his prodigal son Mali to whom he is immediately attached and whom he pampers, although the boy does not quite care for his father. As long as Jagan's wife Ambika lived, the relationship between the father and son was more or less normal. But since her death, when Mali was still a boy, they have drifted apart, an ever-widening gap developing between them, resulting in a failure of understanding and total breakdown of communication. But Jagan's indulgent affection for his son persists. He has to go through many ups and downs before he becomes keenly aware of the delusion of attachment.

Thus at the beginning of the narrative Jagan, who is still far away from the puzzles and crises to be created by Mali, naively and complacently assumes that he has mastered himself. This is obliquely revealed in his pontific exhortation to the cousin: "Conquer taste and you will have conquered the self."[18] In fact the rest of the novel may be read as an ironical comment on this opening sentence. By now, it is true, Jagan has successfully conquered his taste, though he vends delicious sweets everyday. That he fancies that he has conquered his self too is implicit in his reference "with a glow of triumph" (14) to his ascetic dietary practices, and other austerities. The worldly-wise cousin sees at once and points out the contradiction in Jagan's position, when he says that he cannot understand why one who has "perfected the art of living on nothing" should still go on "working and earning" (16) and be a flourishing businessman. The cousin not only draws attention to the contradictions in Jagan, but in a seemingly casual way introduces the theme of renunciation, which assumes great importance in the second half of the novel. Jagan, who now has the "outlook of a soul disembodied, floating above the grime of the earth," (14) for all his pride in his life of high thinking and simple living and devotion to the *Gita,* not only does not entertain even remotely the idea of renouncing the world, but he does not even envisage the possibility of his considering such a step at a later date in his life.

The tranquillity of Jagan's everyday life is not disturbed until the adolescent son brusquely announces one morning that he "can't study any more." (129) The father is naturally aghast as Mali never spoke to him in this fashion before. But he soon reconciles himself to the situation and worries himself over the prospects of his son as a writer, but Mali is as idle as ever.

Jagan gets his second shock when he learns from the cousin that Mali has made all preparations to go to America to learn the art of story-telling. That he should have gone about them without his permission hurts him. The very thought that he will have to live alone in the house when the boy goes away depresses him.

It is with the sudden return of Mali from America that Jagan's problems in relation to his son not only multiply but become more complex and complicated. In fact the real challenges of his life begin from now on, and his professed faith in the teachings of Gandhi and more particularly of the *Gita* are put to test. Till then he thinks that he has solved every problem of his life and even conquered his self. The imposing spectacle of Mali as he lands in Malgudi overwhelms Jagan and fills him with a feeling of inferiority. He is thrown into "complete confusion" (64) when his son casually informs him that he and Grace, his half-Korean and half-American companion, are "married."

His problems begin in right earnest when Mali, ably assisted by Grace from behind the scenes, tries to make him invest his money as a major shareholder in his absurd project of manufacturing story-writing machines.

It is at this psychological moment when Jagan is groping in confusion that he apparently by chance, comes into contact with Chinna Dorai the bearded sculptor. Actually Chinna Dorai comes to seek the other's patronage, so that he could complete the image of goddess Gayatri left unfinished by his late master, and install it. In the light of Jagan's subsequent experiences, this turns out to be the most momentous and vital contact and a god-send for him. It reminds us of the contact that Krishnan the English teacher makes with the person who initiates him into psychic experience. Not only does Chinna Dorai open up an entirely new and fascinating world of gods and goddesses to Jagan, whose "fixed orbit" for years "had been between the statue and the shop" and whose mental operations were confined to Mali, the cousin and frying, (112) but helps him unintentionally to look at himself and his problems from a new angle, and to discover eventually an answer to his questions. He yields to the other's suggestion that it would do him good to have a "retreat" like the grove. This earnest suggestion elicits from Jagan an immediate and spontaneous response: "Yes, yes. God knows I need a retreat. You know, my friend, at some stage in one's life one must uproot oneself from the accustomed surroundings and disappear so that others may continue in peace." (126) These words prove prophetic in course of time, although Jagan is not aware of their implications. Endorsing Jagan's words enthusiastically, Chinna Dorai says: "It would be the most accredited procedure according to our scriptures – husband and wife must vanish into the forest at some stage in their lives, leaving the affairs of the world to younger people." (126)

Thus towards the close of chapter eight of the novel, the traditional Hindu ideal of *vanaprasthya* is explicitly introduced into the novel, and Jagan himself comes upon it unexpectedly. The remaining five chapters of the novel show how under the pressure of painful experiences he moves gradually towards this ideal of withdrawal.

In his naivete Jagan does not know or envisage the hazards involved in the process of transformation. Therefore he returns home from the grove in a state of excitement and turmoil. As he sits spinning on the *charkha*, he has a feeling that his "identity" is "undergoing a change" and that he has become a "different man, at the moment," no longer "committed" to his shop and his family, although he still cares for them. (127) With a touch of complacency he reflects: "One enters a new life at the appointed time and it is foolish to resist. He was no longer the father of Mali, the maker of sweets and gatherer of money each day; he was gradually becoming something else, perhaps a supporter of the bearded sculptor – or was he really his ward." (129) He feels a sudden pity for his son who looks forlorn and puzzled, and curses the barrier which has sprung up between them.

Jagan seems self-possessed enough so that he is able to remain unruffled when Mali once again rejects with repugnance his renewed offer of his prosperous business. One evening, reluctant to return home which looks "sinister and silent" in the dark, because of Mali's doings, Jagan sits alone on the pedestal of the statue of Sir Frederick Lawley, brooding rather nostalgically over the different phases of his life in the past. He recalls the good old days. This exercise of brooding over the past drives home to Jagan how changed is his home, how changed the times and the values are. Mali, he finds, has rejected uncritically and with contempt every value and belief he has cherished in his life. Jagan feels totally estranged and lonely. He realizes that it is beyond his ability to change or mould his son for the better. While he may live for ten or fifteen years more, Mali has to live for many more years with or without his absurd story-writing machine. (181) The thought of withdrawal from one's familiar surroundings which had occurred to Jagan momentarily during his visit to the grove now comes back to his mind with renewed force and urgency: "I have probably outlived my purpose in this house. If I live for ten or fifteen years more, it will have to be on a different plane." (182) If he is fit "only for retirement, then he should earnestly try to shake off things" "unmistakably, completely," leaving Mali to live his life as it may please him. (182) Memories of an earlier time bright and clear, instead of leading Jagan to a sentimental conclusion, enable him to think and analyze clearly about himself and his problems with some detachment. An observation made by Lakshmi Holmstrom in this context is worth-noting. She says: "It is characteristic of Narayan that he uses Jagan's happiest memories not to a sentimental end, but only to strengthen his resolve to leave Mali alone."[19] The special relevance of Chinna Dorai's counsel dawns upon him now. In fact Jagan is now better qualified to enter a new *janma*, to retire into a retreat, than he was at the time of his visit to the grove.

Fortified by thoughts of renunciation, Jagan starts acting briskly upon his resolve to retire. He gathers into a little bundle his things including his *charkha*, and leaves home. Narayan's insight into Jagan's mind is seen in his observation that "the sunlight, the cold bath and the gruel he has had, mitigates somewhat the ardour of his renunciation." (183)

As if to test the strength of his resolution to retire from worldly attachments a fresh problem crops up again because of Mali. Jagan is nonplussed to know from the cousin, who meets him on the way, that Mali has been taken into police custody for violating the prohibition laws. He is shaken beyond expectation.

With some real effort Jagan recovers his composure and attains enough clarity of mind to consider the scrape Mali has got into, with objectivity and detachment. Even the cousin, seasoned in the art of persuasion, fails to make him take an active interest in Mali's case or change his resolve to retire from worldly engagements. His refusal to return home and be involved again in his son's confusing affairs is firm and final. Even the cousin who has known Jagan through and through is amazed at the transformation in him. The parting words of Jagan, as it is obvious, are truly in the spirit of Gandhi and the *Gita*. In unexpected ways his interests in Gandhi, the *Gita*, and Gayatri, which were hitherto separate, bear fruit and are now united in the solution he finds for his personal problems. All events in the novel ultimately lead to the final conclusion, namely Jagan's departure to the mango grove.

The small bundle of possessions that Jagan carries with him into his retirement has in it not only his Gandhian *charkha* but also his "bank book" which, as the cousin is quick to point out, is "a compact way of carrying things." (191) This naturally gives room to doubt the sincerity of his withdrawal. He may appear to be hypocritical. And in going away from home he may even seem to be actually seeking an escape from responsibility and the trials of life. Even such a perceptive critic as S.C.Harrex makes the following observation: "Jagan's selfish attachment turns out to be increasingly troublesome. Therefore Jagan's renunciation of the world is not altogether disinterested or pure-minded: just as he takes his cheque book with him, so the third asrama provides him with a convenient escape from the trials of life with Grace and Mali."[20]

The celebrated West Indian novelist V.S. Naipaul takes the view that Jagan escapes from responsibility. His "is an act of despair" and "he runs away in tears," into "a retreat from civilization and creativity – to magic and incantation."[21] Naipaul seems to miss much of the comic irony in the novel. At the time Jagan decides to go away from his wordly engagements, there is neither regret nor bitterness in him and his zest for life remains intact. The new aesthetic and spiritual interest he cultivates, and his eager desire "to watch a goddess come out of stone," add strength to it. Therefore there is no question of turning his back upon his primary duties and obligations. Much less there is any escape in what he does. As he tells the cousin, he is "not flying away to another planet." (192) There is something positive about his seeking a retreat in the grove. He certainly does not "run away in tears" nor from civilization, as Naipaul thinks. As Santosh Gupta pertinently observes: "His [Jagan's] retreat is a withdrawal from activity directed towards material gain and a turn towards increased interest in spirituality, beyond the 'repetitions of frying and selling' to the task of relating himself to the multifaceted living world of animals and nature."[22] Thus Narayan gives a realistic, psychologically penetrating picture of the sort of personal forces which has made the final stage of retreat a natural part of any life.[23]

Published seven years after *The Painter of Signs* (1976) and sixteen years after *The Vendor of Sweets* (1967), *A Tiger for Malgudi* (1983) shows that Narayan is still resourceful, inventive, and fresh as he was before, and in full command of his creative powers. It is an unusual, and even a challenging novel in the sense that its chief protagonist is a majestic tiger, and its essence is in the tiger – protagonist undergoing an internal spiritual transformation. To begin with, the tiger lives in its jungle home in the Mempi Hills. Then it is captured and trained to become a performing circus tiger under the regal name Raja. Fortuitous circumstances are about to turn it into a cinema-tiger, a film star. But it manages to escape from the film-shooting camp into freedom, but in fact it strays into the busy and crowded streets of Malgudi. Eventually it is once again captured, this time by a hermit, a *sanyasi*, and away into the Mempi Hills to live with him. The hermit discourses to it on philosophical and spiritual matters, as a result of which the tiger is transformed inwardly and attains knowledge about its self.

A Tiger for Malgudi is concerned with *sanyasa* proper. The tiger Raja is the chief protagonist of the novel, and its mentor the hermit, is the second protagonist, though he actually appears in person only in the last part of the novel. But the hermit's presence is felt from first to last, particularly in the autobiographical narrative of the tiger which covers more than half of the total narrative. The hermit strives to achieve non- attachment and quests after self-realization. Even as he seeks an answer to the question "who am I," seized with a passion to understand himself, he also helps the tiger to discover its essential self residing inside its rough exterior. In the case of both the hermit and the tiger there is an inward transformation, though of different degrees and levels, without which there can be no *sanyasa* at all. The novel also finally suggests, among other things that all creatures human and nonhuman, must learn to free themselves from the bonds of attachment and from illusions.

The novel begins with the aged tiger Raja, who, now living a peaceful and retired life in the zoo under the protective care of the zoo-keeper, recounts the story of its life. It is an enlightened tiger which has begun to know itself thanks to the ministry of the hermit, that it reminisces on its long past and vicissitudes, beginning with its life in the jungle from its infancy onwards upto its final parting from its master to live in the safe haven of the zoo. Its account being continuous, we are enabled to follow every changing phase of its life and the inward transformation that takes place in it. Thereby we carry the impression that the tiger at the close of the novel is the same individual as the tiger at the beginning. Every phase of its experience leaves its mark upon it so that when it comes into contact with the hermit it is ripe for internal development. The progress of the tiger may be described as a movement from freedom to captivity and slavery and from thence to freedom (though of a different kind) and liberation.

The novelist gives an authentic account of the jungle life of the tiger, as one who has a reliable knowledge of animal psychology and animal behaviour. The tiger of the novel in its infancy lives in the forests of Mempi under the protective care of its mother feeling confident that its "mother would live for ever."[24] Now as an evolved tiger, it knows that it is "a natural delusion which afflicts all creatures, including human beings." (12-13) With the unexpected disappearance of its mother, it is caught in the struggle for survival. It succeeds and deludes itself once again as having become the "Supreme Lord of the Jungle." (13) Intoxicated by the deference shown by its fellow creatures in the jungle, the young tiger lives through a phase of arrogance, vanity and pride, and of "utter wildness, violence, and unthinking cruelty inflicted on weaker creatures." (13) Even though its notion of its absolute supremacy is continually challenged by the porcupine, the monkey, the crow, and the leopard, it continues to indulge in the self-deceiving illusion of its omnipotence.

Next comes the phase of the tiger becoming a householder, when not only much of its freedom to range about is curtailed but some of its thoughtless violence is mitigated because of the need to care for the young ones and protect them against dangers. Family life results in the tiger developing attachment to the tigress and their four cubs. They too vanish, killed by human hunters. While the tiger is busy trying to take revenge on the villagers for having killed its kin, it gets trapped by the Captain of Grand Malgudi Circus to be trained to perform various feats and become eventually the star perfomer of the circus and be known to the public as "that miracle tiger Raja – the magnificent." (65)

The world of film-making brings out the worst in the Captain. He neither gives Raja rest nor shows any kindness, and drives it to despair by compelling it to stand on its legs even though it is completely tired out. A slight movement of its forepaw intended only to knock out the metal gadget in the Captain's hand has the unexpected result of tearing off his head.

In the pandemonium that follows the fall of the Captain, Raja moves gladly into freedom and strays into the streets of Malgudi after months of degrading captivity. By chance it gets into the school and goes off to sleep in the headmaster's room. At this stage of the narrative in the novel, the hermit appears in person, although he has been a presence in the tiger's autobiographical narrative from the start. Even the mere presence of the hermit in the vicinity begins to affect the tiger though locked up in the headmaster's room. From this moment begins the final stage of its life. Raja, who feels both helpless and uncomfortable under the new influence, becomes aware of some change coming inside itself and tries to resist it, though in vain. But the hermit, who understands the turmoil in Raja's mind tells it: "A change is coming, you will have to start a new life, a different one. . . . I will take you out. Let us go together, it'll be safer." (147) After the headmaster is helped out of the room, the hermit and the tiger come out and vanish towards the mountains. Choosing a suitable spot for shelter on the Mempi Hills, together they settle down to a quiet and peaceful life, away from all the din and bustle of a crowd of human beings. Although to be with the hermit may appear to be a new kind of captivity to Raja, paradoxically it becomes the means for its final freedom and liberation brought about by an awakening of its soul. It is clear from his discourses to the tiger and his mode of life that the hermit is entirely a man of genuine piety, a seeker and a true *sanyasi,* a man of renunciation in appearance as well as spirit. He has tried to put his past behind and be occupied with the living present, as a *sanyasi* is expected to do but has not altogether obliterated memories of his past which he reveals briefly to satisfy the curiosity of his disciple Raja. The hermit never forgets his ordinary humanity. He objects strongly to his visitors regarding him as a "great" man and coming to him for his *darshan*. When they tell him, "we are small men, but you are great," he retorts:

> How? Because I'm unshaven and shirtless? I don't shave because I find it easier not to. I don't wear a shirt because I don't have one. But for these, I go about with the tiger because it is God's will. I am not different from you, we are equals and no need to pay homage to me. It has no meaning. You may prostrate only before God. You should seek only God's *darshan*. (164)

These words are also a measure of his development in the direction of renunciation.

In yet another way the hermit's essential ordinary and average humanity is established, when he is visited by a lady who was his wife before he renounced his family and all his worldly engagements. At first indirectly and later on directly she accuses him for deserting his family and home for no reason. The hermit faces the challenge successfully, though with some effort. Patiently he explains to her, in the third person, that she should have no reason to regret the loss of such a husband, "especially when he has left for [her] and [her] children a comfortable home, all the money he had, and every kind of security in life." (171) Further, he explains to her that her husband "left home not out of wrath, there was no cause for it, but out of an inner transformation." (171)

He manages to remain composed in spite of her repeated entreaties to return home with her. But her visit does disturb the hermit so much that he was to meditate continuously for five days before he recovers his composure fully and resume his routine as a *sanyasi.*

As time passes by both the hermit and the tiger evolve inwardly, though on different levels. The hermit realizes that the concern he feels for the tiger is a form of attachment and bondage from which he has to free himself, if he should be a fully non-attached man. Before he turned a new leaf he was no different from any other human being, and was as much self-centred and eccentric as any one else would be. It is an irresistable inner urge to know his self and to seek spiritual enlightenment that propels him towards *sanyasa*. The novel implies that there is nothing unusual or unnatural in such an urge possessing an individual. It fills him with such determination that once he leaves behind his former self and seeks the path of non-attachment, he does not return to it. It is the decision of a mature man who has experienced the different phases of life. The *sanyasa* of the hermit thus conforms to the teachings of the *Gita*.

The theme of renunciation, once again appears in the latest novel of Narayan, *The World of Nagaraj*. Nagaraj, the protagonist of the novel comes upon an ochre-robed *sanyasi* in the vicinity of the Town Hall library, and asks the *sanyasi* where he can get the cloth similar to the one the *sanyasi* is wearing. When questioned by the *sanyasi* as to what prompted in him a desire to wear the holy men's garb, Nagaraj explains: "I thought it would give me greater peace of mind at home if I wear a sanyasi's dress in the puja room, at least."[25]

Nagaraj meets the *sanyasi* at the same place two days later and the *sanyasi* hands him a packet of ochre dye, telling Nagaraj to soak his clothes in it overnight and that when the morning comes he will acquire the look of a sage. To this Nagaraj's reply is that he does not want to parade it but wear it only when he performs a *puja*. The *sanyasi* tells him:

> When you are wearing this ochre your mind should be only on God, not on money or the family. Your thought must be away from all sensual matters, free from kama, krodha, lobha and moha, you must observe silence, become deaf to other people's voices, never pay attention to it. (12)

Everyday after his bath he takes up his ochre robes, enters the *puja* room, prays for sometime and, feels as if he is in a "haven of peace, silence, [and] isolation." (13) He leaves with his wife strict instructions not to be disturbed while in the *puja* room. She has to conduct herself "as if he has ceased to exist" because wearing the garb of a *sanyasi* and withdrawing from the world, however temporary it may be is a kind of death in itself. As his *guru*, the Town Hall *sanyasi* has explained to Nagaraj: "It's good to experience death a little each day so that when your time is up you will slip into the state effortlessly. You will realise how noble and welcome it is – then Death will not be dreaded and avoided. You will overcome death itself." (12)

But however much he may congratulate himself on his having acquired a measure of detachment, though temporarily, Nagaraj remains as much involved in the worldly affairs as any other human being. His involvement with and worry over his nephew Tim, his absurd affection for the boy, all speak about his worldliness. Therefore it can be said that his is only a temporary withdrawal and not the renunciation of a *sanyasi*.

The novelist also makes a mention of the great sage, Narada which is relevant to the theme of renunciation in the novel. Nagaraj is obsessed with the thought of "Sage Narada," based on whom he wants to write a great *kavya*. A renouncer of the world, Narada moved with ease among gods and demons. He is able to traverse at a thought the skies and space, through galaxies, and is welcome in all the fourteen worlds above and below. He creates strife no doubt, by passing disturbing gossip from one quarter to another, but always to benefit the world in the long run, with an eternal perspective. Thus Narada proves himself to be a real *sanyasi* who truly renounced the world and all that it implies and lives only for the sake of others and for the benefit of humanity in general.

The foregoing analysis shows how renunciation is an ideal inseparable from the Indian consciousness, way of life, and values and how Narayan looks at the ideal of renunciation—not from the point of view of strict adherence to the traditional *asramadharma*. He considers on the contrary its psychological, moral and spiritual implications. He finds in true renunciation a positive ideal, which makes for life rather than go against it, and which affirms both life and society.

NOTES

1. Meenakshi Mukherjee, *The Twice Born Fiction* (New Delhi: Arnold Heinemann, 1974), p. 97.
2. S. Radhakrishnan, *The Hindu View of Life* (London: George Allen and Unwin, 1964), p. 65.
3. R.K. Narayan, *The Bachelor of Arts* (Mysore: Indian Thought Publications, 1985), p. 107.
4. Haydn Moore Williams, "*Precarious Innocence*," *Perspectives on R.K. Narayan*, ed. Atma Ram (Ghaziabad: Vimal, 1981), p. 4.
5. R.K. Narayan, *The Dark Room* (Mysore: Indian Thought Publications, 1986), p. 111.
6. K.K. Sharma, "The English Teacher: An Evaluation," *Perspectives on R.K. Narayan*, p. 94.
7. K.Venkatachari, "R.K. Narayan's Novels: Acceptance of Life," *Indian Literature*, VIII, 1 March 1970, p. 56.
8. R.K. Narayan, *The English Teacher* (Mysore: Indian Thought Publications, 1984), p. 109.
9. R.K. Narayan, *My Days* (Mysorc: Indian Thought Publications, 1975), p. 167.

10. S.C.Harrex, *The Fire and the Offering: The English Language Novel of India: 1935-1970* (Calcutta: Writers Workshop, 1977), vol. II, p. 113.
11. R.K. Narayan, *The Guide* (Mysore: Indian Thought Publications, 1985), p. 5.
12. Lakshmi Holmstrom, *The Novels of R.K. Narayan* (Calcutta: Writers Workshop, 1973), p. 67.
13. Meenakshi Mukhaerjee, *The Twice Born Fiction*, p. 120.
14. Lakshmi Holmstrom, p. 67.
15. In *My Dateless Diary*, Narayan writes: "Graham Greene liked the story when I narrated it to him in London. While I was hesitating whether to have my hero alive or dead at the end of the story Graham was definite that he should die. So I have on my hands the life of a man condemned to death before he is born and I have to plan my narrative to lead to it."(pp. 105-6)
16. R.K. Narayan, *Waiting for the Mahatma* (Mysore: Indian Thought Publications, 1984), p. 17.
17. H.M. Williams, *Studies in Modern Indian Fiction in English* (Calcutta: Writers Workshop, 1973), vol. I, p. 86.
18. R.K. Narayan, *The Vendor of Sweets* (Mysore: Indian Thought Publications, 1981), p. 13.
19. Lakhshmi Holmstrom, p. 75.
20. S.C. Harrex, pp. 131-32.
21. V.S. Naipaul, *India: A Wounded Civilization* (New Delhi: Vikas, 1977), pp. 40-43.
22. Santosh Gupta, *The Journal of Indian Writing in English*, XVI, 1, p. 29.
23. Bruce F. Macdonald, "Humanity and Aesthetic Order in *The Vendor of Sweets*," *Perspectives on R.K. Narayan*, p. 155.
24. R.K. Narayan, *A Tiger for Malgudi* (Mysore: Indian Thought Publications, 1983), p. 12.
25. R.K. Narayan, *The World of Nagaraj* (Mysore: Indian Thought Publications, 1990), p. 11.

A Thousand Years Ago . . .: The Use of Myth

"Writers are interested in myths primarily because they comprise literature itself,"[1] and "because they illustrate essential principles of story-telling."[2] In literature myth is significant for its timelessness. "Despite its remoteness from contemporary reality it has a fundamental significance for that particular group of community from which it has sprung."[3]

The ancient mythology provides an inexhaustible source of inspiration for literary artists. And writers such as Melville, Eliot and James Joyce have used myth to reflect their essentially human experiences in a symbolic form.

And Indian people more than any other people are still closer to their mythology, which indicates their adherence to tradition. It has contemporary relevance all over the country and is even today a "living tradition."[4] As Meenakshi Mukherjee points out: "If a world view is required to make literature meaningful in terms of shared human experience, then the Indian epics offer a widely accepted basis of such a common background which permeates the collective conscious of the whole nation."[5]

"The impact of life, the material and substance of our thought are the same everywhere, in any state. Traditionally, India is the *Ramayana*, the *Mahabharata* and the *Puranas*. The values remain the same in every village, town or city,"[6] says Narayan. It is for this reaaon that he gives a new interpretation to ancient myths and legends of India, in the modern context. This does not mean he tries to escape from the actual and the real, on the contrary he reasserts the permanence of the traditional Indian values.

Mythology helps the writer make the contemporary reality more real. As the epic characters are prototypes of humanity they are valid for all time "*Rakshasas, apsaras*, and heroes have the virtue of never growing old"[7] and for this reason the myth is applicable for all times, as every story has a moral and philosophic significance, implicit in it.

It is in this context that Narayan uses Hindu mythology and interprets the modern or contemporary life through a mythical parallel. Narayan himself explains why he does so: "With the impact of modern literature, we began to look at the gods, demons, sages and kings of our mythology and epics not as some remote concoctions but as types and symbols, possessing psychological validity even when viewed against the contemporary background."[8] That is why one clearly feels the contemporariness in the modern interpretation of his use of myth.

Even in an early episodic novel like *Swami and Friends* there is a reference to fables and legends of India. Narayan's acceptance and appraisal of the literary values from India's past is seen here. It is also implicit in Swami's actions and reactions. To quote an instance, Swami believes the myth that God can turn even sand into money and buries two pebbles in the backyard and asks the Gods to convert them into real money—three pie coins. He prays to God fervently but finds that the pebbles remain as they are and kicks them away in anger and frustration. But fearing the retribution of Gods he immediately picks up the box he has kicked a minute ago and puts back the leaves and pebbles into it. "This incident is narrated in the folk-key and on the basis of the Indian folklore."[9] Invigoratively it invokes subtle laughter.

Another instance is that of Swami's launching of a paper-boat in the gutter with an ant seated in it. As Swami watches: "The boat made a beautiful swerve to the right and avoided destruction. It went on and on. It neared a fatal spot where the waters were swirling round in eddies. . . . The boat and its cargo were wrecked beyond recovery. He took a pinch of earth, uttered a prayer for the soul of the ant and dropped it into the gutter."[10] The influence of the myths and legends and fairy tales becomes clear. The grandmother's recounting of the fairy tales and legends, certainly has a strong impression on the mind of the young boy, and gods, demons and fairies inhabit his world.

In fact Swami himself is named after Lord Subrahmanyaswami who as a child performs many miracles.[11] This can be traced as a mythical in the novel, for, Swami too, like his mythical prototype parallel, is engaged in endless adventures. Swami is a school-going pampered child with all the dreams and enchantments of his age. No terrible tragedy can happen to him. His world is populated by the school teachers, classmates and friends and assignments and cricket clubs. And the fanatic Christian teacher Ebenezar seems to be the villain in Swami's world, because he condemns and criticizes the Hindu Gods and idolatry. Swami, also like his mythical counterpart, does all kinds of funny things but still remains the darling of the family.

For a young boy like Swami, the epic characters like gods and fairies are as real as anything else. In this context one can recall Swami's reaction when the scripture teacher Ebenezar condemns Hindu Gods. Ebenezar turns purple with rage as he thinks of Lord Sri Krishna: "Did our Jesus go gadding about with dancing girls like your Krishna? Did our Jesus go about stealing butter. . . . Did our Jesus practice dark tricks on those around him?"[12] Infuriated and outraged beyond capacity Swami asks, "If he did not, why was he crucified?" Moreover for Swami "Jesus could not be a god since he was not a brahmin."[13] And Ebenezar tries to wrench his ear off for saying it. Thus this simple episodic novel can be read as myth of innocence.

Chandran of *The Bachelor of Arts* is the boy Swami grown up. He is a young man now, soon to be a Bachelor of Arts studying at the Albert Mission College. He is a representative of college-going youth with all his ambitions and aspirations. He gets elected as the cultural secretary, struggles hard to arrange and manage cultural programmes, presents a paper in the seminar, learns to tread warily with his European teachers and finally appears for the end exam, and comes out of the college.

Awaiting the results, and having planned nothing in particular, Chandran goes for a walk and sees Malathi, on the banks of river Sarayu and falls in love with her at first sight. He tries to marry her but the horoscopes mismatch and the parents decline to proceed with the marriage.

According to K.V.S. Murti, it is here that one notices the mythical parallel—that of Tara and Sasanka (The Moon God).[14] Sasanka or Chandra as he is more commonly known, falls in love with Tara, wife of his *guru,* which is out of bounds of the ethical code and hence unsuccessful. Chandran too falls in love with Malathi, a phenomenon which is unheard of in a society where marriages by parental consent and arrangement are common. The love-affair, if one can call it that, is doomed to be a failure from the beginning. Chandran frustrated goes out of Malgudi and becomes a *sanyasi* for a while, thus entering the fourth stage of the *varnasramadharma*, advocated by the *Vedas*, a stage to be entered only after going through the first three—that of *brahmacharya* (bachelor), *garhasthya* (householder) and *vanaprasthya* (renouncer of the world). Because Chandran is not at peak with himself and is not ready for *sanyasasrama* he fails to become a real *sanyasi*. After a short period, he realizes that he has not fulfilled his other duties and responsibilities as a son and householder, and that his renunciation was really an alternative to suicide. He returns home, sets up an office as an agent of *The Daily Messenger* and marries Susila, a girl of his parents' choice, falls madly in love with her and settles down happily. Towards the end of the novel he is seen leaving for Talapur, his wife's place since he failed to get a letter from her for almost a week.

The English Teacher takes up the growing up theme of the two earlier novels, *Swami and Friends and The Bachelor of Arts.* Krishnan of *The English Teacher* is no one but Chandran of *The Bachelor of Arts.* He takes up where Chandran leaves off, working as a lecturer at Albert Mission College. He is happily settled with his wife Susila and his little girl, Leela.

The novel is divisible into two parts. The first part comprises Krishnan's "life of bliss" with his wife and daughter, whereas the second part consists of his lonely and miserable life after her demise. His life becomes a void after his wife's death. He finds out that "There is no escape from loneliness and separation. . . . The law of life can't be avoided. A profound unmitigated loneliness is the only truth of life. All else is false."[15] He is haunted by the shadow of the past, his present is chaos, and the future is blank.[16]

It is here that the mythical parallel becomes clear. In the *Uttara Ramayana* Lord Sri Rama, an incarnation of Vishnu, abandons Sita – an incarnation of Goddess Lakshmi, for the sake of *dharma* and Sita, unable to withstand the separation renounces the earthly body and reaches her abode, *Vaikuntha*. Sri Rama rehabilitates his sons Lava and Kusa and performs his duty towards his sons and his people, however much he suffers from utter loneliness. It is only after his sons attain the age of coronation that he crowns them and leaves the earth to find peace and solace with Lakshmi as Vishnu in *Vaikuntha*.[17] Like Sri Rama, Krishnan too bears his loneliness and unhappiness. He realizes that loneliness is the law of life and one can neither go against it nor fight it and that one can only accept it. Gradually he reconciles himself to the circumstances. He fails to find any meaningfulness in his work as a lecturer at Albert Mission College, resigns the job and finds another more meaningful vocation – that of teaching small children, a world of innocents which he finds to be serene and peaceful providing him solace. Towards the end he is able to communicate with his wife Susila and is at peace with himself and the world, having achieved "spiritual communion" with her.

The Dark Room, though comes earlier than *The English Teacher* chronologically, is a study in domestic discord. It is the tale of a tormented housewife. Savitri is a traditional wife, submissive and meek. She makes her annoyance known by retiring to the "dark room" which only lasts for a short period of time. And she comes out of the "dark room" sooner or later never being one to resist firmly.

The man-woman relationship, one of the important themes of Narayan is thus the major concern of *The Dark Room.* Savitri is a contented housewife with three children and fifteen years of marriage. She lives happily enough till Shanta Bai the new probationary assistant enters the scene. Ramani, the arrogant and egotistical "self-made" husband of Savitri, becomes enslaved by her charms and has an affair with her. Savitri comes to know of the affair through her friends and repulsed by the very thought rebels against it and leaves her husband's house to commit suicide. Rescued by a lock-repairer and burglar she stays with his wife Ponni who is a complete contrast to Savitri. After only a couple of days, longing for her children brings Savitri back home and she realizes her weakness.

In this tale of domestic disharmony, H.M. Williams finds "faint echoes of Sakuntala."[18] But K.V.S. Murti interprets the novel to be a Savitri and Satyavan myth of the *Mahabarata.* Savitri, the daughter of king Asvapathi, falls in love with Satyavan, marries him and when *Yama*, the God of Death, comes to claim his life, pursues *Yama*, fights and wins a verbal battle and regains her husband alive. Murti also finds traces of Kaikeyi-Dasaratha myth in the novel. In the *Ramayana*, Kaikeyi the Queen of Dasaratha gets into the *kopagriha* (the dark room) exposing her ire over the proposed coronation of Sri Rama as the King of Ayodhya.[19] He says these two legends appeal as the mythical soul of the novel in the modern context. Apart from this one can also find a parallel with Sati Sumati, who suffers the vagaries of a womaniser husband in the *Mahabharata.*

It is ironical that Savitri, named for the legendary heroine who captured her husband from the clutches of God *Yama* and is reunited to him thus standing as an example of wifely devotion, leaves her husband's house in a mood of rebellion as a protest of her husband's violation of the sanctity of marriage and marriage vows. While the legendary Savitri embodies wifely duties and devotion entrusted on a woman by the *Dharmasastras,* Narayan's Savitri is another Nora trying to assert her self-identity and existence.

Mr. Sampath published in America as *The Printer of Malgudi* is an individual's quest for identity and self-knowledge. The novel seems to advocate the doctrine of *Nishkamakarma*—disinterested action. In the *Mahabharata* and in the *Bhagavad Gita,* Lord Krishna preaches to the shirking hero Arjuna of "disinterested action" with the "spirit of dedication," *Nishkamakarmayoga,* for the sake of *dharma.*[20] One also notices in the novel the myth of *Kamadahanam*—The Burning of Kama, which advocates the restraint of passion.

The two main characters Srinivas and Sampath enact the above-mentioned myths in the novel and are drawn in the wake of their mythical prototypes. Srinivas hails from a traditional Hindu joint family, from Talapur, comes to Malgudi, and finds his vocation as the editor of *The Banner.* He aims to improve society through his journal and finds Sampath to be the printer of his weekly. Srinivas tries to reform the society through *The Banner.* He writes a series of articles for this purpose in his journal. But he is still bothered for, while he thunders against municipal or social shortcomings a voice goes on asking: "Life and the world and all this is passing—why bother about anything? The perfect and the imperfect are all the same. Why really bother? He had to find an answer to this question."[21] But he soon comes to realize that "one certainly retains a critical concern in the affairs of the world one lives in; nevertheless, it becomes easier to detach oneself from the struggle."[22]

Srinivas seems to think that the problem of self-identity or quest for self-knowledge can be solved by mere abstract speculation. He does not worry about his social and moral responsibilities which he thinks to be petty. But he comes to know a strange "dissatisfaction" which probably arises from the shelving of his responsibilities. Soon he realizes that he has to fulfil his obligations, familial and social, but with non-attachment. Because of this realization Srinivas is able to survive the experience of film-making.

Even when drawn into the stormy film world, "a world dominated by commercial values, self-interest and illusion,"[23] he watches with disinterest that distortion of his interpretation of the script and accepts it with detachment. "He saw without much flutter, the mangling that was going on with his story." (178) After the disaster and disastrous results of the film-making, ending in Ravi's lunacy, he returns to his journalistic career and prints the journal in another press, renders as much help as he can to Ravi's family and steers clear of the printer and takes care not to cross him again. Thus putting into practice what he has learned that "detachment . . . is both a defence and an assertion and yet not so detached as to forget the calls of humanity."[24] He comes to terms with himself as a social being. He realizes that he cannot achieve self-identity in isolation and only by becoming involved in the web of human relationships and activities without losing personal integrity can one acquire true detachment.

At another level the novel can be said to be a parallel of *Kamadahana* myth. It is the myth of Lord Shiva (also known as Nataraja, King of Dance) who opens his third eye of destruction and burns to ashes Manmatha or Kama (God of Desire) for kindling *kama* (desire) in Him for Parvathi especially when He is in meditation.

Significantly Srinivas possesses a sandalwood image of Nataraja, given to him by his grandmother, who in her turn got it from her own father, who, "discovered it in a packet of saffron" (19) to whom he prays. He never starts his day without spending a few minutes before the image, which is symbolic in the novel. The story centres around the traditional tale of "The Burning of Kama." Sampath is the printer of Srinivas's journal. Not satisfied with playing the role of the printer he becomes a partner in the Sunrise Pictures and is to produce an "epic film" "The Burning of Kama." He also draws Srinivas into the world of film-making, by asking him to be the script writer for the film. There Srinivas encounters Shanti the heroine of the film who is to act as Parvathi and a young artist Ravi employed in the Studio. Ravi discovers his dream girl in

Shanti, a young widow with a son, and falls "madly" in love with her. The actual truth is he is infatuated with her. Sampath also finds Shanti desirable and the irony is that they fail to realize the very message or moral they are trying to enact—that passion should be restrained.

"Narayan is aware of the often laconic humour (sometimes overlooked by oversolemn commentators), which lies at the heart of the Indian fable."[25] Srinivas, Sampath and Ravi provide the novelist greatest scope for comic. The film stars a pot-bellied Shiva and a Parvathi in see-through stuff—against South American background music. When a dispute develops between the actor Shiva and Sampath the producer, Shiva descends from Kailas angrily and demands his money.[26] Sampath, already infatuated with Shanti, elects himself to play the role—ironically enough of self-restraint. Soon afterwards Srinivas realizes his mistake in entering the "commercial valued" film world. During the picturization of the climax, Ravi's selfcontrol breaks down when he sees the danger of Shiva (Sampath) embracing Parvathi (Shanti) and unable to withstand it, carries her away. Much damage is caused and the film-making turns out to be a failure. Sampath runs away with Shanti, Ravi goes mad and Srinivas returns to his own vocation, freed at last from the "Mad, unreal world." He resumes his journalistic career and decides to serve society through his journal. He has learnt the moral message of the fable enacted—to "strengthen his own moral resolution"[27] and act with restraint. After a brief period Shanti escapes from Sampath to go back to her own son and bring him up. Sampath having "lost his identity with his family"[28] escapes towards the railway station to start life anew. Only Srinivas who achieves self-detachment resumes his life as usual. He seems to have attained "a knowledge of his true identity which would bring no depression at the coming of age, nor puzzle the mind with conundrums and antitheses." (138)

The next novel of Narayan, *The Financial Expert* is a get-rich quick fable. The novel is built entirely around Margayya—the financial expert.

The mythical analogy is drawn from the story of Kubera, King of *Alakapuri* (the celestial city) and the "wealthiest and most resourceful cashier of gods."[29] The temple priest narrates and relates the story to Margayya. Further, there is the tale of the prodigal son *Nigama Sarma* in the *Panduranga Mahatmayam* which is similar to that of Margayya and his son Balu.

Margayya begins his career as a petty money-lender, opposite the Co-operative Land Mortgage Bank. Insulted by the Secretary of the Bank he realizes for the first time the value of money. At the same time his career of financial transaction comes to a sudden halt by his son's throwing away his account book into the "eternal Malgudi gutter."

He becomes obsessed in the pursit of wealth and riches. He thinks that "Money was men's greatest need, like air or food. People went to horrifying lengths for its sake."[30] In proving the virtue of money and glorifying it he is not unlike Volpone who says:

> Thou art virtue, fame,
> Honours, and all things else.
> Who can get thee,
> He shall be noble, valiant, honest, wise.[31]

Wandering aimlessly he meets the temple priest who tells him: "Wealth does not come the way of people who adopt half-hearted measures. It comes only to those who pray for it single-mindedly with no other thought." (29)

Margayya takes up the advice of the priest and performs a forty day puja. Here Narayan uses two symbols for wealth: milk and lotus. When the priest offers him milk at first Margayya declines. The priest warns him that he is showing disrespect to Goddess Lakshmi, for, milk is one of the ways in which the Goddess appears. Then Margayya grabs the milk and greedily drinks it all. He develops a deeply devotional attitude to milk and is richly rewarded at the end as a result. As for the lotus it is with this flower that Margayya performs the *puja* which results in his acquiring wealth. Also there are two contrasting mythical symbols in the novel namely Lakshmi (Goddess of Wealth) and Saraswati (Goddess of Knowledge) with Margayya and Pal as their respective devotees.[32] Ironically, Margayya stands in the end where he leaves off—under the banyan tree when his financial empire crashes.

The novel is an allegory about "the insignificance of money in life"[33] and warns people not to think of money as the be-all and end-all of life.

Waiting for the Mahatma gives expression to the earlier theme touched in *The Bachelor of Arts*—that of youthful infatuation or love for a girl. It is viewed through a new dimension against the backdrop of the Gandhian freedom movement. The novel also depicts the Gandhian myth of freedom struggle, preaching *Nishkamakarma* (disinterested action) of the *Bhagavad Gita* for the sake of society and for the liberation of mankind.

The protracted love[34] finds a mythical parallel in the Dushyanta and Sakuntala myth found in the *Mahabharata*. The legend of Princess Chudala who purges her husband, Prince Sikhidhvaja gradually of sensual love and chisels him into a *jivanmukta* of spiritual love,[35] also appears to be the mythical parallel of the novel.

The love-theme of the novel is woven round the central mythical figure of Mahatma Gandhi. The novel deals basically with the theme of Gandhian impact, like Raja Rao's *Kanthapura* but with a difference. In the earlier novel this impact is felt by an individual, in the latter, by a community. *Kanthapura* tells the tale of how the *satyagraha* or national freedom struggle comes to a small South Indian village. The narrator is an old woman who also has been a participant in the struggle. Towards the end the people look forward to *Rama Rajya.* And "The hope is collective while the loss has been individual." On the other hand at the end of *Waiting for the Mahatma* there is a loss at the national level but there is a sense of fulfilment in Sriram's personal life."[36]

Raja Rao tells the tale of Kanthapura and its slow awakening to and participation in the Indian freedom movement. Kanthapura is a typical village in the province of Kara. It lies slumberous like a curled-up child on its mother lap, until it is awakened to the freedom struggle of Gandhi. Murti brings about this awareness and gradually the whole community takes up the cause and believes the myth of Gandhi – that he is an *avatar* (reincarnation) of Lord Sri Rama come to rescue them from the clutches of the foreign rule. It is with this faith that the village enters the nation's freedom struggle with a strong desire to establish *Rama Rajya* – a free and ideal country. Raja Rao's portrayal of the small sleepy community, its awakening and participation in the national freedom movement is admirable.

Unlike Raja Rao's *Kanthapura,* Narayan's *Waiting for the Mahatma* is the story of a young man – an individual, his ups and downs in life and Gandhi's influence on him. The story centres round the love theme of Sriram and Bharati. But it is also about Gandhi and his influence on people and nation as a whole. For, Bharati the disciple of Gandhi, with whom Sriram falls in love, is an embodiment of Bharat – India. The novel can be said to be the Gandhian *Kuṛukshetra* for the sake of his own nation. Gandhi advocates the *Nishkamakarma yoga* (non-attached action) of the *Bhagavad Gita.* In a country seething with discontent and frustration Mahatma symbolizes the eternal spiritual faith and non-violence. Therefore Gandhi remains the central figure in the novel.

Narayan sees Gandhi essentially "as a simple, kindly human being."[37] Hence his interest in Sriram and Bharati affair. In fact Bharati has been brought up by Gandhi and that is why she waits for the Mahatma's permission to marry Sriram. Gandhi's presence is felt throughout the novel. Narayan is concerned with Gandhi as Mahatma, the Great Soul, one who renders selfless service to the country and dies (Gandhi falls a victim to his very ideals), as a martyr for its sake. It is here one sees the mythical parallel with Lord Krishna of the *Bhagavad Gita.* Lord Krishna gives up his incarnation through an arrow of a hunter – representative of the humans for whose salvation and *dharma* he has directed the *Mahabharata* movement leading to the battle of *Kurukshetra*. Likewise Mahatma too gives up his incarnation by the revolver of a representative of the Indians for whose freedom and salvation he has led the national movement. Thus Gandhi is "an embodiment of selfless action and love, moral integrity and universal harmony," and he attains his identity in the identity of India. Narayan thus charges the novel with "epic dimensions and significance"[38] just as Raja Rao does in his *Kanthapura.*

At another level the novel can be interpreted as Chudala and Sikhidhvaja myth. The novel opens with Sriram turned twenty. Being an orphan Sriram has been brought up by his grandmother. He meets Bharati when she comes to collect donations for the national movement. Sriram falls in love with Bharati instantly but finds that she is a woman of strong will. She is dedicated to Gandhi and his ideal, that of liberating the real *Bharata Bharati* – the mother country. In order to be close to her, he wants to take part in the freedom struggle. Bharati advises him to get Bapu's blessings. Gandhi asks him to get his grandmother's permission. He does so and joins the camp. Together Sriram and Bharati take an active part in the campaign and start spreading Gandhi's message and even amidst the hardship of touring the remote rural areas "delight is each other's company."[39]

Sriram proves to be an eager lover – concerned only with his love for Bharati and wants to marry her. But Bharati first wants to seek Gandhiji's permission. For her marriage alone is not an end to self-identity and fulfilment. Her "double" concern is liberation of India, and then marriage with Sriram. Hence her love is more spiritual and platonic than physical. "Her waiting for the Mahatma's permission is only a means of chiselling Sriram into an ideal patriot-lover-husband,"[40] just like Chudala of the myth.

Sriram gradually is drawn to the activities of Jagdish a terrorist. It is from Jagdish he learns that Bharati is in prison. He goes there, comes to know about his granny's illness, goes home and finds his granny very much alive, and is arrested for his terrorist activities, spends his time in the prison and loses track of everything. While in jail he realizes his folly and deviance from his chosen path. After sometime, he hears the news of India attaining freedom and is released from the prison. He goes and meets Gandhi and confesses that he is not worthy of Bharati but the Mahatma forgives him and gives his blessings for their marriage. Bharati thus "becomes an ideal for modern women: every woman is to be a symbol of selfless love . . . in guiding man in the right manner, achieving her identity in selfless service."[41]

The deliberate or conscious use of myth occurs in *The Guide* as in the other novels. The novel appears to be the myth of the primitive—that of an act of "ritual for rain."

The novel is "firmly focussed on the social and cultural tradition"[42] and is a realization of "a symbiotic relationship between the individual and society."[43] The protagonist Raju reflects the central theme of "sincerity and self-deception."

Raju a tourist guide meets Rosie at the Malgudi railway station and becomes enchanted by her beauty, comes to know of the lack of compatibility between husband and wife, finds out that she is a dancer, admires her art and thus is able to gain Rosie's interest. After a while Marco, her husband, finds out about their liasion, leaves Rosie and walks away. She comes back to Raju and lives with him at his house. Raju encourages her to dance. With his encouragement Rosie gives a dance performance as "Nalini" and gains recognition, which in its wake brings riches. Consequently Raju becomes possessive of Rosie and in order to keep her away from Marco, forges her signature on a document for the release of her jewellery box which is in possession of Marco and is arrested. He is convicted and imprisoned. Thus he is punished because society does not permit an individual to transgress the natural limits.

After his imprisonment, Raju, unable to face the people of Malgudi, takes refuge in an old ruined temple of Mangala, "where the process of his rebirth begins."[44] He sits there on a slab cross-legged "as if it were a throne." Immediately after his release from the prison, he had gone to a barber's shop where he is made to "look like a Maharaja."[45] Both these words "throne" and "maharaja" indicate that: "this shrine will become his new-found kingdom where he will acquire a new stature, a new authority and a new awareness."[46]

Thus "Raju perched in the sacred place, the peasant (cleansed after his journey but also perhaps ritually purified) sitting respectfully below, the ambiguity of the relationship on Raju's side, the certainty of it on the peasant's"[47]—all this gives us an inkling of what is to happen later. But Raju is blissfully unaware of what is going to happen in future.

In the last phase of the novel, a few days after Raju is established in the role of a saint the village is stricken with a severe drought. Seasonal rains fail and the previous year's food stores get depleted. People come to blows with the shopman and seek Raju's guidance. His advice is misinterpreted. The villagers understand the message quite differently—that Raju is going on a fast to bring rains to the village.

Raju now finds himself nicely trapped in his own web. "He commits the cardinal Hindu mistake of falling into the trap of *Maya,* becoming imprisoned by his passion for attachments and the illusory bonds of self."[48] And when he declares "Tomorrow I'll take my usual food," Velan innocently and naturally enough asks: "Do you expect it to rain tomorrow, sir?" (95)

The people of the village believe him to be their "Saviour": "the Saviour was expected to stand in knee-deep water, look to the skies and utter the prayer for two weeks completely fasting during the period – and lo, the rains would come down, provided the man who performed it was a pure soul, was a great soul." (95) The solemnity of Velan's tone brings tears to Raju's eyes. The blind and immense faith of the innocent villagers has its effect on Raju: "he feels a moral duty not to insult the villagers' faith in him; and so he becomes absorbed into the communal archetype."[49] This is the first step towards his self-knowledge and self-identity. Raju himself had spoken of such a penance, its value and technique. It is important to keep in mind that quite early in life Raju gathered from the traditional accounts he had heard his mother narrate, and he had said that when the time came even the man "who would bring you the rain will appear all of a sudden." The villagers interpreted the words and applied them to the present context.

Raju remembers what his mother used to tell him: "if there is one good man anywhere, the rains would descend for his sake and benefit the whole world." (97) He feels that the time has come for him to be serious to attach value to his own words. He decides to avoid food and help the villagers if he could, that way and feels a new strength to go through the ordeal. The strength comes from the "hitherto untapped reserves of the stories of good men that sacrificed themselves for others."[50] The fourth day of his fast found him quite sprightly: "He went down to the river, stood facing up stream with his eyes shut, and repeated the litany. It was no more than a supplication to the heavens to send down rain and save humanity." (213) And on the twelfth day, exhausted he sags down with the prophetic words that it is raining in the hills. As C.D. Narasimhaiah observes: "Raju's death viewed symbolically, means that the individual by losing his life in water brings rain (and life) to his fellowmen, and his death, a 'death by water' is really not death but a means of self-purification and self-realization."[51] C.D. Narasimhaiah further comments: "Here is India from the inside. Raju is India itself – its astonishing power, and deep inner reserves to revitalize itself and work its way to fulfilment. For like the fallen Phoenix he rises from his own ashes."[52]

In India, where with all the degradation (one) may have suffered, the criterion of greatnes is still the stature of the spirit. Therefore the ending is smooth and inevitable. India's undying faith in God and goodness, holymen and miracles is rendered quite credible by the novelist's art even to the sceptical and questioning mind.[53]

In *The Man-Eater of Malgudi* the central theme is the "exploration of evil." Melville, Milton, Dante, Shakespeare and in fact all great writers were occupied with this theme and Narayan too explores the perpetual struggle between good and evil using the Bhasma myth from classical Indian mythology. "Through his use of the Bhasma myth Narayan is able to covey in terms of fictional art the traditional Indian belief regarding evil, its destructiveness as well as self-destructiveness."[54]

The polarity between Nataraj, the meek, gentle, considerate, friendly, ineffectual printer and Vasu, the self-centred egotist, a man of action is too obvious to be overlooked. Whereas Nataraj is mainly passive and incapable of controlling what happens to him, Vasu is an aggressive man devoted to the goal of "individual achievement." It is because of this implicit allegorical structure, Edwin Gerow comments that the novel follows "the classical pattern of Sanskrit literature."[55]

Apart from the Bhasmasura parallcl there are also references to Vishnu as the destroyer of evil, especially as the saviour of the mythical elephant Gajendra in the *Bhagavata,* a parallel of the "temple elephant" in the novel.

Implicit in the diametrically opposed characteristics of Nataraj and Vasu is the allegorical or mythical conflict between good and evil, *satva* and *rajas,* the *sura* and *asura.* The *sura* and *asura* is a recurrent motif in Hindu mythology. The *asuras* were powerful, sometimes even more than the gods, and many times they triumphed, threatening god Indra in heaven with chaos and confusion. But every time Indra's throne was saved by some miracle or divine strategy whereby the demons caused their own destruction and order was restored in the cosmos again.[56]

In the *Man-Eater of Malgudi* Narayan follows the same *Puranic* pattern, rendering the ancient myth with credibility using both parallelism and ironic contrast—Nataraj, the gentle, friendly printer, the representative of all that is good and cherished in the tradition, and Vasu, the self-centred, power-thirsty individual.

Nataraj is the printer of Malgudi. He owns a printing press, stationed behind a "sanctimonious" blue curtain. The curtain normally keeps the goings on there hidden from the view of the visitors and clients. Nataraj is very much a family man, deeply involved and embedded in the secure fold of the society. The description of his friends who frequent his press, and have made it into a meeting point provide us a glimpse into the communal life of Malgudi. The poet who is "writing the life of God Krishna in monosyllabic verse" and Sen, the journalist who "held forth on the mistakes Nehru was making"[57] represent the social fabric of the peaceful Malgudi world. "Into this world of composed shades and subtleties of relationships, of traditions, complex feelings, of hallowed objects, of modes of conduct and habits of thought which are both ritualistic and homely, there intrudes the abstract and brutal will of "H.Vasu, M.A., Taxidermist,"[58] which is indicated by his violating Nataraj's privacy, for, the curtain stands as a remembrance of Nataraj's right to privacy. And "so binding are the observable proprieties in Nataraj's little society that none has tried to pierce the curtain." But this normal pattern of existence is disrupted by Vasu. For, he brushes the curtain aside in order to state his purpose. Then he establishes himself in the attic of Nataraj's press. From the very beginning he seems to affect the peaceful, ordered universe of Malgudi. Even physically Vasu intimidates Nataraj and his friends and, his appearance corresponds to that of a *rakshasa*. The "black halo" simile is the first hint of Vasu's demoniac character. He sets up his business as a taxidermist, ravaging the forests of Mempi Hills, rich in wild life. He kills animals and brings them to the attic, stuffs and exports them, all single-handed. Soon the whole place becomes filled with the stinking smell of the carcasses and sickening odours of the chemicals. Nataraj's neighbours complain about the increasing stench and the insanitary surroundings in a residential area; he goes to Vasu and tells him to do his tanning and curing of the animal skins elsewhere. He requests Vasu to look for a new house and advises him to let others live in peace. Vasu's reply to this is "we are not lone dwellers in the Sahara to live self-centred lives, and there is no point in living like a recluse." (30) It should be noted, however, that in spite of his insistence on man being a social animal, it is Vasu himself who is anti-social in his isolation and egoism. It is he who tries to evict Nataraj unlawfully, frightens children, kills dogs, disturbs people, and flouts every convention.

Vasu becomes a menacing presence in the normal flow of life. For example he sets the house-rent controller onto Nataraj, without any gratefulness for providing him shelter, which reveals the negative potentiality of Vasu as an evil force. He derives a devilish pleasure in processing and bringing animals back to life. Viewed thus, he is rightly nick-named "man-eater" by Nataraj. Nataraj observes: "Now it was like having a middle-aged man-eater in your office and home, with the same uncertainties, possibilities, and potentialities." (34)

That he is anti-social is revealed also by his disgust for Nataraj's friends, and representatives of the Malgudi community at large. He says, "Your whole crowd sickens me! You are a fellow without any sense. Why you are so enthusiastic about a poet – as obsessed with monosyllables I don't know. And then that local Nehru. Who does he think he is? All of you joining to waste every one's time and money! If I had any authority I'd prohibit celebrations of this kind as a waste of national energy." (165)

It becomes clear that he does not hold good any of the cherished values of the society. He goes against every ethical code and even goes to the extent of bringing home temple prostitute Rangi, and a procession of other women. All these acts set him apart from the ordinary humanity. He has no regard either for man or for beast. He does not consider any institution sacred. He is the lord of the universe; he had no use for other people. For him society is something to be exploited, and not to be contributed.

In spite of the fact that Vasu oppresses and harasses him Nataraj still feels a strange mingling of dread and admiration for Vasu and does not want to lose him. Though he is a terrible specimen of human being Nataraj wants to be on talking terms with him. This strange fascination for Vasu and his attempt to re-establish friendly relations with the taxidermist indicates that "evil is not merely stronger but also more attractive than goodness."[59]

Sastri's definition of Vasu corresponds to that of a *rakshasa*: "a demoniac creature who possessed enormous strength, strange power, and genius, but recognized no sort of restraints of man or God." (95) Unable to solve the problem of his menacing presence the people at large, like the poet, "develop the art of surviving Vasu's presence." But society cannot tolerate such evil presence and the end must come.

With the strict vigil of the guards, the Mempi forest becomes inaccessible to Vasu. He starts shooting pet dogs and animals. He even shoots a circling eagle – a *garuda* "the messenger of God Vishnu," and announces to Nataraj that he wants to sell stuffed *garudas* each for fifty rupees. (66)

Vasu plans to kill the temple elephant "Kumar." Nataraj comes to know about the plan through Rangi. He is appalled at the thought of destroying the sacred temple elephant. By now the image of *rakshasa* is complete. Vasu is too confident of himself, too sure of his superiority. As Sastri wisely remarks: "Every *Rakshasa* gets swollen with his own ego. He thinks he is invincible, beyond every law. But sooner or later something or other will destroy him." (95)

Nataraj tells his friends of Vasu's plans to shoot Kumar and incensed they seek the help of the Deputy Superintendent of Police who is rendered helpless by Vasu. He dislocates the inspector's wrist. This scene makes it explicit how the strong man of evil continues to be reckless until he is destroyed by the tempo of his own misdeeds. Evil has in it, buried subtly, the infalliable seeds of its own destruction and however frightening a demon may seem, his doom is implied in his own evil propensities.

Nataraj thinks it his moral duty to save the elephant, since it is he, who borrowed it for the temple festival. Deciding to deal with Vasu himself, he visits Vasu and entreats him not to harm the elephant and the reply he gets is: "Has it occurred to you how much more an elephant is worth dead." (167) Crestfallen Nataraj returns and realizes that it is too late to stop the celebrations. He tries either to postpone or to change the route of procession, only to be laughed at by the people. Helpless to do anything he goes back to the temple and watches the *puja* being performed. He is reminded of the Gajendra myth. Gajendra, the elephant of the myth steps into a lake and has his leg caught in the jaws of a mighty crocodile. The elephant struggles helplessly, and in desperation calls on Lord Vishnu, who immediately appears and gives him stength to come out of the jaws of the crocodile. According to the *Bhagavata*, Gajendra was in its former life a human being named Indradyumna, King of Dravila. Cursed by sage Agastya for the poor reception given to him, the king was born as a king elephant and his servants as the elephants of its herd. The crocodile which gripped Gajendra's leg was in its previous birth a *gandharva*, (a semi-divine being) named Huhu. The intervention of Vishnu brought redemption to both the elephant and the crocodile. So it is obvious that the Gajendra story has an added relevance to the meaning of the novel. Nataraj believes that like Gajendra, the temple elephant could be saved by Lord Vishnu. He prays: "Oh, Vishnu! Save our elephant, and save all the innocent men and women who are going to pull the chariot. You must come to our rescue now." (175-76) This is a struggle against the evil and negative force of life that is Vasu.

The festival has another and larger mythical dimension. It is a symbolic reaffirmation of the community itself. And the festival despite Nataraj's apprehensions, proceeds smoothly, uneventful. "The God answered Nataraj's call."[60]

Also Kumar is not just an ordinary elephant, but a temple elephant and elephants in India are considered divine with religious sanctity that Nataraj feels anxious to save Kumar. Kumar's survival means the survival of religion apart from the triumph of good over evil. That is why Nataraj reverts to stealing of Vasu's gun. He holds the gun on supposed-to-be sleeping Vasu and to save the mankind from annihilation, he is ready to give up his life without hesitation. But the procession passes and Nataraj makes a dash for the landing.

Vasu is found murdered during the night. The man-eater of Malgudi is dead. Nataraj is suspected of having committed the murder, but there is no allegation against him because of the lack of evidence. He becomes a social outcast. Thus "the *rakshasa* lives on for a while after his death; the inconvenience he embodies continues as "error" . . . and the power of the rakshasa is so great that even after Nataraj has accomplished the feat which should reintegrate the world of printshop, that world is irretrievable."[61]

Nataraj thinks: "This was the greatest act of destruction that the man-eater had performed, destroying my name, my friendships and my world." He appears to be hopelessly lost. But soon the truth about Vasu's death comes to light. Sastri finds out the truth from Rangi, that "The man [Vasu] had trapped a couple of mosquitoes which had settled on his forehead by bringing the flat of his palm with all his might on top of them." (231) Thus Vasu, the mighty taxidermist, the hot-headed and self-willed manifestation of evil, who threatened to defy all cherished human values to fulfil his own selfish needs, is ultimately caught in his own trap and dies at his own hands. It is Sastri who draws the parallel once again. He brings out the moral fable underlying the mythical structure of the novel: "Every demon appears in the world with a special boon of indestructability. Yet the universe has survived all the *rakshasas* that were ever born. Every demon carries within him, unknown to himself, a tiny seed of self-destruction, and goes up in thin air at the most unexpected moment. Otherwise what is to happen to humanity?" (231) "The settled order of the cosmos, the fundamental ontological fact"[62] is re-established. At the end there is a reconciliation, and restoration of order.

Actually the action of *The Man-Eater of Malgudi* reveals that "events are often fortuitous and the final resolution comes about as a transcendent act. That, it seems to be suggested, is the result of divine intervention."[63]

Vasu happens to be the only total villain in Narayan's fiction.[64] And Narayan is not unaware that he is creating an *asura* in the person of Vasu, because in a radio interview he said: "The man-eater is a man, not a tiger, an ego-centred man for whom the objective world is non-existent – a modern *rakshasa* who wants to kill the elephant that belongs to the local temple."[65]

The novel follows the *Puranic* pattern and has a powerful allegorical component where good and evil are set in a precarious balance. It recreates the ancient Bhasmasura myth in contemporary terms.

Vasu "the invincible" is the man-eater of Malgudi. He takes his place in the Malgudi community as a *rakshasa* – a demon. Rangi, the temple *devadasi* is the parallel of Mohini, the seducer and destroyer of Bhasmasura. This concept Sastri illustrates from the mythic story:

> Bhasmasura . . . acquired a special boon that everything he touched should be scorched, while nothing could destroy him. He made humanity suffer. God Vishnu was incarnated as a dancer of great beauty, named Mohini, with whom the *asura* became infatuated. She promised to yield to him only if he imitated all the gestures and movements of her own dancing. At one point in the dance, Mohini places her palms on her head, and the demon followed this gesture

> in complete forgetfulness and was reduced to ashes that very second, the blighting touch becoming active on his own head. (96)

To quote William Walsh, "the deeply serious idea which sustains *The Man-Eater of Malgudi,* namely the opposition between influences fostering life and those hostile to it, the quarrel between the god Vishnu and the *rakshasa,* is filtered through some of the lightest and yet most solidly established comedy in Narayan."[66]

Thus in *The Man-Eater of Malgudi* R.K. Narayan uses myth as a technique to illustrate his moral vision and he gives the reason for doing so. Lecturing at Columbia University in 1972, Narayan said:

> At some point in one's writing career one takes a fresh look at the so-called myths and legends and finds a new meaning in them. After writing a number of novels and short stories based on the society around me, some years ago I suddenly came across a theme which struck me as an excellent piece of mythology in modern dress. It was published under the title *The Man-Eater of Malgudi.* I based this story on a well-known mythical episode, the story of Mohini and Bhasmasura.[67]

In the way indicated, Narayan "wanted to come into contact with the original purity of Indian fantasy and folk and epic reality."[68] We can clearly feel the position of our contemporary life in Narayan's interpretation of heroic spirit and events of the legendary past.

Through centuries, writers and thinkers have reflected deeply on this problem of the existence of evil and its consequences. Narayan suggests in the novel through Vasu, that evil may be triumphant temporarily, but ultimately, like Bhasmasura, turns out to be a self-destroying and destructive force. Vasu ultimately seals his own doom because anything that mars the rhythm of life must cease to exist in God's creation. N.J. Nanporia has this to say about Narayan's epic theme and his handling of it: "In such a recreation of mythological incident and situation there is considerable promise of the hidden poetry and unrestrained laughter in which Narayan has so successfully located the truth."[69]

Discussing about the novel's effective rendering of the myth M.K. Naik observes: "An intensive analysis of a novel like *The Man-Eater,* however, reveals quite a different Narayan . . . a writer who not only asks some fundamental questions about good and evil and their roles in human life, but also finds his own answers to them. Furthermore, in doing so, he grafts a realistic narration of modern South Indian life in an ancient Hindu myth, thus answering that his questioning solutions are firmly rooted in his own cultural ethos."[70]

The Vendor of Sweets is a variation on the father-son relationship, a popular theme with Narayan. Once again he comes back to and picturizes an indulgent father and a pampered son in the novel. And this story also has its mythic parallel in the epic of *Mahabharata*. The *Mahabharata* tells us the tale of the blind Kuru King Dhritarashtra, a fondly-foolish father who remains helpless, as his stupidly arrogant son, Duryodhana runs into his own ruin.[71]

The novel also deals with the theme of self-identity in the sense, that the entire novel is about Jagan's quest for self-knowledge. Jagan by virtue of the circumstances of his life, engages himself in different kinds of search. But "he is not a deliberate and self-conscious quester."[72]

Jagan the protagonist of the novel is Mali's father. A sixty year old sweet-vendor and an advocate of "Gandhi, the *Gita* and Gayatri." His whole world centers round his son Mali. When the novel opens Jagan is living all alone with his only son Mali, his wife having died ten years ago. Jagan divides his time between his sweet shop and his son – the two levels of his existence. Jagan is absurdly affectionate towards his son Mali, which results in his defying his father. Jagan fails to establish a rapport – any meaningful relationship with his son. There is hardly any communication between the father and the son and neither tries to bridge the gap. Mali does not desire to spend any time with his father and, when he is at home locks himself in his room. As per Jagan he remains satisfied as long as he could get "a glimpse," of his son.

Jagan is indulgent towards Mali and whatever plans Mali makes he tries to go along with them. Even when Mali refuses to go to college, Jagan fails to reprimand him. "He tries to get completely identified with Mali's fantasies."[73] When Mali reveals his desire to be a writer, immediately, Jagan thinks of Kalidasa and others of the great literary tradition. But Mali does not answer Jagan as to the literary form he is attempting, except for vague replies, and becomes a puzzle for him. Jagan is hopelessly lost trying to solve the puzzle called Mali. "He is mired like Dhritarashtra in the narrow grooves of the world."[74]

Jagan is shocked when Mali suddenly declares his intention of going to America to study creative writing. When he comes to know through the cousin that Mali had already made preparations to go to America, he takes a certain pride in his son's self-reliance. "The boy is very practical, he said with feeling." (54)

He feels proud of his son. "My son is in America," he says to all and sundry. The day he gets an airline letter from America, he is atop the pinnacle of joy. He relishes whatever piece of news he gets from Mali. "If it is possible he would have bound them into a neat little volume at Truth

Printing." (61) As it is, gradually his reading of the *Bhagavad Gita* was replaced by the blue air mail letters. (61) Soon after, Mali arrives home and a greater shock awaits Jagan. Mali brings with him Grace, a Korean-American girl and introduces her as his wife. Jagan accepts Grace as his daughter-in-law and even comes to like her and appreciate the feminine touch she brings to the household.

But Mali has a new plan to disrupt the even tenor of life. He comes out with an absurd project, "to manufacture story-writing machines" in India with American collaboration. Jagan is asked to contribute fifty thousand dollars for the project. He refuses to do anything with it. For, "Mali's story-writing machine is the ultimate profanity in the realm of art. He rejects his own culture,"[75] a culture which Jagan affirms. He tries to ignore the whole business by "non-violent non-cooperation." But it does not work for long. Mali confronts him one day, and demands an answer. Jagan tries to wean Mali away from his project by offering him to hand-over the sweet shop. But Mali reacts contemptuously.

Jagan is deeply hurt because it is the very same business that had provided the money for Mali to fly to America and do all sorts of things there (98) and comes to the conclusion that "money is an evil" and makes a drastic reduction in the price of sweets. It is at this phase of life he meets Chinna Dorai the sculptor and hair-dyer, who comes to seek Jagan's patronage to complete the image of the Goddess.

All is not over and yet another shock awaits Jagan. He discovers that Mali and Grace are not married. His moral sensibilities are shocked and he feels that they have polluted his ancestral house. Recovering himself he suggests they both get married but Mali laughs at the idea. Jagan is baffled. And even at his shop his mind works on one theme only—the puzzle created by Mali. Jagan is reminded of the concept of *Viswarupa* that he has read about in the *Bhagavad Gita* but he is "rational enough to realize the irreverence of the comparison." (153) As Barry Argyle observes: "The irreverence occurs not in the comparison, but in Jagan having made of his son a god. Like his father, Mali is many-sided but he remains a man. Man can create both gods and sons, but there is only confusion in trying to combine them."[76]

Thus Jagan finds out that "puzzling over things was enervating" and reading a sense in Mali's actions was fatiguing like the attempt to spell out a message in a half-familiar attempt. He comes to the realization that he was fit only for retirement. He recollects Chinna Dorai's advice to develop an interest in the making of the Goddess's image. He makes up his mind to retire to his chosen retreat.

But before he leaves a final shock awaits Jagan. The news of Mali's imprisonment for violating prohibition laws, is brought to him by the cousin. Jagan is initially disturbed, but is able to recover his composure. He is not any more blind to his son's faults. "A dose of prison life is not a bad thing. It may be just what he needs now. If what you say is true, well, truth will win." (191)

If circumstances force Jagan, to withdraw from the world and take up a life of renunciation, Daisy voluntarily gives up the bonds of the family and society. The relationship of Daisy and Raman in *The Painter of Signs* is based on the legendary relationship of King Santhanu and Goddess Ganga of the *Mahabharata.* Raman and Daisy relationship resembles that of Sriram-Bharati of *Waiting for the Mahatma* but in a more refined way. The pair also reminds one of Rosie and Raju of *The Guide,* Ravi and Shanti of *Mr. Sampath* and also Chandran and Malathi of *The Bachelor of Arts.*

The novel is built around Santhanu-Ganga myth of the *Mahabharata* as already mentioned. Raman a sign-painter meets Daisy, a staunch believer and upholder of the cause of the family planning at the Family Planning Centre. Not a believer in any kind of relationship that ties down a woman, she agrees to marry Raman on certain conditions.

After a brief period of togetherness, Daisy, realizing that married life is not for her, leaves Raman for intensive family planning work at remote villages. This is the mythical parallel. There are also references to other legends like Lord Krishna and Rukmini, where Krishna abducts Rukmini and marries her. Mohini-Bhasma myth, Mohini alluring Bhasma to his self-destruction, is also mentioned in the novel. While Raman is likened to Santhanu, Daisy is first likened to Mohini luring Raman and next to Ganga wishing to give away each child she may beget.[77] The novel appears to have as its context these three myths.

The legend central to the novel, taken from the *Mahabharata*, runs as follows: Santhanu was fond of hunting and passed much of his life in the woods. One day, as he was wandering along the banks of the river Ganga, he saw a lovely maiden. The monarch then in soft words addressed her: "O slender-waisted one, O thou of celestial beauty, I solicit thee to be my wife."

Of faultless features, the damsel replied: "O King, I shall be your wife and obey thy commands. But thou must not interfere with me in anything I do, be it agreeable or disagreeable. . . . I shall certainly leave thee the moment thou interferes with me or speaks to me an unkind word." The King answered: "Be it so! True to his promise, he refrained from crossing her in anything and the Lord of Earth, Santhanu, was exceedingly gratified with her conduct, beauty and attention to his comforts. And the goddess Ganga also . . . lived happily as the wife of Santhanu. . . . Eight children were born unto him. But those children, as soon as they were born, were one after another thrown into the river by Ganga, who repeated. 'This is for thy good.' The king could not be pleased with such conduct. But he spoke not a word about it lest his wife should leave him. When the eighth child was born and his wife as before was about to throw it into the river, the King, anxious to save it, addressed her and said: "Kill it not." The wife, thus addressed, replied "According to our agreement the period of my stay with thee must now end. . . . I leave thee." And that child of Santhanu known as both Gangeya or Deva-vrata was left to live.[78]

Raman, a bachelor, is a signboard painter. He regards his profession as a "means of communication" between the people without which they will wallow in isolation. He profeses to be a rationalist. He wants to think none of money and sex as he regards them as the twin evils of society. He wishes to establish that "there are other things more important in life than sex and that man-woman relationship is not inevitable. Yet he is obsessed with them.

Raman meets Daisy when he is commissioned to write a signboard for the Family Planning Centre. Daisy asks Raman to paint a board for her clinic, "Family Planning Centre, Free Advice." He falls passionately in love with her and immediately gets lost in erotic thoughts. His determination to remain a bachelor disappears in thin air the moment he sees her. He determines to give her the "best possible service," finds excuses to meet her and gets familiar with her but is discouraged by "a calculated coldness in her look."[79] Thus the rationalist is completely infatuated by Daisy. He analyzes his behaviour and realizes that he is "obsessed."

Daisy with her "non-denominational" name poses a problem to Raman from the start. He fails to understand her missionary zeal for family planning. He tries to resist the attraction of Daisy but fails. Daisy becomes Mohini the temptress luring him to his very downfall. Even though "he had determined to give sex its place . . . somehow the gods didn't seem to like it." (34) They establish a friendship and come together as lovers but the association proves to be brief. Raman proposes marriage but Daisy is not for it, as she sees nothing extraordinary for a man and a woman beginning to live under the same roof. (131) But for Raman's sake she agrees to a *gandharva* type of marriage, thinking it most suitable for them. "That was the type of marriage one reads about in classical literature." (124) Raman even goes against his aunt's wishes, as a result of which she leaves for Benares. Thus "Raman's *dharmic* responsibilities are seriously eroded by his passion for Daisy,"[80] even to the point where work is relegated to a second place and where he lets his aunt leave his home. Narayan brings out the inherent irony in the situation—"the serious obligations in his life, now appear less serious to Raman in the light of his great passion."[81]

Despite his aunt having left him, Raman intends to bring home his bride. He accepts her decision of the *gandharva*-style marriage, but she, "the final deciding authority" in their relationship, lays down two conditions to marriage: "one, that they should have no children, two, if by mischance one was born she would give the child away and keep herself free to pursue her social work." (124) She further warns him: "If you want to marry me you must leave me to my own plans even when I am a wife. On any day you question why or how, I will leave you." (124) Raman enslaved by her agrees to let her have her own way. It is Raman himself who brings in the Santhanu-Ganga myth and likens himself to King Santhanu, "whatever you say I will never interfere. I won't question you, I will be like the ancient King Santhanu." (125)

In spite of his promise to Daisy to let her lead her own life even as his wife, he could not help having serious doubts about their relationship. But Daisy remains indifferent to all his plans of making "a home together" and plans for future. She leaves everything to Raman and does not care much about the domestic arrangements.

When Raman insists that she move to his house, she suddenly realizes that she is not cut out for married life. Not "interested in making a home,"[82] she makes it clear to Raman that she "cannot afford to have a personal life" and that she would not swerve from her chosen purpose. Daisy, the "kindred soul," thus leaves Raman to pursue the family planning campaign. "Like Celia in Eliot's *Cocktail Party*, she has chosen her destiny."

Faced with Daisy's missionary zeal and rendered helpless Raman reflects: "May be we will live together in our next *janma*. At least then she will leave people alone, I hope" (143) just on the lines of King Santhanu.

Once more in *A Tiger for Malgudi* Narayan takes up one of his favourite themes – that of renunciation as an ideal. But unlike *The Guide* where he presents the concept ironically, here in *A Tiger for Malgudi* he portrays the theme "in its ideal focus against the ridiculous perspective in humorous hues."[83] But this does not mean that he confines himself to exploring the theme in these two novels only. Actually even in his first novel *Swami and Friends* Narayan shows his interest in the concept of *sanyasi* and touches upon this theme in all his novels – from *Swami and Friends* to *A Tiger for Malgudi* and *The World of Nagaraj,* his latest. The difference lies in that whereas in the earlier novel "the ridiculous is presented conspicuously suggesting the ideal, in the later ones the ideal is conspicuously portrayed leaving the ludicrous fade away into insignificance."[84]

The novel is a blend of myth and fable. It belongs to the lore of

Panchatantra – the great Indian classic for all times, written by Vishnusarma. Vishnusarma wanting to instruct the three princes of the King Amarasakthi in the principles of policy and worldly wisdom, taught by means of stories enacted by animals. He chooses as his characters the animals like a lion, a monkey, a bull and a jackal to compose entertaining as well as edifying fables. The *Panchatantra* is a unique source of instruction and entertainment with "visions and concepts that are true for all times and elements projecting the spirit and reality of its origin."[85] Narayan follows the literary tradition of *Panchatantra* where animals act and behave as human beings, being the protagonists.

A Tiger for Malgudi, as Narayan himself says is the story of salvation. It is a myth of *sanyasi*[86] preaching the *Karmayoga* of the *Bhagavad Gita* and upholding the *guru-sishya* or teacher-disciple relationship of Lord Krishna and Arjuna as an ideal to attain salvation.

The novel tells us the tale of a tiger "with a soul." It is the autobiography of the tiger. The tiger ruminates over its past starting from its early days to the spiritual awakening in the hermit's hands. The tiger starts its life as a cub living with its mother in a cave in the forest. One day, the mother disappears and fails to return. But the tiger gets used to its mother's absence, learns to fend for itself and in time grows up. The realization of its mighty power gives the tiger supremacy over the animal kingdom and it achieves an identity as the Supreme Lord of the Jungle. Later it becomes the husband of the tigress and the father of four cubs. One day the tigress strays into human habitation and is shot dead along with her four cubs. The tiger sees the carcasses of its wife and cubs being carried by the hunters and, wanting to wreak vengeance, it is caught in the trap of the villagers and is captured by the Captain. The Captain, the owner of the "Grand Malgudi Circus" tames and trains him and makes him perform in the circus. The tiger resigns itself to its fate in the circus until the Captain uses the metal gadget to satisfy the whim of the eccentric film director, Madan. Unable to bear the humiliation any more the tiger tries to warn the Captain but in the process kills him accidentally. Freed and released from bonds of captivity, it walks through the streets of Malgudi and takes shelter in the room of the school headmaster. The hermit now appears on the scene and brings the tiger under his hypnotic spell. Being unaware of the spiritual power of the hermit the tiger tries to resist him. But subdued spiritually and rendered helpless, it follows the hermit (like a disciple). The hermit names the tiger "Raja" and they retire to Mempi Hills and pass their days in philosophical and spiritual discourses on the teachings of the *Bhagavad Gita*. Time passes and the "beautiful old age" descends on them both, compelling them to part from each other. The hermit realizes that the time has come for him to part company with the tiger, and attain his *samadhi.* He entrusts the tiger to the care of a zoo and hopes to meet him again in the next life.

Narayan's use of animal allegory has a definite purpose. He intends to show, through the tale of a tiger possessed with the soul of an enlightened human being, that "deep within, the core personality is the same in spite of differing appearances and categories, and with the right approach you could expect the same response from a tiger as from any normal human being."[87] "That the Atman in Man is the very same vital force in the elephant, in the gnat, the ant, the four quarters of the world; in short, the Atman in Man is part and parcel of the whole universe."[88] Here Narayan is referring to the traditional belief, which reinforces the central theme of the novel touched upon even in an earlier novel *The Man-Eater of Malgudi.* The reference is to the belief in the doctrines of transmigration of souls into other bodies, human as well as non-human, and rebirth and reincarnation. Belief in these doctrines is well-rooted in the minds of the poeple and is shared by Hindus, Buddhists and Jains with slight variations and modifications. And these doctrines "can be traced back to the earliest times in the history of Indian thought."[89]

According to the belief of transmigration and rebirth, one is born high or low, or as a human being or an animal or any of the lower order creatures, all due to one's *Karman*, one's deeds and conducts, in the course of the cycle of births. Thus, "Each human soul goes through a continuous series of reincarnations reaping the fruits of thoughts, desires and actions done in the past and generating, during the process of reaping, new causes which will bear fruits in this or future lives."[90] *The Chandogya Upanishad* says: "Those whose conduct here has been good will quickly attain a good birth, the birth of a Brahmana, the birth of a Kshatriya or the birth of a Vaisya. But those whose conduct here has been evil, will quickly attain an evil birth of a dog, the birth of a log or the birth of a *Chandala*."[91] *The Katha Upanishad* says on the theme: "Some souls enter into a womb for embodiment; others enter stationary objects according to their deeds and according to their thoughts."[92] The *Manu Smriti* puts it thus:

> Action, which springs from "Action, which springs from the mind, from speech, and from the body, produces either good or evil results. By action are caused the various conditions of men, the highest, the middling, and the lowest. A man obtains the result of a good or evil mental act in his mind, that of a verbal act on his speech, that of a bodily act in his body. In consequence of many sinful acts committed with his body, a man becomes in the next birth something inanimate, in consequence of sins committed by speech,

> a bird or a beast, and in consequence of mental sins he is reborn in a low caste.[93]

In the *Ramayana* and the *Mahabharata* also one finds a number of instances of Gods and human beings transformed, under curse, into subhuman creatures like tigers, elephants, birds and snakes.

That is why Narayan chooses a "tiger as the central character" in the novel. And the novel is the story of a tiger – punctuated in four *asramas* (stages) of life – *brahmacharya* (bachelor), *garhasthya* (householder), *vanaprasthya* (detached life) and finally *sanyasa* (renunciation). Raja, the tiger, passes through all these stages and attains "the ideal spiritual identity in selfless service[94] like his *guru* -- the hermit.

The tiger in the novel is a "tiger with a soul" endowed with intelligence and human personality, unlike Vasu, the "metaphorical" man-eater. Spiritualized by the hermit the tiger behaves in a much more "humanly way than human beings." The tiger follows its *guru* to the foot of the Mempi Hills and there they lead a life of peace and serenity trying to attain the heights of spiritual enlightenment. The tiger and his *guru* following the *guru-sishya* tradition, hold long discourses on the preachings of the *Bhagavad Gita.* The tiger now "redeemed" is able to understand "yoga, life and existence of death" (157) and even has his own conception of God as an enormous tiger, spanning the earth and the sky and even feels remorse for having killed the animals for his sustenance. Raja too along with its *guru* looks forward to attain salvation. The enlightenment of the tiger which says: "You are not likely to understand that I am different from the tiger next door, that I possess a soul within the formidable exterior. I can think, analyse, judge, remember and do anything that you do, perhaps with greater subtlety and sense, (11-12) is not too far-fetched if one thinks of the tales of *Panchatantra* and especially *Jataka* tales. For, the *Jataka* tales are nothing but stories – depicting various reincarnations of Bodhisattva as deer, monkey or elephant, before he becomes Buddha the Enlightened one. Also the hermit is likened to Buddha (hence the Buddha image) whose reincarnations are described in the *Jataka* tales. The inference here is, that, he too might have been in his previous birth a tiger. He and Raja might have been brothers then. Hence his brotherly feeling and association with Raja. Therefore the enlightenment of the tiger may be due to his *karma.* According to the traditional Hindu thought one is not doomed to suffer for ever. The soul has chances of acquiring merit and thereby advancing to eternal life. And this is what exactly happens to Raja. The tiger is redeemed through its spiritual transformation and selfless service to society. That is why it is said that "one who is born as a bird or beast, can in the course of the series of births and deaths redeem himself by his *Karma* and rise again in the hierarchy of creation."[95]

Hence it is not at all difficult to accept the miracle of the spiritual transformation of a tiger from "the subhuman to the superhuman sphere"[96] because he is simply meeting his preordained destiny.

The theme of renunciation thus finds full expression in the novel. The hermit is a true *sanyasi*, one who considers it his duty to serve the society. Hence he walks into Malgudi to subdue the tiger before it harms anyone. He takes the tiger back with him, gives it a name (Raja) and spiritualizes it with a brotherly sympathy. The hermit realizes that the "soul is universal" and recognizes the same in the tiger also. This belief or brotherly feeling the hermit expresses towards the tiger can be traced back to the doctrine of transmigration. One can say that Narayan, by an enchanting combination of myth and fable, brought home the centuries-old religious and philosophical beliefs.

Talkative Man (1985) is one of the latest novels of Narayan. After a break of several years Narayan once more tells the tale of an abandoned wife. Narayan seems to take up where he left off several years ago, for, he takes up the theme of a suffering wife. Savitri of *The Dark Room* appears as the Commandant Sarasa in *Talkative Man.* The times have changed, Malgudi has become modernized and the impact of modernity is clearly seen. Even the attitudes of the people change to a certain extent and all modern amenities are there. But the plight of these two women remains the same. Both suffer because of the immorality of their husbands and both are humiliated at the hands of their husbands. Both have womanizing husbands. Both have differences in their capabilities and outlook. Savitri of yesteryears in *The Dark Room* remains incapable of earning her livelihood, but today's woman Sarasa is economically independent. There is yet another difference between the two, that is the difference in their outlook. Savitri, though a traditional housewife tries to become a liberated woman and fails whereas Sarasa though modern in the sense that she is able to fend for herself and is economically independent, appears to be more traditional in her values. For it is she who goes after her husband, however bad he may be. Thus upholding the traditional values, while Savitri comes back to her husband and family grudgingly because she has no other go, and because of her mental makeup and her attachment to her children. Sarasa would willingly give up everything if only she could retain her husband.

Rann in the *Talkative Man* is none other than Ramani but more sophisticated. Both are smooth and incurable womanizers, disloyal to their wives but with one difference. Where Ramani confines himself to Malgudi in his philandering activities, Rann operates on a "global scale."

In the novel, Narayan seems to recount the legend of Savitri and Satyavan of the *Mahabharata* fame. The myth appears as a parallel in the story. Sarasa is the wife of Dr. Rann, the "futurologist" whom talkative man (TM) befriends at the Town Hall Library and gives shelter in his own house in Kabir Street. Everything goes on smoothly until the arrival of Sarasa from Delhi. She meets TM and asks him about Rann, whom she claims to be her husband. TM, unable to believe what is being said about Rann escapes from her saying that he met Rann only briefly and at the time he was enquiring about some long distance buses. However, Sarasa comes searching for TM, to find out Rann's whereabouts. TM denies any knowledge about Rann. It is then that Sarasa narrates her story, about her past life with Rann. Having met Rann as a paper boy how she has fallen in love and married him against her parents' wishes having run away from home, how they set up their family, how they were found out by Sarasa's parents, and how a law suit had been brought against Rann for having abducted a minor girl; and how a lawyer, a customer of the library where Rann works, helped clear the case, and how the court declared the couple to have been properly married; how after having undergone a change of personality, Rann failed to come home one evening, and how, after having traced him through the Travel Agency of the Kuwait Air Counter she lost trace of him. After having seen the photograph in the newspaper she has come all the way from Delhi to find him and as she puts it emphatically "to get at that man."[97]

Later, finding that her search for Rann is futile, she leaves for Delhi. But after some time she receives a telegram from TM asking her to "come immediately." As soon as she receives the telegram Sarasa arrives from Delhi and having been instructed by TM's letter abducts Rann. However, six months later she comes in search of TM, and tells him that Rann has "vanished again," (136) ten days ago. There are many parallels in the novel of Savitri-Satyavan myth. Sarasa meets, falls in love and marries Rann against her parents' wishes, like the legendary Savitri, who after having fallen in love with Satyavan marries him against her parents' wishes. Thus with her relentless pursuit Sarasa reminds one of the legendary Savitri who follows *Yama*, the God of Death, when he takes away her husband's life. She wins him back but the modern Sarasa captures her husband only to be deserted by him once again.

It is Varma, the proprietor of The Boardless Hotel, who brings out the mythical paralled in the novel. Varma is very much impressed with the wife's determined pursuit and capture of her husband:

> It reminds one of Savitri and Satyavan of our legends. How Savitri persistently followed Yama, the God of Death, when he plucked

> away her husband's life; how Savitri dogged his steps as he tried to move off, pleading and pleading until he yielded, and how Satyavan whose body had lain inert in the forest, revived and joined his wife. I think this commandant is a similar one. (136)

The most recent of Narayan's novels, *Grandmother's Tale*, biography of a great Grandmother, could be called personal fiction. Narayan himself says: "The borderline between fact and fiction, between biography and tale wears thin and ultimately vanishes in the following chronicle." Further one does not know "how much of it is history and how much is fiction." [98] That it might not all be imaginary would be concluded from the fact that the descendants of the couple in the story are present in our midst in different walks of life scattered here and there, with this author (Narayan) being one.

It is the tale of Narayan's great grandmother who lived in the later period of the East India Company. Bala, the central character, was married at the early age of seven to Viswa a boy of ten. One day, he just left bidding her good-bye, joining a group of pilgrims going to Pandaripur. Years go by and there is no trace of him. Bala, now a young woman finds life extremely difficult with the entire *Agraharam* gossiping about her husband's fate. She leaves house, determined to find him. The arduous journey she undertakes to Poona, her success in locating Viswa and persuading him to return to the South and their lone, happy life in Kumbakonam, where five children are born to them, Bala's death and eventually Viswa's death due to poisoning by his cook form the narrative.

As in the earlier novels of his, Narayan takes up the theme of an abandoned wife. Once again there is a parallel between the Savitri-Satyavan legend of the *Mahabharata* in the story line of the novel. The same theme occurs in the *Talkative Man* (1988). The protagonist is Sarasa, the commandant, a modern woman from Delhi who comes to Malgudi in search of her errant husband. Likewise in *Grandmother's Tale*, the protagonist Bala is also a deserted wife. She too goes searching for her missing husband, who with no thought for her renounced the family and left for Pandaripur. But the difference lies in that whereas Sarasa fails to capture her husband and keep him with her, Bala quite succeeds in doing so. She goes to Poona, finds her husband, pursues him relentlessly and brings him back home and settles down to a happy married life in Kumbakonam.

Thus Bala of *Grandmother's Tale* is none other than Sarasa of the *Talkative Man* in another guise. But whereas Sarasa is a modern woman, Bala belongs to that period of later East India Company rule in India. She is married quite young to Viswa. Her life changes after her marriage.

She could not go out freely, or join her friends playing in the street. She could not even meet her husband except on special occasions such as the New Year and other festival days when Viswa was invited to visit his wife's house with his parents.

After their first meeting, during which they felt shy, they discover an interest in each other. But it is not easy for them to meet publicly in front of the elders. Instead, Viswa finds out that his wife is more accessible at the backyard and takes to meeting her there. They would not meet normally as husband and wife. Bala being only ten years old, must attain puberty and then go through an elaborate nuptial ceremony before she could join her husband. But Viswa has other plans. He comes to see Bala and announces: "I am going away. Keep it a secret." (22) When she asks him where he is going, he simply says he does not know. As to why he is leaving: "I have to go away – that is all." (22) That is the last Bala sees her husband for a long time – in fact many years to come.

Bala remains indifferent for a week and then full of anxiety informs her mother and in-laws. But their search for Viswa proves futile. As time passes, Bala comes of age and finds her existence a "sore trial." People of the *Agraharam* persist in demanding news of Viswa. When they fail to do so they believe Viswa to be no more and ask Bala to shave her head and observe the rules of a widow. Unable to bear the humiliation, Bala vows: "I'll not rest until I come back with him some day and shame you all."

In course of time, Bala reaches Poona and finds Viswa residing there but with his other wife Surma. Bala gains the sympathy of Surma who is kind enough to provide shelter for her. After a few months at Poona, Bala confirms the identity of Viswa, confronts him and threatens to reveal his true identity to Surma unless he goes away with her. He pleads for time but eventually gives in to her demands. Accompanied by Surma, they undertake the journey but on way Bala ruthlessly gets rid of Surma, even though she is all sympathy for Surma. She admits, "You have been like a goddess to me, but I cannot go home with you. Our village will not accept you. You see this *thali* was knotted by him. He is my husband, I can't share him with you." (62) Bala remains unmoved by all the pleadings of Surma and Surma turns back towards Poona. Thus finally Bala wins Viswa from Surma.

The parallel to the Savitri-Satyavan legend of the *Mahabharata* fame is thus clear to us. As Savitri pursues Yama, so Bala wins her husband from his other wife Surma. There is a direct reference to the myth in the novel. The narrator, the grandmother of the author says: "what else could a poor woman like her do to recover her husband. Only a woman can understand it. To a woman, her husband is everything. She cannot lose him. Remember in what condition Bala had left home and what trials she must have gone through to reach Poona and how much misery she faced before she could reach him. Everything is justified, all means are justified in her case. Did not Savitri conquer Yama himself, and trap him into promising her a boon? And the boon she asked for was to beget children and he had to give her his blessing that she could have children. After accepting the boon, she asked how it would be possible when he as the God of Death was carrying away her husband's life, leaving his inert body in the forest . . . and then Yama had to yield back Satyavan's life. You should not imagine a greater woman than Savitri for austerity and purity of mind." (65-66)

In this way the art of story-telling has a long antiquity in India. And the myths and legends of the *Vedic* times have been followed by the stories of the *Upanishads* and epics and the *Jatakas* which merge into history blurring the frontiers between history and fiction. Narayan thus belongs to a great tradition; a tradition which had been arrested for a few hundred years though all the while the oral tradition had a vitality and a continuity among the masses and has now been revived, and through which he suggests the nature of his characters and the meaning of their acts and perhaps his own attitude towards them in relation to his vision of life.[99] As he himself says "the hold of religion and the conception of gods ingrained in us must necessarily find a place in any accurate portrayal of life."[100] For this reason one also sees Narayan the novelist as a "moral analyst"[101] depicting his own vision of life through the mode of comic. It can be said that Narayan writes not merely with an intense social awareness of his own age but with the past of India in his bones, and one feels one's social sympathies are broadened and one's moral being considerably heightened.[102]

NOTES

1. Richard Chase, *Quest for Myth*, quoted by Meenakshi Mukherjee, *The Twice-Born Fiction*, p. 130.
2. Northrop Frye, *Fables of Identity: Studies in Poetic Mythology* (New York, 1963), p. 27.
3. Shyam M. Asnani "The Use of Myth in R.K. Narayan's Novels," *Literary Endeavour*, vol. I, nos. 3 and 4, April-June 1982, p. 19.
4. *Ibid.*, p. 20.
5. Meenakshi Mukherjee, "Myth as Technique," *The Twice-Born Fiction*, p. 31.
6. R.K. Narayan, *Gods, Demons and Others* (Delhi: Hind Pocket

Books, 1979), p. 43.

7. H.M. Williams, "Precarious Innocence," *Perspectives on R.K. Narayan*, ed. Atma Ram (Ghaziabad: Vimal, 1981), p. 6.
8. R.K. Narayan, "English in India: The Process of Transmutation," *Aspects of Indian Writing in English*, ed. M.K. Naik (New Delhi: Macmillan, 1979), p. 21.
9. Shyam M. Asnani, p. 22.
10. R.K. Narayan, *Swami and Friends* (Mysore: Indian Thought Publications, 1983), pp. 32-33.
11. K.V.S. Murti, "Monkey and Hanuman," *Studies in Contemporary Indian Fiction in English* (New Delhi: Sterling, 1987), p. 127.
12. *Swami and Friends,* pp. 5-9.
13. H.M. Williams, p. 7.
14. K.V.S. Murti, p. 128.
15. R.K. Narayan *The English Teacher* (Mysore: Indian Thought Publications, 1984), p. 203.
16. K.V.S. Murti, p. 130.
17. *Ibid*.
18. H.M. Williams, p. 7.
19. K.V.S. Murti, p. 130.
20. R.K. Narayan, *The Mahabharata* (Mysore: Indian Thought Publications, 1979), pp. 142-48.
21. R.K. Narayan, *Mr.Sampath* (Mysore: Indian Thought Publications, 1985), p. 30.
22. Ron Shepherd, "The Sublime and the Ridiculous: Allegory and Irony in R.K. Narayan," *R.K. Narayan: A Critical Spectrum*, ed. Bhagwat S. Goyal (Meerut: Shalabh, 1983), p. 84.
23. Shirley Chew, "A Proper Detachment: The Novels of R.K. Narayan," *Readings in Commonwealth Literature* (Oxford: Clarendon, 1973), p. 65.
24. *Ibid.*, p. 66.
25. Ron Shepherd, p. 80.
26. *Ibid.*
27. *Ibid.*, p. 81.
28. K.V.S. Murti, p. 8.
29. *Ibid.*, p. 134.
30. R.K. Narayan, *The Financial Expert* (Mysore: Indian Thought Publications, 1984), p. 22.
31. Ben Jonson, *Volpone*, I, i, 25-27.
32. Shyam M. Asnani, p. 25.
33. K.V.S. Murti, p. 135.
34. R.K. Narayan, *Gods, Demons and Others,* cf. *The Mahabharata*, pp.

150-68.

35. R.K. Narayan, *The Mahabharata*, pp. 187-94.
36. Meenakshi Mukherjee, p. 42.
37. Rameshwar Gupta, "The Gandhi in Narayan," *Perspectives on R.K. Narayan,* p. 55.
38. K.V.S. Murti, p. 137.
39. R.K. Narayan, *Waiting for the Mahatma* (Mysore: Indian Thought Publications, 1984), p. 59.
40. K.V.S. Murti, p. 136.
41. *Ibid.*, p. 137.
42. S.C. Harrex, "*The Guide* as a Guide to Narayan's Art," *R.K. Narayan—A Critical Spectrum*, p. 107.
43. Bhagwat S. Goyal, "From Picaro to Pilgrim: A Perspective on R.K. Narayan's *The Guide*," *Indo-English Literature*, ed. K.K. Sharma (Ghaziabad: Vimal, 1977), p. 142.
44. William Walsh, "Sweet Mangoes and Malt Vinegar," *Indo-English Literature*, p. 148.
45. R.K. Narayan, *The Guide* (Mysore: Indian Thought Publications, 1986), p. 8.
46. Bhagwat S.Goyal, p. 148.
47. William Walsh, p. 131.
48. S.C. Harrex, p. 109.
49. *Ibid.*, p. 110.
50. C.D. Narasimhaiah, *The Swan and the Eagle* (Simla: Indian Institute of Advanced Study, 1969), p. 157.
51. C.D. Narasimhaiah, R.K. Narayan's *The Guide*, p. 198.
52. *Ibid.*, p. 192.
53. *Ibid.*
54. R.A. Jayantha, "*The Man-Eater of Malgudi*: Some Aspects of Its Narrative Strategy," *Literary Endeavour*, vol. III, nos. 3 and 4, June 1982, p. 96.
55. Edwin Gerow, "Quintessential Narayan," *Considerations*, ed. Meenakshi Mukharjee (New Delhi: Allied, 1977), p. 71.
56. Meenakshi Mukherjee, p. 147.
57. R.K. Narayan, *The Man-Eater of Malgudi* (Delhi: Hind Pocket Books, 1979), p. 2.
58. William Walsh, "R.K. Narayan," *A Manifold Voice* (London: Chatto and Windus, 1970), p. 14.
59. Meenakshi Mukherjee, p. 148.
60 Edwin Gerow, p. 79.
61. *Ibid.*
62. *Ibid.*, pp. 68-69.

63. David Scott Phillip, "The Reinvented Traditionalist," Perceiving India through the Works of Mulk Raj Anand and Raja Rao (New Delhi: Sterling, 1986), p. 119.
64. Uma Parameswaran, *A Study of Representative Indo-English Novelists* (New Delhi: Vikas, 1976), p. 6.
65. R.K. Narayan, Interview on Sept. 8, 1961, Writers Workshop Miscellany, p. 50.
66. William Walsh, *R.K. Narayan: A Critical Appreciation* (New Delhi: Allied, 1983), p. 139.
67. R.K. Narayan, "Gods, Demons and Modern Times," *The Literary Criterion*, Winter 1972, pp. 47-48.
68. E.J. Kalinnikova, "Indian Myths and Legends in R.K. Narayan's Interpretation," *Perspectives on R.K. Naryan*, p. 19.
69. N.J. Nanporia, cited by Kalinnikova, p. 22.
70. M.K. Naik, "Theme and Form in R.K. Narayan's *The Man-Eater of Malgudi*," *The Journal of Commonwealth Literature*, no. 3, April 1976, pp. 65-72.
71. R.K. Narayan, *The Mahabharata*, pp. 128-31, 141, 151-66.
72. R.A. Jayantha, "Gandhi, *The Gita* and Gayatri in *The Vendor of Sweets*," *Triveni,* April-June 1985, p. 62.
73. R.K. Narayan, *The Vendor of Sweets* (Mysore: Indian Thought Publications, 1981), p. 39.
74. Som P. Sharma, "*The Vendor of Sweets*," *Perspectives*, p. 163.
75. Bruce F. Macdonald, "Humanity and Aesthetic Order in *The Vendor of Sweets*," *Perspectives*, p. 157.
76. Barry Argyle, "Narayan's *The Sweet Vendor*," *The Journal of Commonwealth Literature*, July 1972, p. 38.
77. K.V.S. Murti, p. 143.
78. E.J. Kalinnikova, p. 24.
79. R.K. Narayan, *The Painter of Signs* (London: Penguin, 1985), p. 32.
80. Ron Shepherd, p. 86.
81. *Ibid.*
82. Anthony Thwaite, "The Painter of Signs" in *Times Literary Supplement,* June 20, 1976, pp. 6-7.
83. K.V.S. Murti, p. 145.
84. *Ibid.*
85. R.M. Varma, *Some Aspects of Indo-English Fiction* (New Delhi: Jainson, 1985), p. 2.
86. K.V.S. Murti, p. 145.
87. R.K. Narayan, *A Tiger for Malgudi* (Mysore: Indian Thought Publications, 1983), pp. 9-10.
88. Quoted by Betty Heimann, "Introduction to Hinduism," *The Eleven*

Religions and their Proverbial Love, ed. by Selwyn Gurney Champion (London: George Routledge, 1947), p. 139.

89. C. Kunhan Raja, *Some Fundamental Problems in Indian Philosophy* (Delhi: Motilal Banarasidas, 1974), p. 338.
90. I.K. Taimni, *The Science of Yoga* (Madras: The Theosophical Publishing House, 1974), p. 157.
91. S. Radhakrishnan, *The Principal Upanishds* (London: George Allen and Unwin, 1974), p. 433.
92. *Ibid.*, p. 638.
93. Cited by Louis Renou, *Hinduism* (London: Prentice-Hall International, 1961), p. 117. The fourth chapter of the *Atri-Smriti* lists out at length the kinds of bodies human and non-human, that different kinds of unrepentant sinners will acquire during transmigration and rebirth, according to their *Karma.*
94. K.V.S. Murti, p. 145.
95. R.A. Jayantha, *The Man-Eater of Malgudi*, p. 97.
96. Jayant K. Biswal, p. 115.
97. R.K. Narayan, *Talkative Man* (Mysore: Indian Thought Publications, 1985), p. 65.
98. R.K. Narayan, *Grandmother's Tale* (Mysore: Indian Thought Publications, 1992).
99. C.D.Narasimhaiah, R.K. Narayan's *The Guide.* p. 198.
100. R.K. Narayan, "English in India: The Process of Transmutation," p. 22.
101. William Walsh, "Nataraja and the Packet of Saffron," *Readings in Commonwealth Literature*, p. 54.
102. C.D. Narasimhaiah, R.K. Narayan's *The Guide*, p. 198.

How Much Lies in Laughter

Narayan's world is a world of comedy, where he presents the predicament of the middle-class individuals in a changing, growing society. Hence his being called a born story teller, with a fine sense of the tragicomic. As William Walsh observes "Narayan's novels belong to a difficult genre, the serious comedy."[1] And his outlook is essentially comic, that of a man who believes in the affirmation of life with all its oddities and imperfections, follies and foibles.

And it is this comic realism that makes him capable of weaving an intricate web of patterns of life, where, each minute detail and event, however insignificant and absurd it may seem on the superficial level, turns out ultimately to be meaningful.

Gentle irony pervades all his novels with an underlying recognition that the follies and foibles of the ordinary human beings can be accepted and looked at with amused tolerance and sympathetic reality. There is a realization towards the end that the discomfiture of the individual's life is of his own doing – a direct result of his absurd aspirations and ambitions in a world where the individual loses his importance and merges with the wider system. And all this is done through a deep sense of humour rooted in the incongruities of life.

Moreover, Narayan not only presents the protagonist's constant struggle with the unfriendly world but also the oddities and absurdities of other men and women in various walks of life. Thus Malgudi becomes real and stands for reality based on certain stable social values which enfold all these irregularities, passions and emotions.

Malgudi has a vivid presence and the atmosphere is evoked not only by geographical details but also by its authenticity and living presence or reality. "The thousand small comedies of man's dreams and aspirations, of his revolts and retreats glow in their typical humanness"[2] against the backdrop of the intimate and eternal presence of Malgudi. And it is here that Narayan's protagonists are able to laugh at themselves, with indomitable ego, despite their painful experiences and obvious suffering.

Narayan's comic vision not only deals with the humorous side of life and its joys and delights but also with the serious aspects of life. But despite dealing with the serious side of life in lighter vein, Narayan's novels are not tragic in the sense that the evoked atmosphere is not gloomy but is full of life and warmth. Therefore the individual's aberrations are viewed sympathetically.

The comic realism of Narayan requires the realistic presentation and detail of the actual world, which he is able to fulfil in that he captures and presents the real world with admirable documentation. The minute details regarding the ways of people, their likes, dress, food, rituals and other things are described with rich detail so as to create an authentic fictional locale and reality. The protagonists are, therefore, "provided with a context of particularity much like that which we define ourselves and others in the real world; they have names, parents, possessions, occupation etc., ordered in such a way as not to violate our sense of probability derived from the empirical world."[3]

Narayan's concern is to depict realistically the comic aspect of life in an imaginary town and he creates an authentic locale, that of Malgudi, to serve his purpose where he lets his characters enact their human drama in various moods and manners. Malgudi is rendered real in this sense. It is a living presence and blends with the lives of the individuals and plays an important role in their lives. The topographical details merely provide authenticity to the human comedy. The river, the hills, the statue and the streets together with the people and their thousand small events and aspirations provide a vivid rendering of life, a community existence, bound not only to one another, but also to the Mempi Hills and the Sarayu river in an age-old emotional attachment. Sarayu is not only a fact of the immediate present but it also has its own history stretching from the remote past to the present. As Srinivas of *Mr. Sampath* muses, it is formed by Lord Srirama's arrow. Thus the abiding spirit of the Sarayu brings a sense of the eternal before which the serious transactions of the temporal world of Malgudi appear to be funny and meaningless. The society which Narayan presents is a traditional society in transition. The age-old values, beliefs, customs, superstitions, gods and goddessess, cricket clubs and night clubs, circus, the family planning centre and so on exist simultaneously. But the values that sustain the Malgudi society remain the same over the times. Further, there is a sense of awareness of life, which is realized not through preaching but through a sense of meaningfulness. It is an accepted fact that there is a certain moral concern in Narayan's novels, but it is presented with a gentle and sympathetic irony and good humour.

Narayan draws widely from the real and ordinary everyday life, from hopes and passions and emotions, all of which are permeated by the comic sensibility. Narayan presents his fictional characters with a vivid detail and while doing so touches upon their own peculiarities. Even the trivialities are described to enrich the comic realism of the novels because even the trivialities have their own place in the scheme of life. Narayan recognizes that everyday and ordinary life holds and unfolds much of the drama. Thus Narayan's world of Malgudi is marked by a spirit of amused tolerance. As Malgudi is a fictional town based on a real life model, his comedy is the comedy of real life. The "universal captured in the particular," one can say, as Malgudi is India in microcosm.

Narayan is often compared with great writers like Chekhov. His minute observation and depiction of life gained him this likening to the great masters, which is what Graham Greene finds in him. "A humour strange to our fiction, closer to Chekhov than to any English writer, with the same underlying sense of beauty and sadness."[4] And it is apt here to quote what Chekhov himself comments of his own art, as it is equally applicable to Narayan. "We? Wc paint life as it is and beyond that—no 'gee-up' nor 'gee-down'. . . . Beyond that, even if you lashed us with whips, we could not go. We have neither immediate nor remote aims."[5]

The warmth and compassion that suffuses Narayan's novels make him a moderate writer. He has no strong missionary zeal and that is why his comic is nowhere cutting or acerbic. He does not move to the extremes. He views life's lapses with understanding and wisdom as one who admits to life's various compulsions. That is why Raju with the comic defiance of all his misfortunes is still admired and the moral condemnation of all his sins is not so severe. Even Vasu, a man-eater is basically human and comic despite his demoniac qualities. Narayan is never pedantic. "He has no axes of any kind: he is that rare thing in India today, a man of letters pure and simple."[6] Hence his being likened to Aristophanes and Jane Austen who possess the same enduring quality of amused tolerance and sympathy for all human frailties, follies and foibles and incongruities and idiosyncrasies.

Narayan's comic vision is noticeable even in his first novel *Swami and Friends* which Compton Mackenzie calls "an entirely delightful story." The novel is full of boisterous humour, which springs mainly from the situations, the situations which involve Swami and his friends Somu, Mani, Samuel—the Pea, and Rajam. The comedy springs from these innocents trying to imitate the adult world, a world which looks bizarre to the innocent eyes of Swami. And thus provides occasion, giving rise to laughter where none exists. This instinct is something that he shares with Samuel—the Pea. "The bond between them was laughter. They were able to see together the same absurdities and incongruities in things. The most trivial and unnoticeable thing to others would tickle them to death,"[7] which can be said to be fair representation of Narayan's own approach to life.

In the comic world of Swami, the fanatical scripture teacher Ebenezar appears to be an extremely bizarre figure. "Tears rolled down Ebenezar's cheeks when he pictured Jesus before him. Next moment his face became purple with rage as he thought of Sri Krishna—" (4) Likewise Swami's description of his baby brother is extremely comic and picturesque: "this thing has a wonderful pair of hands, so small and plump, you know! But I tell you, his face is awful, red, red like chilli." (4) Nothing and no one escapes Swami's comic vision, whether it be the coachman's son who acquires nightmarish proportions or Mani's uncle who is called the Bushy-Eyebrows. Even his teachers and Headmasters do not escape Swami. And the game of cricket too contributes to the humour and Narayan's description of the game is quite picturesque. The Malgudi Cricket Club needs all the paraphernalia attached with the game and Rajam being the captain of the team writes to the Messers Binns at Madras promising that "we shall send you money afterwards. Don't fear. Please be urgent." (115) Naturally, they do not receive anything but somehow they manage and Swami even becomes "Tate." Swami's astonishment and abhorrence at his grandmother's ignorance of the cricket and his attempts to educate her as he feels it his duty to save granny from stagnating and appalling ignorance, provide a rich "comic duet"[8] and provoke much laughter. Apart from all this, the problems that Malgudi Cricket Club faces—that of getting Swami exempted from the evening drill sessions and in the process seeking Headmaster's permission, which is of course refused, and Swami's request to the Doctor to certify him as suffering from "delirium"—some kind of stomach-ache which provokes "a great fit of coughing threatened to choke him [the doctor]" (137) are all instances of much hilarity. Despite all the troubles, Malgudi Cricket Club has Swami the "Tate" and Mani the star one who "could be depended upon to stop with his head, if necessary, any ball. He had a peculiar style. With his bat he stopped all reasonable approaches to the wicket and brought the best bowlers to a fainting condition."[9] Which of course, proves that "Narayan is surprisingly, one of the few Indian novelists to exploit the humour as well as the epic nature of Indian enthusiasm for this English game."[10]

But the simple story of the childhood chronicles is not without its pathos. Swami has his own troubles and in his own world the troubles seem real for him. Swami's agony over having fallen out of grace with Rajam as a result of missing the vital cricket match, his bidding farewell to Rajam, as Rajam is leaving for the town, his "parting present" and Mani's assurance that all is not lost, all these seem to have a sense of deep sincerity and poignancy. And Narayan is able to move one to tears through this simple tale.

The Bachelor of Arts – the "story of a young Indian in his last year at college, and his first year of freedom"[11] gives a "charming, unusual and amusing account of youth and early manhood and all that it entails." The tone of the novel is tragi-comic in the sense that while it gives an amusing picture of Chandran's life at college and home, it also depicts the young man's tragedy in love. But all this is depicted with such delicate pathos that one is apt to remember what Graham Greene says in this regard: "Some readers will admire it for its humour, some for its sense of implicit – I was going to say tragedy, but that word is too blatant for a pathos as delicate as the faint discoloration of ivory with age. . . . But it would be wrong to emphasize more deeply than Mr. Narayan himself this sad and poetic background: the humour of the book is enough to enchant." (viii-x)

The college life and incidents of Chandran give rise to much of the humour in the novel. Chandran is to speak as the prime mover for a debate which causes him unnecessary tension and he has "dreams of picking up a hatchet and attacking his history professor, Raghavachar" (14) for having involved him in the debate. For young Chandran even going to a cinema is a great event. It was an aesthetic experience to be approached with due preparation. One has to chew the betel leaves, light a cigarette and then go to watch the cinema and, while coming back should enjoy a hot cup of coffee and then go home and sleep. This seems to be "the ideal way to set about a night show." (14)

Likewise, Chandran's encounters with and descriptions of his professors at the college is something humorous. Gajapathy "the Elephant Master" is approachable, the history professor Raghavachar is formidable and Chandran indulges in fanciful dreams at humanizing the professor: "Remove those spectacles, the turban, and the long coat, and let Raghavachar appear only in a loin-cloth, and Mr. Raghavachar would lose three-quarters of his appearance. Where was the sense in feeling nervous before a pair of spectacles, a turban, and a black coat." (14) And Principal Brown towards whom Chandran is slightly antagonistic because of his being a foreigner, has nothing much to recommend except a sense of humour and power to hold the audience's interest "with nothing very serious, nothing profound, but with the revelation of a personality, with delicious reminiscences, touched with humour and occasional irony." (14) Chandran's eccentric friends Mohan, the poet and Veeraswami, the revolutionary also add to the humour.

The gentle irony with which Narayan treats the human fallibility and gullibility comes through in the situation where Chandran and his father try to catch the flower-thief. The whole family organizes the operation to the last detail only to find that the flower-thief is none other than an ochre-robed *sanyasi,* who wanted the flowers for worship. Irony permeates the whole situation where the "thief" is honoured and left free to take the flowers and go, all because of the garb of a *sanyasi.*

Chandran's infatuation for Malathi is humorously dealt with. He feels he does not have room for anything else in his mind. The one-sided affair has rich comic overtones in Chandran's fervid romantic fancies of having Malathi in his arms and fervently praying God for success in his romance. However, the affair comes to an end when horoscopes mismatch. The whole affair of Chandran's infatuation and his failure to marry Malathi is treated by Narayan with an amused tolerance which marks his comic vision.

Chandran's disillusionment makes him leave Malgudi for Madras where he spends a short time with Kailas, a drunkard and womanizer. Horrified Chandran leaves the place, renounces the world, and becomes a *sanyasi.* "He was a *sanyasi* because it pleased him to mortify his flesh. His renunciation was a revenge on society, circumstances, and perhaps, too, on destiny." (14) The faith of the innocent villagers in him which resembles the situation in *The Guide* where it is more elaborately dealt with, makes Chandran realize his falsity. The sight of the gifts given by the credulous villagers pierces his heart. (119) He feels that he is a cad, fraud, and a confidence trickster. Thus "the facade of ironical humour rests on a sad seriousness which constitutes the blend of beauty and sadness in Narayan's humour."[12] Chandran's return to Malgudi and his rehabilitation symbolize the triumph of the comic over the tragic in life. Normalcy returns at the end, significant in Chandran's marriage to Susila and his being "madly" in love with her. Thus one can say that *The Bachelor of Arts* reveals Narayan's comic realism and gentle irony which pervade through the whole story and make it a success.

The English Teacher reveals the further growth and maturity of Chandran as Krishnan. The novel, though intensely autobiographical is amusing and gently comic. The novel is a fine blend of humour and pathos and the earthly and the mystical-supernatural.

The humour springs from the perception of incongruity where unrelated objects are juxtaposed. The alarm-clock which Krishnan possesses provides a fine example of this kind of humour. "It lets out a shattering amount of noise, and it sometimes went off by itself and butted in a conversation, or sometimes when I had locked the room and gone out, it started off and went on ringing till exhaustion overcame it. There was no way of stopping it, by pressing a button or a lever."[13] Amusing as the description of the clock is, it becomes even more humorous with Krishnan's unusual discovery of stopping it: "One day I learnt by some sort of instinctive experiment that if I placed a heavy book like Taine's

History of English Literature on its crest, it stopped shrieking." (5) As R.K. Kaul comments: "The thought of using a solemn, self-important French literary historian to muffle the noise of an unmanageable clock seems rich in its incongruity."[14] Thus the world of academics proves to be a rich source of humour.

Another instance of humour is the incident of Krishnan's house-hunting business acompanied with a mental dialogue. When he fails to find a house of his liking, he thinks: "The builder of this house must have been dead-drunk while doing the latter portion of the house. This house must have been designed by a tuberculosis expert so that his business may prosper for the next hundred years. This house is ideal for one whose greatest desire in life is to receive constant knocks on his head from door posts. A house for a twisted pigmy." At last after much house-searching Krishnan finds a house of a "palsied patriarch," one of the eccentric characters like cousin in *The Vendor of Sweets*. The landlord holds Krishnan in much reverence saying: "I revere college teachers, our *gurus*. Meritorious deeds in previous births make them *gurus* in this life." (22)

Krishnan with his constant worry and anxiety on the arrival of his wife and infant provide a beautiful touch of humour. "How many infants were damaged and destroyed by careless mothers in the process of coming out of trains? Why couldn't they make these railway carriages of safer dimensions? It ought to be done in the interests of baby welfare in India." (25) It would be appropriate to note that underneath the humour there is a seriousness of purpose in all these descriptions. Likewise, even Susila's reactions to Krishnan's reproduction of Wordsworth's poem, though full of fun and frolic, also serves to underline the future events:

> "My true love hath my heart and I have his." Susila would laugh till she became red in the face. "Why can't each keep his own or her own heart instead of this exchange?" She then put out her hand and searched all my pockets saying: "In case you should take away mine.". . . And then another line that amused her very much was "Oh, mistress mine, where are you roaming?" She would not allow me to progress a line beyond, saying: "I shall die of this poem some day. What is the matter with the woman loafing all over the place except where her husband is?" (31)

Narayan's perception of the absurd shows clearly in the situation where Leela's Headmaster, who is supposed to be dead turns up alive only to be harassed by his wife. The amused tolerance which marks his comic sense can be seen also in Krishnan's confrontations with Gajapathy, who places much importance on the correctness of spelling and pronunciation. "Mr.

Gajapathy, there are blacker sins in this world than a dropped vowel. . . . Let us be fair. Ask Mr Brown if he can say in any of the two hundred Indian languages 'The cat chases the rat.' He has spent thirty years in India." (45) And further over the need for teaching history of literature. "Why do they make so much of the history of literature? They have to make a history of every damned thing on earth – as if literature could not survive without some fool compiling bogus history." (3) And again at the end where he owns that his work at college does not provide or give any satisfaction to him. "What I am doing in college hardly seems to me work. I mug up and repeat and they mug up and repeat in examinations. . . . It is a fraud. I am practising for a consideration of a hundred rupees a month." (203) One can see Narayan criticizing the educational system through Krishnan. Thus *The Bachelor of Arts* and *The English Teacher* are tragi-comic portrayals of life reflected in Chandran's "involvement, dissociation and rehabilitation and Krishnan's preternatural culmination."[15]

The Dark Room is the sad story of the plight of a traditional Indian housewife. Though all the characters in the novel are sketched with a comic touch, all of them represent serious aspects of life. Especially, Mari the locksmith-burglar and umbrella-repairer and his wife Ponni provide rich source of humour. Despite his chosen career Mari has his own code of conduct. "Opening a lock in the correct manner, and locking a house again when leaving it was, Mari felt, a piece of courtesy which a man owed the absent householder."[16] The incident of his rescuing Savitri from drowning with the resultant dialogue is quite comical.

The way the cook handles the unhappy children in the absence of their mother shows Narayan's comic ingenuity in handling even the sadness and depression of life. "The belief was that a person who looked into the cook's eyes at certain moments would be turned to stone. They had been told that many of the furlong and milestones in the place were once human beings who had dared to look into the cook's eyes; after they became stones the government people came along, chiseled them into shape, and carved miles and furlongs on them." (195) As H.M. Williams observes: "The comedy of the novel is of two kinds: ironical social comedy in Narayan's depiction of Ramani's uneasy affair with the lighthearted comedy in his desperate attempts to keep his children amused during his wife's desertion by taking them every night to the new "Palace Talkies" cinema, another feature of Malgudi's modernisation."[17]

Mr. Sampath, the novel not much acclaimed by Narayan's critics has rich comic overtones and is published under the title *The Printer of Malgudi* in America. The printer, "Mr. Sampath is the first of a line of comic eccentric villains to enliven Narayan's world."[18] The novel is a serious comedy and much of the comic springs from Sampath and his enactment of various roles such as printer, actor and producer. Also Srinivas's comic involvements with Sampath and the hypocritical and illusory film-world. Then there is Ravi's hopeless infatuation for Shanti which drives him mad. Sampath also is infatuated with Shanti at the same time. And Srinivas becomes involved in both though unwittingly: "Narayan uses the myth of the burning of Kama to bring out the comic implications of involvements."[19]

Though much of the humour in the novel arises from Sampath and his involvement in the film-world with all its unusual and odd characters, there are others in the novel like Srinivas's landlord, who proves to be a perennial source of ironical humour. The incongruity in the human conduct is brought out when the old man professing pious and abstemious living becomes incoherent with joy at the sight of coffee and tiffin. Likewise, Sampath cracking a groundnut pod in the court to foil the terrible gloom of the place; the famous actor V.L.G., the "pot-bellied" Shiva climbing down from the Kailas in anger at not having received his cheque; the producer, the director and financier going round one another in a funny chase to protect their interests; dance scenes and horseplay comedy being "scattered like spice all along the story to ruin some of the most sublime moments" in the screen play; the studio-lights x-raying the diaphanous Parvathi with the lightboys looking down from their platforms as if privileged to witness the amours of gods; and then the passion-demented Ravi, "rushing between Shiva's extended arms and Parvathi, and knocking Shiva aside with such violence that he fell amidst his foliage in Kailas in a most ungodly manner"[20] – these are some of the highly comic situations of the novel.

The novelist's depiction of the film-world is ironical: "Narayan mocks Srinivas's high-mindedness, while at the same time pillorying the absurd activities of the film-makers who unite Hollywood's meretricious glamour with Indian confusion."[21]

Thus *Mr. Sampath* depicts the mad whirlwind events in which Sampath tries to play various roles trying to dominate and live by his wit and tact, by disregarding the others in the society and ends up where he started, having lost in the battle between an individual and society. Ravi ends up in madness owing to his passionate involvement and infatuation with Shanti, and Srinivas the mere spectator to what has happened learns his lesson – that one should restrain passion and develop an attitude of non-attachment. That is why when he meets Sampath again he checks himself and feels that "he was once again in danger of getting involved with him if he asked him too many questions." (219) *Mr. Sampath* thus is a serious comedy depicting a world that is real through comic realism.

Quite a few Dickensian or Wodehousian characters crowd the canvas of *Mr. Sampath*. Srinivas, aged 39, with wife and children, but an unpractical idealist, founder-editor of *The Banner* and later script-writer of *The Burning of Kama*; Ravi, still in his twenties, engrossed in a vision of Beauty once seen in the Ishwara temple and lost, a gifted but unrealized artist; the old landlord shark, a self-styled *sanyasi*, a hesitant financier and an intolerable bore; Somu, as partly as he is rich, an ex-President of the District Board (we should now have called it Zilla Parishad;) and one of the promoters of Sunrise Pictures Limited; Sohan Lal, the calculating financier imported from outside; De Mello, with his Hollywood affiliations, a supposedly technical wizard; "V.L.G" the "Shiva" of a hundred pictures; Shanti the predestined "Parvathi," and, above all, Mr. Sampath himself. What a menagerie? The only "normal" people are Mrs. Srinivas with her domestic budgetary problems, Mrs. Sampath with her cross to bear, and Ravi's mother with her mental anxieties."[22]

The Financial Expert is quite an achievement and in creating Margayya "a type which is unique in world literature,"[23] Narayan proved his remarkable powers of portraying memorable characters. Der Kuries recognizes the universality of Narayan's humour in the novel: "This is a precious book. It is full of hidden irony and hidden humour. . . . Humour knows no national boundaries. Only jokes have national boundaries."[24] The novel is full of comic episodes and "the chief characters are little better than caricatures"[25] which is truly Dickensian. The primary source of humour in the novel is, of course the protagonist, Margayya, who, with all his money-mindedness and obsession for wealth, is still a rather endearing and likeable character, full of naivete. The novelist tells the story of meteoric rise and fall of Margayya with a tragi-comic tone. As Graham Greene observes, "Margayya—the sad ambitious absurd financial expert—is perhaps the most engaging of all Mr. Narayan's characters. In his ambitions for his boy, his huge dreams, his unintended villainies and his small vanities, his domestic tenderness, he has the hidden poetry and the unrecognised pathos we so often find in Chekhov's characters who on the last page vanish into life."[26]

Margayya is a rich comic figure and is the source of much of the humour in the novel. Sitting under the banyan tree with his tin box, coaxing and cajoling the innocent villagers to get unending loans from the bank he defeats the very purpose of the bank, until humiliated by the Bank Secretary. Shaken by the confrontation he decides to acquire wealth and makes desperate attempts. Advised by the temple priest, he takes up *Lakshmi-puja* for forty days and after the penance or as a result, one should say, gets hold of Dr. Pal's manuscript of "Bed-Life" (renamed later as Domestic Harmony) inspired by *Kamasutra* and Havelock Ellis, as the journalist-sociologist claims it to be. Margayya's involvement with the priest, who suggests the ritual and is a vague figure, even without a name (he is simply a tall gaunt man), Dr. Pal a journalist-sociologist, and Madan Lal the publisher, is fun-evoking and humorous. In the later phase of his career, Margayya having become a rich man is obsessed with money and money-making schemes. He fails to find any happiness at home. He disregards his obligations and responsibilities as husband and father, and the realization occurs only with the final crash. Thus one finds ironic overtones in Margayya's financial career which is also marked by an underlying sadness.

The comic vein of the story is noticeable in the depiction of the father-son relationship too. Balu, clever enough to exploit any situation and any one to his own advantage, even as a child gets round his father "exacting various levies" even for a slight burn on a finger. And one cannot fail to notice the humour in the hilarious situation where Balu throws away his father's account-book in the gutter (thereby bringing Margayya's career to a standstill, unknowingly). The neighbours and passers by become onlookers and find fault with Margayya for trying to thrash a small child and Margayya finds it helpless in face of such opposition to mete out any punishment to Balu, and feels as if he is a victimizer instead of a victim. There are many such situations in the novel which prove to be highly amusing. Margayya's encounter with the priest at the temple is one such. "Margayya began to tremble slightly. . . . Perhaps he is a sorcerer, or a black magician or an alchemist. He threw a frightened look at the shack in which he usually dwelt. Perhaps he has hidden human bodies in that shack, and extracts from the corpses some black ointment, with which he acquires extraordinary powers." (29)

More often than not it is Margayya's naivete that gives rise to humour. When someone asks him about some technical specifications he wonders what it is all about. "Body? Points? Ten and Eleven? What was it all about?" Margayya said: "Ah, that is interesting. . . . I should like to see your eleven-point body." He has grotesque visions of a torso being brought in by four men on a stretcher. (84)

Margayya always managed to survive through his sheer wit and tact in the world of business. And his wit is able to carry the day any time for him. One such incident occurs when he boards the train to go to Madras to bring back his wayward son to his house. "The moment he had shot in through the window, the impact of his arrival displaced someone who was already seated." Margayya just let himself down there before the other could recover. He was a villager.

> When he did recover he cried: "Get out of my seat." "Why don't you learn better manners?" Margayya said in his habitual masterful

way with villagers. "I have been sitting here from Trichinopoly," the other began. "Well, you must be tired of sitting—a change will do you good" replied Margayya. (133-34)

Narayan's expertness in creating eccentrics comes to the fore once more in *The Financial Expert* in the creation of the priest, who is a vague figure, and the wealthy mad man of "The House of Enlightenment" who writes letters to President Roosevelt, Stalin and Churchill, particularly and takes it as his mission in life to inform at least ten mortals about death each day and educate them.

Thus *The Financial Expert* reveals Narayan's comic genius at its highest ranging from "situation comedy, comedy of characterisation, farcial humour, wit and irony to mild satire."[27] Margayya's passion for money leads him to his downfall and Narayan's depiction of Margayya's achievement of financial wizardry and subsequent catastrophe, despite its seriousness is done through comedy. The satire of course is there but toned down by comic detachment. Towards the end Margayya escapes from being a monster only by remaining essentially human even in his weakness. Rajeev Taranath observes: "Margayya as a human entity is preserved all through his changing fortunes as a financial expert, by his unchanging, slightly awkward tenderness towards his wife, son and, later the daughter-in-law and grandson."[28]

The Vendor of Sweets like *The Financial Expert* concentrates mainly on the father-son relationship. Though it does not find as much favour as the earlier novel, *The Man-Eater of Malgudi* did, it still is and can be read as an amusing story which depends for its comedy on the improbable and fantastic.

The novel is Narayan's most sophisticated and attractive presentation of a character and relationship. "Jagan, the sweet vendor, is a more finely developed human version than Narayan's purely comic characters, namely Nataraj the printer, Margayya the financial expert and the versatile and roguish Mr. Sampath."[29] Jagan is a typical comic creation of Narayan and along with the unnamed "cousin," is dexterously delineated. The prosperous vendor of sweets advises every one: "Conquer taste, and you will have conquered the self." When the listener asks "why conquer the self?" he admits, "I do not know, but all our sages advise us so."[29] Thus the tragi-comic note of uncertainty is struck in the beginning itself along with the harmless hypocrisy and pseudo-idealism. He would not shave regularly "feeling that to view oneself daily in mirror was an intolerable European habit. He claims to be a follower of Gandhi and "professes simple living and high thinking" and has made it a point ot wear only "non-violent footwear. . . . Sandals made of the leather of an animal which had died of old age."[30] He wears only *khaddar* and is very much an enthusiast for nature cure and naturopathy. He declares that one who has "come under the spell of Gandhi could do no wrong," (45) but evades the tax and accumulates wealth. All these make him an eccentric and rather a comic figure. As A.N. Kaul has pointed out, "Jagan's spiritualism and idealism are constant targets of Narayan's comedy and irony."[31] The purpose of the comic irony is to remind us that Jagan is of the ordinary and average humanity, both in his weaknesses and strengths.

Narayan's unerring instinct for the extraordinary and comic in the ordinary and commonplace is once again evident in his recounting of Jagan's past, especially his marriage and the circumstances leading to the birth of Mali, after so many years of frustration. The cart journey from the railway station in the company of his elder brother and future brother-in-law, the self-conscious and nervous manner with which he behaves under the strict ceremonial protocol, all underline a strictly Indian sensibility. "The humour latent in a perfectly normal situation in the Indian context has been brought out,"[32] with some deft strokes. When asked if he had a comfortable journey, he waits for a signal from his brother before giving a reply, for he has been instructed not to be too communicative, "as a certain mysteriousness is inevitable in a son-in-law."[33] When in a prospective bride's home the bridegroom's party always has to say "Oh why all this? I cannot eat. We have just had coffee and everything in the train," even if one was maddeningly hungry. This episode displays all the gifts of Narayan for interweaving tragedy and comedy, and for comic but sympathetic treatment of Indian traditional institutions.[34]

The "cousin" who remains unnamed throughout the novel is one of Narayan's nameless and eccentric characters. A "cousin" to everyone he is a "man-about-town" and visits many places and houses in the town, arrives at Jagan's shop everyday at four-thirty, throws a brief glance at Jagan, passes to the kitchen and comes out in ten minutes wiping his mouth with the end of a towel on his shoulder and comments: "The sugar situation may need watching." He acts as a buffer between the estranged father and son and it is only through the cousin that Jagan comes to know of Mali's intention to go to America and later, the various schemes. And it is towards the end that he makes his picturesque though important presence felt. Jagan decides to renounce the world and "when passing Sir Frederick Lawley, he saw his cousin riding down clumsily on a bicycle, his tuft flying in the wind, his wheels zig-zagging perilously on to the edge of the storm drain and retracting miraculously to the centre of the road. Jagan stood arrested by the spectacle for he had never seen the cousin on a bicycle before. The wheels seemed to come straight for him. Shouting incoherent enquiries Jagan stepped aside. The cousin helplessly dashed past him a dozen yards, and fell off the saddle, leaving the bicycle to bolt away by itself to a ditch." (155) The appearance, though extremely funny and ludicrous, is timed perfectly and is very effective as it happens when Jagan is renouncing the world, as he is the messenger of the shocking news of Mali's arrest, in whom "the comic eccentricity and absurdity, bordering on the monstrous behaviour"[35] is to be found.

The master stroke of irony is yet to come. Jagan with all his worldly renunciation still retains his cheque book!

The Guide and *The Man-Eater of Malgudi* have a mythical framework. Anthony West has this to say regarding *The Guide*: "Narayan has written under the surface of the flashing light comedy that is his signature, a story that has the grandeur of the Indian scene and is a tragedy worthy of it."[36]

H.M. Williams remarks that "Here his comedy is at its most serious; and irony is effectively used."[37] The title itself indicates clearly "the all-pervading irony which informs the entire action, by indicating the moral dilemma in the life of the protagonist."[38] The novel is full of irony and is evident particularly in the characterization of Raju, the guide, who is prone to self-deception. Raju drifts along in life, always a "public figure" struggling to cope his best with circumstances, living upto others' expectations, ending up in enforced sainthood and becoming a martyr.

The irony of it all is that it is of his own doing. He is caught in the web of his own making and the game of make-believe becomes horrifyingly real very soon. That is why Raju at the end is a picture of irony not unmingled with tragic grandeur. "He stands at the end up to his knees in water, utterly isolated from the enormous crowd, and yet it is his collaboration – uneasy, desperate and finally total – with the expectations of the people that turns their immense illusion into something like truth."[39]

The Guide thus proves to be "a remarkable example of the especially difficult genre to which most of Narayan's work belongs, the serious comedy."[40] Though the theme dealt with is that of renunciation, it is a serious one, the treatment meted out is particularly comic and ironic. The very tone and narrative technique underline the fact.

Narayan's perception of the comic becomes clear when a dead crocodile becomes the target. "When its belly was ripped open they found in it ten thousand rupees worth of jewellery. Did this mean that the crocodile had been in the habit of eating only women?"[41]

We have yet another comic character, apart from Marco, in Velan's brother. One of the lesser intelligences of the village, he unwittingly becomes the cause of Raju's enforced penance to bring down rains. Misunderstanding what Raju said he blabbers incoherently to the whole village, what he thinks to be the Swami's message and lands Raju in the role of the Saviour.

Towards the end even through the impending tragedy, "The underlying comic irony continues." The telegraph master of Mangala strikes a comic note with his jitters at the sight of a telegram.

James J. Malone, the film-maker from California, is yet another character who provides an immense comic relief from the impending tense and tragic situation where he tries to comprehend the esoteric oriental mind through an interview:

> "Will you tell us something about your early life?"
> "What do you want to know?"
> "For instance, have you always been a Yogi?"
> "Yes; more or less." (218-19)

Raju's affirmation of having been a Yogi all his life sounds ironical yet is meaningful when looked at in view of Narayan's perception of the comic as a mode of detachment.

The world of *The Man-Eater of Malgudi* is suffused with the spirit of irony. Nataraj the meek and naive protagonist with his eccentric friends – the "monosyllabic" poet, the inveterate Nehru critic, Sen, the journalist, and the philosophic Sastri – all prove to be a rich source of amusement. Even Vasu the man-eater, is not without a given comic stroke with his morbid fear of mosquitoes. "Night and day, I run when a mosquito is mentioned."[42] The demoniac, turning into the grotesquely comic is often to be seen in the Indian mythology. Evil perhaps could not receive a more comical treatment.[43]

The most hilarious incident in the novel is Nataraj's efforts to bring the sick temple elephant Kumar to Malgudi for treatment. His desperate and humorous attempts to make the sick elephant rise and the refusal of the temple committee to allow Kumar to be taken to Malgudi, and finally Kumar responding to the green switch of the mahout – the whole episode is of high comic order and simply unforgettable.

There is rich tragi-comedy as well as moral symbolism in the curious relationship that develops in this novel between Vasu and Nataraj, the wild slayer and stuffer of animals and the gentle printer of labels, school magazines and calling-cards. Curiosity and awe and sheer physical fear on the part of the down-trodden Nataraj who is under the thumb of his own typesetter and whose wife "wears the pants" are matched in Vasu by a mixture of friendliness, threatening power, patronage and exploitation of Nataraj's weakness.[44] The serene life of the peace-loving Malgudians is disturbed by Vasu and his taxidermy operations become obvious. But the impact and intrusion is felt more by Nataraj and his friends, the poet and the journalist Sen, who are helpless onlookers in the presence of Vasu. "Vasu is terrifying because he cancels out, by brutally refusing to acknowledge their existence, the values implicit in the life which Nataraj and his friends live."[45]

Some of the best of the spry and mellow comedy of *The Man-Eater of Malgudi* depends, as William Walsh puts it, on "Nataraj's increasingly frantic efforts at rendering the oppressive presence of Vasu at least tolerable. But anything Nataraj can think of is hopelessly inadequate to effect the deeper reconciliation that his nature and indeed the character of the community call for."[46] And things come to an end when Vasu threatens to kill the temple elephant Kumar. The community is outraged at the intended sacrilege and the "climax" of the comedy and the resolution of the problem of an assimilation come together in Vasu's grotesque death[47] which reaffirms the triumph of the positive and brings a comic dissolution.

Waiting for the Mahatma and *The Painter of Signs* deal with the theme of "bitter sweet love." In *Waiting for the Mahatma* the love theme is played against the background of Gandhian politics and Indian freedom movement. The novel may be said to be "a comic perspective on the Gandhian theme, not any way travesting it but giving it a simplistic treatment through Sriram's fervent, though mistaken, following of it as the ardent disciple-lover of Bharati."[48] The humour arises from Sriram's failure to comprehend the National movement in which he participates with over-enthusiasm. The comic incongruity springs from Sriram's passionate love for Bharati and her zealous involvement in the Gandhian freedom struggle, which gives rise to the comedy in the novel.

When the novel opens, Sriram is already in love with a portrait and has his own conception of an ideal girl. The portrait of a European lady in Kanni's shop becomes to him a pleasing object. "Those eyes look at me," Sriram often thought. "For the pleasure of returning that look he went again and again, to buy something or other at the shop." He even asks Kanni, pertinently, "If the lady's husband turns up and demands the picture, what will you do?"[49]

Sriram has his own way of interpreting Gandhi's advice, to be sure in his heart that it is love and not bitterness. Sriram wanting to be near Bharati needs to approach Gandhi and seek his permission to become a follower. Nervous at the prospect, he fumbles "What should I say when I speak to him? I would blabber like an idiot." Quick-witted, Bharati quips, "you are already doing it." Once again, Sriram's attempts at learning to spin provokes her to comment, "you will waste all the cotton in India and Egypt before you make yourself a yard of yarn." (64)

Sriram's musings, when painting Gandhi's message on a wall, are quite comic. Painting the slogan "Quit India" on the wall as part of National Campaign, he wondered if, for economy's sake, he could manage without drawing its tail. "It also seemed to him possible that Britain had imported the letter 'Q' into India so that there might be a national drain on black paint." (69)

There are numerous minor characters who also provoke laughter. For instance the carter, who Sriram talks to. Asked his age by Sriram, he replies:

> "I think I'm twenty."
> "Twenty; more likely you are fifty."
> "Maybe, Sir, a little this way and that. I used to be twenty." (71)

Then there is the incident of Sriram's comic involvement with a shopkeeper at Solur village which is quite humorous. The shopkeeper wanting to show off, declares proudly that he has a very good stock of English biscuits, and lands himself in trouble. Sriram, zealous freedom-fighter and promoter of Swadeshi Khaddar Movement, takes him to task for selling foreign goods and pickets his shop by lying on the ground in front of the shop. People gather around and enjoy the spectacle and the shopkeeper's predicament as he tries his best to get out of the situation.

The uproaringly hilarious scene where Sriram's grandmother is taken and placed on a funeral pyre, after which the Fund Office manager notices a slight movement in the toe and jumps up and lifts her down and places her on the ground, the event at which the priest's anger and outrage becomes explicit, as he refuses to let her be lifted from the pyre, provokes much laughter.

The Painter of Signs, like *Waiting for the Mahatma*, is a tale of love and is sprightly and vivacious. The story of the modern lovers Raman and Daisy is amusing to the hilt. The passionate ardour of Raman is contrasted with the practical reasoning of Daisy and thus gives rise to many incongruous situations. Their coming together and parting again – all these are treated comically. "Raman's romantic effervescence has an obvious touch of absurdity but Narayan's characteristic geniality mellows it to a comic delight."[50] And Raman's final disillusionment and his return to the solid real world of people symbolize once again, as Rajeev Taranath observes, the reaffirmation of "the average as the positive."[51]

The novel is plentiful in comic incidents and episodes. For instance, the launching of the lawyer on his career with all auspiciousness, pomp and ceremony is full of comic ingenuity. The precise timing of the hanging of the signboard owing to astrological reasons, and the lawyer's assumed outrage at some grains of sand on the freshly painted board, and his trying to cheat Sriram over the money for the signboard because of that—"What's this? Am I to start my career with dirt on my name?"[52]—all contribute to the humour of the situation.

The comic vein continues and is evident in his encounter with the Town Hall Professor, who in return for Raman's signboard, passes a message on a slip of paper professing "everything passes" and is also evident in his relationship with Daisy. He accompanies Daisy during the family planning campaign to the remote villages. It is humorous that at one of the villages, people heave a collective sigh of relief at the departure of Daisy and Raman, for they need not be any more guilty for having children. Their journey back to Malgudi is highly amusing. The bullock-cart journey, the breakdown and resulting developments provide hilarious situational comedy and Narayan's treatment of the episode is comical. "The cartman derived the greatest enjoyment out of this situation. He kept turning round and winking at Raman as if to say, 'This is all a part of the game. Keep your side up, as ever.'" (81) Raman, stung by Daisy's indifference tries to molest her thinking that women like aggressive lovers. Daisy saves herself by climbing a tamarind tree and quotes a proverb at Raman, which says that when one is married to the Devil one should be prepared to climb the tamarind tree, thus provoking Raman out of bounds, which of course is highly amusing.

Towards the end, a touch of irony marks the narration culminating in the moment of consummation in their relationship and the mythic parallel of Santhanu-Ganga, and the final parting of ways and Raman's disillusionment and despair that results in his return to the solid world of Malgudi, having shed his illusions. Thus the novel makes it evident of Narayan's comic detachment.

In *A Tiger for Malgudi* Narayan once again takes up one of the favourite themes of his—that of renunciation. The novel, in the tradition of the *Panchatantra* and *Jataka* tales, is about an enlightened tiger possessed of a soul. But the treatment of the novel is comic.

The novel abounds in comic situations. One such is where Narayan touches upon the national policy on language—the three language formula, comically expounded by the tiger Raja.

The comic strain of the novel becomes apparent with yet another example when Raja, the tiger refers to a scene of communal riot. "At another place we went into a rioting mob—groups of people were engaged in a bloody strife, attacking each other with stone, knife, and iron rod and screaming murderous challenges. In their frenzy they had not noticed us, but when they did, they dispersed swiftly." Narayan goes on to explain humorously the causes for the conflicts. "If you are ready to hate and want to destroy each other, you may find a hundred reasons – a division of canal water in your field, two urchins of opposite camps slapping each other, rumours of molestation of some woman, even the right to worship in a temple, anything may spark off a fight if you are inclined to nurture hatred – only the foolish waste their lives in fights."[53]

The tiger, after killing the menacing Captain, calmly walks down the streets of Malgudi – the description of which creates hilarious comedy. The tiger takes shelter in a school, in headmaster's room to be precise. Thus Narayan builds up a comic world where the tiger's transformation would look credible.

Alphonse with all his commotion and preparation to shoot the tiger is a comic figure and while this is going on, "The crowd which watched in silence all along, let out a moan in chorus: "Aiyo; Never thought our beloved headmaster would come to this end." They all looked bitterly at the assistant headmaster, whom they somehow held responsible for all the delay. "The assistant headmaster probably had confused feelings, happy at the thought that after all he was getting his chance to become the headmaster, but also unhappy at the same time. He wailed the loudest at the thought of the headmaster's fate." (137) Alphonse after procuring a ladder and aiming his gun feels that his hands are shaky and the hermit making his timely appearance, subdues and transforms the tiger and saves him.

Much of the comedy in the story also springs from the modern man-woman relationship portrayed, showing a changing trend from tradition to modernity. There is no strong denunciation anywhere, even when Narayan hits out at the bureaucracy that fails to respond immediately and efficiently to the plea of the villagers for relief from the dreaded presence of a tiger that preys on the village. The clerk at the Collectors Office takes their petitions and directs them to other officials who assure the villagers that there would be no delay on their part except to make sure that there is a tiger. Thus *A Tiger for Malgudi* proves to be an avowed example of Narayan's comic genius.

Talkative Man tells the sad and pathetic story of an abandoned wife and her search for her wayward husband. This gentle, funny and intriguing tale, crowded with life and colour, adds a beguiling new chapter to the legends of the fictional Indian town, Malgudi.

Narayan comes back to the theme of a sufferring wife after a long gap. But he treats the story in his usual way as a comedy. It is because of this comic treatment of the theme that the novel abounds in comic situations which provoke laughter. There are any number of characters sketched by Narayan as "comic cameos" – TM, Rann, the Station Master, Sarasa the Commandant, and many others.

TM befriends Rann at the Town Hall Library. Rann with his unusual Oxford suit seems to be "a strange man" to the innocent Malgudians. For people who are unused to anything but a dhoti and shirt sleeves he seems to be an "oddity" who dislikes being stared at and who keeps his own company.

Soon Sarasa the Commandant arrives at Malgudi, looking for her husband. The very sight of her intimidates TM and Narayan excels in his comic sketch of the character "a six-foot (as it seemed at first sight) woman, dark-complexioned, cropped head, and in jeans and a T-shirt with bulging breasts, the first of her kind in Malgudi area"[54] she terrifies the wits out of the Station Master and informs TM rather menacingly that she has come searching for her husband – Rann.

She took out of her handbag a press-cutting of the Timbuctoo Man, with the photograph of Rann she managed to get. She flourished the press-cutting and said, "You wrote this?"

> "Yes Madam," I said meekly. "No one can fool me," she said. The diminutive Station Master tried to shrink out of sight, simpered and stayed in the background. I felt rather intimidated by the woman's manners, (but) still had the hardihood to retort, "what do you mean by it?" "I mean," she said undaunted, "if you know where this so called Doctor Rann is, you will lead me to him." "Why?" "For the good reason that I am his wife perhaps the only one wedded to him in front of the holy fire at a temple." (49-50)

TM denies any knowledge of Rann and his whereabouts. But he informs Rann about her presence in the town who is terrified at the news. However, she finds her way to Kabir Street and corners TM. Her personality and appearance and its impact on the tradition-bound society is described by Narayan quite humorously. "The neighbours viewing her from their pyols must have felt shocked; her dress and deportment were so unusual in our setting, she looked like a Punjabi woman, in her Kurta or salwar kameez or whatever they call it, which seemed to exaggerate her physical stature, which was already immense. In our street where women were used to glittering silk sarees, gold and diamonds, she looked like a visitor from another planet. She wore around her neck white beads in a string, looked like a gypsy, and had around her shoulders a pink muslin wrap – the total effect was startling really. No wonder the spruce tailor-dummy called Rann quailed at the very thought of her." (64) She tells TM that she just wants to "get at that man." She narrates her story of love and marriage with Rann to TM, accepts his hospitality and replete after a packet of biscuits and half-a-dozen bananas, declares: "husband-hunting is a fatiguing business." (69)

Though the mode of presentation is comic, Sarasa's predicament is not without pathos.

The beautiful touch of humour throughout the story becomes evident in the telegram TM sends to Sarasa. "Come immediately. Your husband found. Come before he is lost again. Your only and final chance to rope him. Stay in the Railway Waiting Room. Don't come into town. I've fixed it. Take care not to be seen in town. Will meet you and explain further procedure." (118) Also the Silver Jubilee celebrations of Lotus Club at the Town Hall auditorium, Rann's public lecture in Futurology which creates a havoc, and the abduction of Rann by his wife are extremely hilarious.

The story of Sarasa's search and ultimate capture of her abandoned husband is portrayed in comic terms where the whole exercise is paralleled to the Satyavan myth. Thus *Talkative Man* once again shows Narayan's comic genius at its height.

The World of Nagaraj proves that "he is an enchanter." "It is beautifully written, funny and haunting, evoking in marvellously rich detail the atmosphere of a small town in Southern India and creating a magical world into which the reader is instantly drawn."

The novel tells the story of Nagaraj. Nagaraj's world is quiet and comfortable. He lives in his ancestral house with his wife Sita and his aged mother. He spends his time writing letters, drinking coffee and doing some leisurely book-keeping for his friend Coomar's Boeing Saree Company. His favourite pastime is sitting on the veranda, watching the world and planning the book he intends to write about the life of the great sage Narada.

But his peaceful life is disturbed when Tim, the son of his ambitious landowning brother Gopu, decides to leave home and come to live with Nagaraj. Forced to take responsibility for the boy, he is puzzled by his secret late-night activities and by the strong smell of spirits which lingers behind him. The father gets the boy married in the hope that he settles down. But Tim remains as he is, and leaves Nagaraj's house on some pretext only to return later. Nagaraj finds out that he has to relinquish the thought of the contented tranquillity of his world for ever.

The novel abounds in comic situations. For example, there is the scene where Nagaraj tries to catch-hold of his wayward nephew, who returns at midnight with a trail of alcoholic scent. After sniffing everyday for the smell, finally one evening he could not help asking Tim that he detects a smell when Tim passes him, "something like a spirit stove of a doctor's." Tim explains:

"Some chap sprayed eau-de-cologne on me."
"Why?"
"They play that sort of joke in our club."
"But your breath also smells when you talk."
"Oh, that chap sprayed it on my lips too."[55]

Nagaraj's worry, though absurdly comic is real and he tries to rationalize the boy's behaviour in order to believe him.

Highly comic are his efforts at finding out what is wrong with Tim, from Jesudoss at Albert Mission College. He goes there with the intention of finding something about Tim. Instead, he himself is interrogated by Jesudoss. Jesudoss asks Nagaraj suddenly why he stopped the boy from attending the college. At his wit's end to find an answer while concealing his shock at the news, he tries to defend the boy. But Jesudoss holds Nagaraj responsible, who is quite "cowed" by the former's "flashing eyes." He regrets his meeting the Professor at all: "When he met Jesudoss outside, at the fish market, for instance, the Professor was so mild and friendly. But in his official seat within the four walls of Albert Mission, he sounded terrible. How people assumed different avatars on different occasions, he marvelled secretly." (76)

Narayan's instinct for the extraordinary in the ordinary becomes evident once again in the creation of Kave pandit who insists that one should know Sanskrit in order to write about sage Narada and, who considers Nagaraj to be a dunce because he knows little Sanskrit.

Nagaraj's efforts at trying to protect himself from Saroja's harmonium and music are highly amusing. He tries to stuff his ears with cotton wool. "Thank God the harmonium has no tongue." (142)

There is no strong discrimination of anything except factual delineation. Hence Nagaraj's acceptance of Tim as he is at the end, though revealed in comic overtones. "I'll take him as he is. I do not mind anything except that huge harmonium; when its bellows work, the roof will be lifted off the rafters and beams. I dread it." (184) In order to let the children live in peace he decides to wear ochre robes and remain silent.

Graham Greene observes a strange mixture of humour, sadness and beauty in Narayan's novels. He also comments on Narayan's "complete objectivity, complete freedom from comment."[56] Further, in his introduction to *The Financial Expert*, Greene comments on Narayan's gift of comedy with its undertone of sadness, its gentle irony and absence of condemnation – "a type of comedy virtually extinct in the West, where farce, satire and boisterousness are substituted for true comedy."[57] Success in it calls for a sensibility preserved from ambivalence or fracture, an unusual unity in the point of view as well as a social tradition in which the comic and the sad are not sharply marked off one from the other. It requires too a certain equanimity, an evenness, to hold back both the exaggeration of farce and the one-sidedness of sentimentality.[58]

This gentleness and geniality is the quintessence of Narayan's comedy. There is an inherent awareness of life in his works and his art is never deliberate or didactic. Whatever awareness there is, is realized through not a moralizing stance but an acceptance of reality which gives a meaningfulness to life.

That is why his tone remains mild even while criticizing and he is quick to perceive the absurd and the incongruous in life. Hence his constant juxtaposition of the age-old convention and the modern character. His humour is "sly and poker-faced."[59] Affectation and hypocrisy never escape his keen perception and observation.

Narayan's forte lies in the painting of the ordinary and the commonplace, the events and aspirations of middle-class people in a small town – Malgudi. The world of Malgudi is peopled with Chandran, Krishnan, Raju, Margayya, Jagan, Srinivas and a number of other common characters because the ordinary common man[60] holds the interest of Narayan. He portrays their absurd dreams and aspirations and their ultimate return to normalcy, but without any censoriousness. His attitude remains one of compassion, tolerance and detachment and he is "concerned with those abnormalities of character and ideas which isolate the hero until he is enabled or forced to shed them and rejoin, as it were, the human race which means the society he happens to belong to."[61]

Narayan's writings are marked by a deep sense of humour. As one of the critics remarks, "Narayan certainly entertains but not at a brisk, rollicking pace. On the other hand, the laughter he evokes is not recorded laughter edited into the video-tape but genuine and simple laughter."[62]

Narayan's vision remains essentially tragi-comic and he is intensely aware of the underlying sense of beauty and sadness of human life. That is why even Vasu and Pal are casually dismissed. His tolerance marks his comic vision unsullied by any acerbity. "He has been called a satirist, but it is doubtful whether this bitter role can be assigned to so genial a writer. Yet the melancholy which informs his vision of life and the vein of mockery in his comedy tends to produce an effect not unlike satire."[63] But there are no villains in the real sense of the word, because his vision of life is realistic.

Narayan's ability to unfold the serious and the tragic in life thus makes his comic mode unique. To cite some instances, the predicament of Sampath, the fortunes of Margayya, the detachment of Jagan, the disillusionment of Raman, the philanderings of Rann, all lend themselves to the comic treatment. It is worth-mentioning here that the tragedy of Raju

The Guide, that most acclaimed novel, is treated in terms of comedy as well as irony. "It is here that one witnesses the fusion of the comic and the tragic. It is the surpassing triumph of the art which makes the comic pursue the ends of the tragic, in the attempt to resolve the duality and perceive the hard core of things. The tragic muse who normally grapples with so serious an enterprise is here seen surrendering her privilege in favour of her rival, the muse of comedy, who accepts the opportunity with a daring and demonstrates her possibilities in the hands of a consummate practitioner of art."[64]

Narayan's comic vision is essentially humanistic and his writings are permeated by a warmth which gives him a universal appeal and perhaps is the secret of his abiding strength. The comic mode he chooses requires an absurdly realistic and fantastic treatment where slight exaggeration is unavoidable. "His wit and irony gently pulverize old and young, traditional and modern, but it is the very overdose of amusement which makes it difficult for many Indian readers to accept Narayan as a genuinely serious artist."[65] But the amusement is deceptive and serves only to restitute Narayan's comic objectivity and detachment as the novels prove it.

The achievement of Narayan is unique. His comedy is not all entertainment but has a certain moral concern and levels of reality which is perhaps not obvious, and tells the tale of common humanity. He views the human predicament in terms of "comedy of affirmation."[66]

NOTES

1. William Walsh, *Indian Literature in English* (London: Longman, 1990), p. 79.
2. Jayant K. Biswal, *The Novels of R.K. Narayan* (New Delhi: Nirmal, 1987), p. 120.
3. David Lodge, *Language of Fiction* (London: Routledge and Kegan Paul, 1970), p. 29.
4. Graham Greene, "Introduction," *The Bachelor of Arts*, p. vi.
5. Cited by Shiv K. Girla in *R.K. Narayan: His World And His Art* (Meerut: Saru, 1984), p. 91.
6. K.R. Srinivasa Iyengar, *Indian Writing in English* (New Delhi: Sterling, 1985), p. 358.
7. R.K. Narayan, *Swami and Friends* (Mysore: Indian Thought Publications, 1983), p. 9.
8. H.M. Williams, *Indo-Anglian Literature* (New Delhi: Orient

Longman, 1976), p. 51.

9. *Ibid.*, p. 51.
10. *Ibid.*
11. Graham Greene, "Introduction," *The Bachelor of Arts*, pp. vii- viii.
12. Shiv K. Girla, p. 97.
13. R.K. Narayan, *The English Teacher* (Mysore: Indian Thought Publications, 1984), p. 5.
14. R.K. Kaul, "The Comic Vision of R.K. Narayan," *Essays presented to Amy G. Stock* (Jaipur: Rajasthan University, 1965).
15. Shiv K. Girla, p. 102.
16. R.K. Narayan, *The Dark Room* (Mysore: Indian Thought Publications, 1986), p. 128.
17. H.M. Williams, p. 53.
18. *Ibid.*, p. 57.
19. Lakshmi Holmstrom, *The Novels of R.K. Narayan* (Calcutta: Writers Workshop, 1973), p. 52.
20. R.K. Narayan, *Mr. Sampath* (Mysore: Indian Thought Publications, 1985), p. 189.
21. H.M. Williams, p. 56.
22. K.R. Srinivasa Iyengar, pp. 374-75.
23. Cited by Shiv K.Girla, p. 105.
24. *Ibid.*
25. K.R. Srinivasa Iyengar, p. 376.
26. Graham Greene, "Introduction," *The Financial Expert* (Mysore: Indian Thought Publications, 1984), p. viii.
27. Shiv K. Girla, p. 108.
28. Rajeev Taranath, "The Average as the Positive," *Critical Essays in Indian Writing in English* (Delhi: Macmillan, 1977), p. 372.
29. H.M. Williams, *The Galaxy of Indian Writings in English*, p. 73.
30. R.K. Narayan, *The Vendor of Sweets* (Mysore: Indian Thought Publications, 1981), pp. 15, 45.
31. A.N. Kaul, "R.K. Narayan and the East West Theme," *Considerations,* ed. Meenakshi Mukherjee (New Delhi: Allied, 1977), p. 60.
32. Shiv K Girla, p. 116.
33. *Ibid.*
34. H.M. Williams, *The Galaxy of Indian Writings in Englsh*, p. 74.
35. *Ibid.*, p. 73.
36. Cited by Shiv K. Girla, p. 59.
37. H.M. Williams, *Indo-Anglian Literature*, p. 59.
38. M.K. Naik, *The Ironic Vision* (New Delhi: Sterling, 1983), p. 54.
39. William Walsh, "Sweet Mangoes and Malt Vinegar," *Indo-English Literature*, ed. K.K.Sharma (Ghaziabad: Vimal, 1977), p. 139.

40. *Ibid.*, p. 129.
41. R.K. Narayan, *The Guide* (Mysore: Indian Thought Publications, 1985), p. 212.
42. R.K. Narayan, *The Man-Eater of Malgudi* (New Delhi: Hind Pocket Books, 1979), p. 30.
43. Shiv K. Girla, p. 114.
44. H.M. Williams, *Galaxy of Indian Writings in English*, p. 65.
45. William Walsh, *Indian Literature in English*, p. 83.
46. *Ibid.*, p. 86.
47. *Ibid.*, p. 87.
48. Shiv K. Girla, p. 109.
49. R.K. Narayan, *Waiting for the Mahatma* (Mysore: Indian Thought Publications, 1984), pp. 2-10.
50. Shiv K. Girla, p. 118.
51. Rajeev Taranath, p. 372.
52. R.K. Narayan, *The Painter of Signs* (England: Penguin, 1985), p. 12.
53. R.K. Narayan, *A Tiger for Malgudi* (Mysore: Indian Thought Publications, 1983), p. 165.
54. R.K. Narayan, *Talkative Man* (Mysore: Indian Thought Publications, 1986), p. 49.
55. R.K. Narayan, *The World of Nagaraj* (Mysore: Indian Thought Publications, 1990), p. 60.
56. Graham Greene, "Introduction," *The Bachelor of Arts*.
57. Perry D. Westbrook, "The Short Stories of R.K. Narayan," *The Journal of Commonwealth Literature*, no. 5, July 1968, p. 51.
58. William Walsh, *Indian Literature in English*, p. 79.
59. H.M. Williams, *Galaxy of Indian Writings in English*, p. 47.
60. William Walsh, "Sweet Mangoes and Malt Vinegar," p. 126.
61. H.M. Williams, *Galaxy of Indian Writings in English*, p. 27.
62. Uma Parameswaran, *A Study of Representative Indo-English Novelists* (New Delhi: Vikas, 1976), p. 47.
63. H.M. Williams, *Galaxy of Indian Writings in English*, pp. 47-48.
64. C.D. Narasimhaiah, *The Swan and the Eagle*, p. 157.
65. Stephen Ignatius Hemenway, *The Novel of India* (Calcutta: Writers Workshop, 1975), vol. II, p. 22.
66. Shiv K. Girla, p. 126.

By Way of Summing Up

In the foregoing pages an attempt has been made to trace and study in some detail the world of Malgudi as reflected in the novels of R.K. Narayan. Narayan's fiction is built on certain themes which recur and which are inter-related and interdependent. Therefore only for the sake of analysis they have to be isolated. Of the recurrent themes of his fiction, the family, personal relationships, and renunciation come first and foremost. These are to be found virtually in all his novels, be they early or late. Of course, it goes without saying that they do not have the same importance in all the novels. As a novelist Narayan is very much interested in human beings and relationships, at home as well as outside. Hence his consideration of the above-mentioned themes in relation to the everyday lives and experiences of men and women, and never in abstract. His imaginary town Malgudi which is the locale for all his novels, and the family provide him manageable and convenient context to study different types of people, human relationships, and human behaviour. Just as he limits himself by and large to the little world of Malgudi and its surroundings for the locale of his fiction, he also intentionally limits himself to the middle-class of society which he knows first-hand and intimately. What is more, he chooses for his fictional contemplation men and women who are ordinary and average, whose experience of life appears to grow with our own. Therefore, Narayan's characters appeal to us at once and a sympathetic identification with them is almost immediately established. Occasionally they may become extraordinary. Margayya may almost reach the summit of the world of money; Raju may become a martyr; and even Vasu may become a modern *rakshasa,* just to cite a few instances of the ordinary becoming the extraordinary. But their essential and shared humanity is never in doubt, the solitary exception being Vasu, the 'maneater.' Even in the case of this modern counterpart of the mythical Bhasmasura, his incorrigible demoniac qualities become pronounced only after his human qualities are established. He remains most human in his limitations. It is the distinctive achievement of Narayan that he shows how rich, varied, and engaging even the ordinary and average lives can be. And he is able to present his characters realistically, even when considerable fabulous element gets interwoven with the narrative. Narayan's characters, be they young or old, eccentric or absurd, convince us as human beings. Hence the universal appeal of his fiction.

Malgudi with all the historical and geographical details and the behavioural details of its people convey a vivid impression of its society. The atmosphere of the town is evoked with subtle and delicate strokes. Malgudi's presence is made vivid not only by mere geographical details but by the fact of the continuous awareness of its eternal presence. Hence the legend of Sri Rama and how the river Sarayu is formed. The Sarayu river, the Lawley statue, the grandmother – all these and others convey a sense of the eternal reality of Malgudi. And what is more, the world of Malgudi is based on certain social values which are more traditional than modern. And there seems to be a conflict between these values and sometimes a corrosion of old values. Therefore we see the town slowly awakening to modernity. But, however, the permanence of the traditional values become obvious at the end.

It is the manageable context of the family, concrete and particular, that enables Narayan to keep the focus on character and personal relationships. The family in India has always been a network of personal relationships: parents and children, husbands and wives, brothers and sisters, uncles, aunts, cousins, grand-parents, mothers-in-law and daughters-in-law, and many not easily definable relationships; the 'cousin' in *The Vendor of Sweets* is an instance of the latter. It is not necessary that they all should be living under the same roof. Narayan's imagination finds a fertile ground to operate in the little world of the family. Western readers of his fiction are particularly impressed by this aspect of his writing.

Narayan's handling of the family theme reveals his awareness and understanding of its different aspects, its range, variety and complexity, encompassing the personal, emotional, social, economic, cultural and other factors which operate in the family. Chapter III endeavours to analyze them in the novels chosen for consideration. In *Swami and Friends* and *The Bachelor of Arts,* the significant role played by the family in the lives of their protagonists when faced with a crisis is demonstrated. Growth towards emotional maturity in the boy Swami and the young man Chandran depends very much upon the unbounded and unabated love of their respective parents for them.

The traditional Hindu way of life attaches very great importance to married life or *grihasthasrama*, the second of the four stages in one's life. A loving and harmonious relationship between husband and wife is the cornerstone on which the edifice of the family and of parenthood is built. It also makes for what may be called the mental and spiritual growth of the husband and wife. But in actuality, persistent domestic discord, apart from incidental conflicts and tensions, is at least as common as domestic harmony. Perhaps this is an optimistic view of the prevalent situation. In *The Dark Room* and *The English Teacher*, Narayan attempts a sensitive and perceptive study of this aspect of family life, avoiding at the same time a sentimental and a romantic view of it. In *The Dark Room* he presents with sympathetic detachment the plight of Savitri whose married life is a tale of frustration, and shows how she has to reconcile herself to her domestic situation because of her own limitations. Narayan successfully avoids in this novel the stance of a 'problem' novelist, a temptation to which a lesser writer would have yielded readily. In *The English Teacher,* which is in part a fictional recreation of Narayan's own experience of bereavement consequent upon the premature death of his wife, he has not been able, according to some readers, to achieve his accustomed degree of detachment. But the analysis of the family theme in this novel attempted here, has implicitly shown that the novel needs to be and can be read, without any reference to Narayan's autobiography, as the story of Krishnan and Susila, of their married life and its transcendental quality, and of their sense of fulfilment in spite of bereavement.

Father-son relationship and the breakdown of communication between the successive generations, which is an aspect of the former, form the theme of *The Financial Expert* and *The Vendor of Sweets.* An attempt has been made to show how insightfully Narayan probes the anguished minds of indulgent fathers whose expectations and hopes regarding their sons are disappointed, the possible reasons for the failure of communication between the fathers and the sons, and how in different ways they come to terms with their respective situations.

The three novels, *The Guide, The Man-Eater of Malgudi* and *The Painter of Signs* expose the minds of certain characters who, for different reasons, cannot remain in the fold of the family and abide by its conventions. Raju of *The Guide,* having lived the life of a drifter without a rudder, ultimately finds himself sacrificing his life for the welfare of a rural community. Such a transformation in one who could invent excuses to justify his indifference to his mother, the most sacred of familial bonds, appears nothing short of a miracle. It is Narayan's achievement that he makes this transformation credible. Vasu of *The Man-Eater of Malgudi* who is conceived as being evil straightforwardly, makes himself unfit by his very demoniac nature to be in any society, big or small. Rosie of *The Guide* and Daisy of *The Painter of Signs* are more complex studies of misfits in the family. If in Rosie, we find one who is anxious to live a conventional married life but who cannot do it, in Daisy we have one who deliberately goes out of its bounds being fully aware of the hazards of such a step. What needs to be noted is that they both are sustained by their dedication to a cause, to an ideal. Rosie's devotion to dance and Daisy's dedication to the cause of family planning bring out all the hidden potentialities.

The individual's innate compulsion to find a meaning of life, and to assert his identity to realize the absurd ambitions, which he does not recognize as such at the time, are taken up by Narayan. The individual tries to defy the moral and ethical codes of the society to satisfy his needs. Thus there arises a conflict between the individual and society. The individuals move along erroneous patterns to realize their ambitions and aspirations, and the consequent conflict gives rise to disorder in the tradition-bound society of Malgudi. But the Malgudi society has the unending resilience and withstands the disorder, and finally normalcy or order is restored. In spite of his rebellion against society, the individual is not wholly condemned. Therefore, if disorder is due to man against his society, the ultimate order and restoration is due to his lawful place and absorption in his society. Thus the individual traversing along a path realizes his folly and returns chastened, to the fold of the society.

Renunciation is one of the most important themes of Narayan. Renunciation being very much an Indian ideal in that it is inseparable from the Indian consciousness, way of life and values, it is natural that Narayan should have chosen it as a recurrent theme in his fiction. With his roots deep and firm in Indian traditions and culture, he is fully aware of the value attached to the ideal of *sanyasa* in the traditional *asrama-dharma,* and the place given to the *sanyasi* in the social and cultural milieu of Indian society. He is equally aware of the hypocrisies, frauds, and deceits practised in the name of *sanyasa,* exposure of which has been the preoccupation of several Indian writers. But he does not choose the theme for satirical attack on the frauds and cheats among *sanyasis.* Nor does he try it merely for its fictional possibilities. The study of the novels reveals that a variety of reasons guide Narayan's choice of the theme. First of all, the ideal of renunciation is a part and parcel of the life and social reality around him. Secondly, he is drawn to it because of his own philosophical and spiritual interests. Thirdly, he finds that the ideal of renunciation, in its essence is both psychologically and morally relevant to our lives, although one may not adhere strictly to the four-stage traditional pattern of life. Fourthly, this being the most important, human nature, motives and behaviour being the focus of his interest as a novelist, he sets out to explore in terms of fiction, what factors—personal, psychological and circumstantial, motivate one to think of some form of renunciation, and to examine the frame of mind appropriate to live a life of renunciation, with or without ochre robes.

Therefore Narayan takes a comprehensive view of the theme, though he deliberately restricts himself to the comic mode. He brings under his purview not only the *sanyasi,* holy man or *guru,* genuine as well as spurious, but men and women of different age groups. Thus a young graduate like Chandran growing from late adolescence to emotional maturity, a young idealistic woman like Daisy devoted to an impersonal cause with zeal and determination of a missionary, a betrayed and frustrated housewife like Savitri in her late thirties, a sensitive college teacher like Krishnan, also in his thirties, struggling to come to terms with the death of his beloved wife, the Mahatma who is the very essence of sainthood and renunciation, living and sacrificing his life for his people and his country, a drifter without a rudder like Raju who successfully exploits the gullibility of a rural community, plays the role of a holy man, and gets transformed into a genuine man of sacrifice by the very faith of the villagers, a sixty year old businessman like Jagan, complacent and wealthy, who chooses to withdraw into a grove from his family and his worldly engagements to cultivate an impersonal aesthetic interest, and a well-to-do householder with wife and children who suddenly turns his back upon all worldly attachment to become forest-dwelling hermit in quest of self-realization, and who also takes for his companion and disciple a majestic tiger—all are protagonists in Narayan's study of the theme of renunciation.

Narayan does not look at the ideal of renunciation from the point of view of strict adherence to the traditional *asramadharma*. Nor does he take a dogmatic stand for or against it. He considers, on the contrary, its psychological, moral and spiritual implications. As the analysis of the selected novels shows, Narayan finds in true renunciation a positive ideal, which makes for life than go against it, and which affirms both life and society. Although renunciation does require freeing oneself from attachments, Narayan true to the spirit of the Hindu view of life, does not set it in opposition to the other necessary stages of life, especially that of the householder. The most important thing for the man or woman of genuine renunciation is the achievement of non-attachment, freedom from delusions of all kinds, transcendence of the ego, and serenity of mind, rather than running away from home and family from reason and responsibility. When achieved, genuine renunciation brings out one's hidden potentialities. Since Narayan finds in renunciation a positive ideal, his comedy and irony are not directed against it. The hoax practised by Raju, the guide, is dealt with ironically but not the holy man or *swami* as such. Yet another characteristic of Narayan's handling of the theme is that he avoids any suggestion of solemnity and other worldliness in his protagonists who seek true renunciation. This is as much true of Krishnan who gives up his college job to withdraw into the children's school as of the tiger-hermit who dwells in a forest cave.

Narayan has a strong Indian sensibility and manages to convey this essential Indianness in his writings. He portrays the traditional Indian society, a society which believes in *Karma,* rebirth and *Samsara* (transmigration of soul). Deeply rooted in his culture, Narayan does not merely attempt to draw the picture of an imaginary town; he brings the centuries-old religious and philosophical beliefs of his own country into the fictional narrative, which has its source, as far as form is concerned, in the great epics, legends and folk tales. Fable and myth are the inherited formal patterns in which the Indians from generation to generation find their expression. And it is this that Narayan takes up and renders into fiction. He improvises the traditional myths and legends into modern stories set in the contemporary world. He depicts his moral vision in these stories through the comic mode. For instance *The Man-Eater of Malgudi* is the tale of a modern Bhasma namely Vasu. *Mr. Sampath* is drawn on the lines of the myth Kamadahana (The Burning of Kama). Likewise *The Guide* presents the picture of a man's primitive ritual to bring the rains, to relieve a credulous community from drought.

Narayan's sense of the comic is his distinguishing mark as a writer of fiction. It is something unique and deserves a detailed investigation, which the present study has no pretensions of claiming to have done. Narayan's sense of the comic is never laughs all the way, nor does it depend upon the merely satirical which specializes in the exposure of folly to ridicule, accompanied by indignation or laughter. Indignation of any kind is not known to Narayan the novelist. It does not mean that he compromises easily. His comedy springs from his unillusioned acceptance of people for what they are, even though he is very quick to perceive and poke fun at what is odd, peculiar, ludicrous, ridiculous and absurd in thought and behaviour. What people ought to be is invariably implied in his writings, and is rarely stated overtly. Therefore, irony characterizes his writings. Contrary to the view of some of his critics that he is superficial and merely skims the surface of life with a tickling joke or a witticism, it will be found that the pathetic, the painful, and the tragic are never far away from his comedy. If a label is necessary to characterize his comedy, one may for the sake of convenience use the term tragi-comedy. His comic perspective provides a healthy corrective to the melodramatic, the sentimental, and the narrowly satirical perspective. Rather than make easy concessions to human weaknesses and follies, one would find Narayan implicitly affirming certain values of life which are traditional and Indian.

Glossary

The following terms are formally transliterated on their first appearance in the thesis and thereafter appear in that form only. After each transliterated term, the language and a brief definition are given.

Agastya (Sans.)	A celebrated sage.
Alakapuri (Sans.)	The capital city of Lord Kubera, the treasurer of the Gods.
Amarasakthi (Sans.)	The King of Mahilaroopya, an ancient kingdom in South India. He employed Vishnusarma, a scholar, to educate his foolish sons in the principles and polity of the State, namely *Saama* (using gentle or pacific means), *Daana* (giving presents or bribing), *Bheda* (sowing dissensions among the enemy or dividing his force or strength), *Danda* (waging a war), and *Upaaya* (using tactful means). Vishnusarma achieved his task by entertaining them to stories enacted by animals. These stories later came to be known as the *Panchatantra* (pancha = five; tantra = strategies).
Apsara (Sans.)	Heavenly nymph.
Arjuna (Sans.)	Name of the third brother among the five Pandavas, the heroes of the *Mahabharata*.
Asrama (Sans.)	Stage of an individual's life from the Hindu religious point of view.
Asramadharma (Sans.)	The traditional Hindu view of life which offers a set of duties enjoined for each of the four *asramas* or stages. There are four such stages in one's life, viz., *Brahmacharya* (bachelorhood or studentship), *Garhasthya* (housholder-ship), *Vanaprasthya* (an anchorite) and *Sanyasa* (being a recluse).
Asura (Sans.)	Demon.
Asvapathi (Sans.)	King of Madra State in ancient India. Savitri is his daughter.
Atman/Atma (Sans.)	Soul.
Atri-Smriti (Sans.)	A Law-Digest written by Sage Atri.

Avatar (Sans.)	Incarnation of God; the manifestation of the Divine Spirit in a human form.
Ayodhya (Sans.)	The capital city of the kingdom of Kosala, the land ruled by the Ikshvaku line of kings in ancient India. King Dasaratha belongs to this line of kings. The greatest of these kings is Rama, son of Dasaratha.
Bapu (Hindi)	Father or a venerable man. Father of the Nation, Gandhi, is affectionately called Bapu.
Bhagavad Gita/Gita (Sans.)	A classic of Hindu philosophy—a portion of the epic of the *Mahabharata*. It appears in the form of a dialogue between the hero Arjuna and his charioteer Lord Krishna.
Bhagavata (Sans.)	A celebrated Hindu poem describing the life and incarnations of Lord Vishnu. It is a *Purana.*
Bharata Bharati (Sans.)	Mother India.
Bharata Natyam (Sans.)	A type of South Indian dance.
Bhasmasura (Sans.)	A demon who is a great devotee of Shiva. He gets a boon from Lord Shiva to the effect of turning people into ashes if he placed his palms on their heads. It so happens that he places his palms on his own head and reduces himself to ashes.
Bodhisattva (Sans.)	One who according to the tenets of Buddhism, has only a few births more to attain complete enlightenment or eternal happiness (nirvana). This obviously refers to Buddha, in his previous births.
Bonda (Dravidian)	A popular savoury, either stuffed or unstuffed, in South India.
Brahmacharya (Sans.)	The first of the four *Asramas*. It refers to bachelorhood or studentship.
Brahmana (Sans.)	A member of the priestly class according to the traditional Hindu social order (*varna*).
Buddha (Sans.)	The Enlightened; the founder of Buddhism.
Chandala (Sans.)	An outcaste; an ancient class of downtrodden people considered as untouchables.
Chandogya Upanishad (Sans.)	A philosophical disquisition attached to the *Vedas*, the most ancient religious texts of Hindus.
Chandra (Sans.)	Another name for Moon-God.
Charkha (Hindi)	Spinning wheel.
Chudala (Sans.)	A princess who reformed her husband Sikhidhvaja of sensual love and chiseled him to be a liberated soul of spiritual love even while living (*jivanmukta*).

Darshan (Sans.)	To see a Deity.
Dasaratha (Sans.)	King of Ayodhya, belonging to the line of Ikshvaku rulers. He is the father of Rama.
Devadasi (Sans.)	A temple dancer.
Deva-Vrata (Sans.)	Son of Ganga and Santhanu. Also called Gangeya or Bheeshma.
Dharma (Sans.)	Essential quality or character of one's own nature as stipulated by religious law, custom or duty.
Dharma Sastras (Sans.)	The books of Hindu religious law, setting down the code of life to the minutest detail.
Dhoti (Hindi)	A loin-cloth.
Dhritarashtra	The blind Kuru King, the father of Duryodhana.
Duryodhana (Sans.)	Eldest of the hundred sons of King Dhritarashtra.
Dushyanta (Sans.)	King of Hastinapura who married Sakuntala, the adopted daughter of the great sage Kanva.
Gajendra (Sans.)	King elephant, the ruler of Dravila in the previous birth.
Gandharava (Sans.)	A semi-divine being, who is a celestial singer.
Gandharva Vivah (Sans.)	Marriage by mutual consent of the boy and the girl. It is one of the eight traditional forms of Hindu marriage.
Ganga (Sans.)	Goddess who assumed the form of the river. In her human form she becomes the queen of King Santhanu on certain conditions..
Garhasthya/Grihastha (Sans.)	Householder stage according to Hindu view of life.
Garuda (Sans.)	The sacred eagle, the messenger and the vehicle of Lord Vishnu.
Gayatri (Sans.)	The name of a short prayer addressed to the Goddess of Radiance by the Hindus.
Guru (Sans.)	Teacher.
Guru-Sishya (Sans.)	Teacher-Disciple.
Hanuman (Sans.)	The mythological Monkey-God of the *Ramayana* fame.
Huhu (Sans.)	A *gandharava* cursed to become a crocodile that caught hold of Gajendra, the King Elephant.
Indra (Sans.)	King of Heaven.
Indradyumna (Sans.)	King of Dravila who is cursed by sage Agastya.
Iswara (Sans.)	Another name for Lord Shiva.
Janma (Sans.)	Birth.
Jataka Tales (Pali)	Tales related to the previous births of Buddha.
Jilebi (Hindi)	A sweetmeat made of sugar and ghee.

Jivanmukta (Sans.)	One who attains final liberation or emancipation even when alive in this world.
Jutka (Hindi)	Two-wheeled vehicle drawn by a horse.
Kaikeyi (Sans.)	One of the three queens of King Dasaratha.
Kailas (Sans.)	The abode of Lord Shiva.
Kalidasa (Sans.)	A great dramatist in Sanskrit.. He is the writer of *Abhijnana Sakuntalam* which describes the story of Sakuntala and Dushyantha.
Kama (Sans.)	Desire; another name for the God of Desire.
Kamadahana (Sans.)	The Burning of Kama.
Kamasutra (Sans.)	A Sanskrit text written by Vatsayana. It deals with the principles of love and erotics.
Kapaleeswara (Sans.)	A form of Lord Shiva.
Karman/Karma (Sans.)	Action; Fate; Consequences of good and evil actions performed in this as well as previous lives.
Karma yoga (Sans.)	Performance of the necessary worldly duties, merely by reason of a sense of duty, with no thought of liking or disliking, and of reaping the fruit of action; detached action.
Katha Upanishad	One of the philosophical disquisitions (Sans.) attached to the Vedas.
Kavya (Sans.)	A literary production or composition.
Khaddar (Hindi)	Handspun cloth.
Kopagriha (Sans.)	The sulking boudoir.
Krodha (Sans.)	Anger.
Krishna/Sri Krishna (Sans.)	An incarnation of God Vishnu.
Kshatriya (Sans.)	Member of a warrior class.
Kubera (Sans.)	The God of Riches and the treasurer of the Gods.
Kuru (Sans.)	The line of Kings named after Kuru to which Duryodhana belongs.
Kurukshetra (Sans.)	A famous battle-field on which the *Mahabharata* war was fought.
Kusa (Sans.)	Eldest son of Rama.
Lakh (Hindi)	One hundred thousand rupees.
Lakshmi (Sans.)	Goddess of Wealth.
Lalgudi (Dravidian)	Name of a place on the banks of river Kaveri in Tamil Nadu.
Lava (Sans.)	Younger son of Rama.
Lobha (Sans.)	Greed; avarice.
Mahabharata (Sans.)	An epic of Hindus dealing mainly with the conflict between the Pandavas and the Kauravas.
Maharaja (Sans.)	A sovereign or an emperor.
Manmatha/Kama (Sans.)	Cupid, the God of Desire or Love.
Manu Smriti (Sans.)	Law-Digest composed by Manu.

Mantra (Sans.)	Syllables or formulae with magic potency.
Maya (Sans.)	Psychic power capable of producing deception of the senses; anything unreal; one of the snares that entangle the soul; the divine power of cosmic illusion.
Moha (Sans.)	Infatuation.
Mohini (Sans.)	An incarnation of Lord Vishnu in the form of a captivating siren.
Narada (Sans.)	A celestial sage, great musician, a messenger and newsmonger of the immortals, who is constantly on the move between all the worlds above and below this world of Earth.
Nataraja (Sans.)	King of Dance, another name of Shiva.
Navaratri (Sans.)	The festival of nine nights, celebrated by Hindus in honour of Goddess Durga in September-October.
Nigamasarma (Sans.)	The prodigal son of Sabhapathi, who brings the downfall of his parents.
Nishkamakarma yoga (Sans.)	Disinterested action; a practice in which an individual becomes free from the motive of action bearing fruit.
Pahelwan (Hindi/Urdu)	Wrestler.
Panchatantra (Sans.)	A book of animal stories written by Vishnusarma on principles and methods of Government.
Pandit/Pundit (Sans.)	Scholar.
Panduranga Mahatmyam (Sans.)	A poem in Sanskrit (a part of *Skanda Purana*), translated into Telugu also, in which the story about Nigamasarma the prodigal son of Sabhapathi appears.
Parvathi (Sans.)	Consort of Lord Shiva.
Puja (Sans.)	Hindu ritual worship.
Purana (Sans.)	Source books of mythology and legends of Hinduism. They are the quasi-legendary, quasi-historical accounts of ancient kings with a good amount of symbolism incorporated into them.
Puranic (Sans.)	Adjective of the word *Purana*.
Radha Kalyan (Sans.)	Marriage of Lord Krishna and His favourite devotee Radha.
Rajas (Sans.)	The second of the three qualities (*gunas*). It signifies passion.
Rakshasa (Sans.)	Demon
Rama/Sri Rama (Sans.)	An incarnation of Lord Vishnu. The son of King Dasaratha.
Ramayana (Sans.)	An epic poem of Hindus which depicts the story of Rama.
Ram Dhun (Hindi)	Holy fire.

Ram Nam (Hindi)	Name of Lord Rama, uttered as a prayer.
Rama Rajya (Sans.)	Ideal state as it existed during the reign of Rama, the hero of the epic poem *Ramayana*.
Rishi (Sans.)	Sage; hermit.
Rukmini (Sans.)	Wife of Lord Krishna; she is an incarnation of Lakshmi, the Goddess of Wealth.
Sadhu (Sans.)	Saint or holyman.
Sakuntala (Sans.)	Wife of King Dushyanta and mother of Bharata after whom India is named Bharat.
Samadhi (Sans.)	Profound meditation.
Samsara (Sans.)	Infinite transmigration of souls all according to one's Karma.
Santhanu (Sans.)	Ancient king of Hastinapura who married Goddess Ganga.
Sanyasa (Sans.)	The fourth and final stage of the four *asramas*—that of renunciation.
Sanyasi (Sans.)	Renunciate, an ascetic, a homeless seeker, one who wears ochre-robes.
Saraswathi (Sans.)	Goddess of Learning or Knowledge.
Sasanka (Sans.)	Moon-God also known as Chandra. His teacher is Brihaspathi. His teacher's wife Tara falls in love with him at the time of his studentship.
Sati Sumati (Sans.)	The epitome of suffering Indian womanhood; a housewife who suffered the vagaries of a womanizer husband.
Sattva (Sans.)	The quality of excellence, purity or goodness. It is the highest of the three *Gunas* (qualities).
Satyagraha (Sans.)	Passive resistance.
Satyavan (Sans.)	Son of Dyumatsena and husband of Savitri.
Savitri (Sans.)	The legendary heroine of the *Mahabharata* fame who pursues Yama and gets back the life of her husband. She symbolizes wifely devotion.
Shiva/Siva (Sans.)	The third of the Hindu triad, who is the Destroyer of the world.
Siddhartha (Sans.)	Prince of Sakya Kingdom who later becomes Buddha. He leaves his wife, children and kingdom out of an inner tranformation, in search of eternal happiness (nirvana).
Sikhidvaja (Sans.)	A Prince, husband of princess Chudala.
Sita (Sans.)	Consort of Lord Rama.
Sthithaprajna (Sans.)	Balanced intellect; one who is firmly established in wisdom.
Subrahmanyaswami (Sans.)	Second son of Lord Shiva.
Sura (Sans.)	Immortals; Gods and Goddesses.
Swadeshi (Sans.)	Of one's own country.

Swami (Sans.) — Hindu religious teacher; spiritual guide or preceptor.

Tara (Sans.) — Wife of Brihaspathi, the High Priest and the preceptor of gods. She falls in love with her husband's disciple namely Sasanka.

Upanishads (Sans.) — Spiritual Treatises in Sans.; they are the most sacred Hindu mystical texts which are records of the personal spiritual instruction to deserving disciples by perfect masters.

Uttara Ramayana (Sans.) — The later part of the epic *Ramayana*.

Vaisya (Sans.) — A member of trader class according to traditional social order (*varna*).

Vaikuntha (Sans.) — The abode of God Vishnu.

Vanaprasthya/Vanaprastha (Sans.) — The stage of withdrawal from active worldly life to the forest to pursue a life of total spiritual discipline; the third of the four *asramas*.

Vedas (Sans.) — Scriptures of Hindus.

Vedantic (Sans.) — That which is related to Hindu philosophy based upon the major *Upanishads*.

Vijayadasami (Sans.) — A festival during which Durga, the Goddess of Initiation is worshipped; in celebration of the triumph of good over evil.

Vishnu (Sans.) — The second deity of the Hindu triad, who is the Preserver of the world.

Vishnusarma (Sans.) — The author of the book *Panchatantra*.

Viswanatha (Sans.) — Another name of Lord Shiva.

Viswarupa (Sans.) — Universal form; multiformity; manifestation or display of one's own real form; he who exists in all forms, is Lord Vishnu.

Yadavagiri (Sans.) — A small town near Mysore in the State of Karnataka.

Yama (Sans.) — The God of Death.

Yoga (Sans.) — A system of Hindu philosophy showing the means of emancipation of the soul from further migrations and union with the supreme being; any of a number of systems of physical and mental disciplines by means of which such emancipation is attained; yogic exercises.

Yogi/Yogin (Sans.) — A Hindu ascetic who practises the yoga system, consisting of the withdrawal of the senses from external objects.

Zilla Parishad (Hindi) — The erstwhile District Board.

Bibliography

Works by R.K. Narayan

Novels

Swami and Friends. Mysore: Indian Thought Publications, 1983. First Published in London: Hamish Hamilton, 1935.

The Bachelor of Arts. Mysore: Indian Thought Publications, 1985. First Published in London: Nelson, 1937.

The Dark Room. Mysore: Indian Thought Publications, 1986. First Published in London: Macmillan, 1938.

The English Teacher. Mysore: Indian Thought Publications, 1985. First Published in London: Eyre and Spottiswoode, 1946.

Mr. Sampath. Mysore: Indian Thought Publications, 1985. First Published in London: Eyre and Spottiswoode, 1949.

The Financial Expert. Mysore: Indian Thought Publications, 1984. First Published in London: Methuen, 1952.

Waiting for the Mahatma. Mysore: Indian Thought Publications, 1984. First Published in London: Methuen, 1955.

The Guide. Mysore: Indian Thought Publications, 1984. First Published in New York: Viking, 1958.

The Man-Eater of Malgudi. Delhi: Hind, 1979. First Published in London: Heinemann, 1962.

The Vendor of Sweets. Mysore: Indian Thought Publications, 1981. First Published in London: The Bodley Head Ltd., 1967.

The Painter of Signs. London: Penguin, 1985. First Published in New York: Viking, 1976.

A Tiger for Malgudi. Mysore: Indian Thought Publications, 1983. First Published in London: William Heinemann, 1983.

Talkative Man. Mysore: Indian Thought Publications, 1986.

The World of Nagaraj. Mysore: Indian Thought Publications, 1990. First Published in London: William Heinemann, 1990.

Grandmother's Tale. Mysore: Indian Thought Publications, 1992

Short Story Collections

Malgudi Days. Mysore: Indian Thought Publications, 1986. Originally Published, 1941.

An Astrologer's Day and Other Stories. Mysore: Indian Thought Publications, 1968. First Published in London: Eyre and Spottiswoode, 1947.

Lawley Road and Other Stories. Delhi: Orient Paperbacks, 1982. Originally Published, 1950.

A Horse and Two Goats. Mysore: Indian Thought Publications, 1982. First Published in New York: Viking, 1970.

Retold Legends

Gods, Demons and Others (Tales from ancient Indian epics). Delhi: Hind, 1979. First Published in London: Heinemann, 1965.

The Mahabharata. Mysore: Indian Thought Publications, 1979. First Published in New York: Viking, 1978.

The Ramayana. Mysore: Indian Thought Publications, 1973.

Other Works

My Dateless Diary. Delhi: Orient Paperbacks, 1969.

My Days: A Memoir. Mysore: Indian Thought Publications, 1975. First Published in New York: Viking, 1974.

Reluctant Guru. New Delhi: Orient Paperbacks, 1974. Originally Published, 1964.

Books on R.K. Narayan

Agnihotri, G.N. *Indian Life and Problems in the Novels of Mulk Raj Anand, Raja Rao and R.K. Narayan*. Meerut: Shalabh,1984.

Girla, Shiv K. *R.K. Narayan – His World and His Art*. Meerut: Saru,1984.

Goyal, Bhagwat S. *R. K. Narayan: A Critical Spectrum*: Meerut: Shalabh, 1983.

Biswal, Jayant K. *A Critical Study of the Novels of R.K. Narayan*. New Delhi: Nirmal, 1987.

Holmstrom, Lakshmi. *The Novels of R.K.Narayan*. Calcutta: Writers Workshop, 1973.

Naik, M.K. *The Ironic Vision: A Study of the Fiction of R.K. Narayan*. New Delhi: Sterling, 1983.

Pontes, Hilda. *R.K. Narayan: Man and Writer*. A Bibliography of Indian Writing in English, ed. Nissim Ezekiel. New Delhi: Concept, 1983.

Ram, Atma. ed. *Perspectives on R.K. Narayan*. Ghaziabad: Vimal, 1981.

Rao, Vimala, ed. *The Literary Endeavour.* Special Issue on R.K. Narayan, vol. III, nos. 3 and 4, 1982.

Sundaram, P.S. *R.K. Narayan.* New Delhi: Arnold Heinemann, 1973.

Walsh, William. *R.K. Narayan: A Critical Appreciation.* New Delhi: Allied, 1983.

Critical Articles on R.K. Narayan

Alphonso, Karakala John B. "Symbolism in *The Financial Expert.*" *Indian Writing Today,* II, January-March, 1970.

Amur, G.S. "The River, the Lotus Pond and the Ruined Temple: An Essay on Symbolism in R.K. Narayan's Novels." *Indian Readings in Commonwealth Literature.*

Argyle, Barry. "Narayan's *The Sweet-Vendor.*" *The Journal of Commomwealth Literature,* vol. VII, no. 1, June 1972.

Asnani, Shyam M. "The Use of Myth in R.K. Narayan's Novels." *Literary Endeavour*, vol. I, nos. 3 & 4, April-June 1982.

Berry, Margaret. "R.K. Narayan, Lila and Literature." *The Journal of Indian Writing in English,* vol. 4, no. 2, July 1976.

Bhardwaj, S.P. "*The Painter of Signs* – An Analysis." *Perspectives on R.K. Narayan.*

Bhatnagar, O.P. "Love, Non-Violence and Freedom in *Waiting for the Mahatma.*" *Literary Endeavour*, April-June 1982.

Chew, Shirley. "A Proper Detachment: The Novels of R.K. Narayan." *Readings in Commonwealth Literature.*

Croft, Susan E. "Interview with R.K. Narayan." *R.K. Narayan: A Critical Spectrum.*

Dhawan, R.K. "The Anima Animus: Interaction in *The Guide.*" *Perspectives on R.K. Narayan.*

French, Warren. "Preface." *Perspectives on R.K. Narayan.* ed. Atma Ram.

Gerow, Edwin. "The Quintessential Narayan." *Considerations*, ed. Meenakshi Mukherjee.

Greene, Graham. "Introduction." *The Bachelor of Arts*. London: Pocket Book Edition, 1951.

____. "Introduction." *The Financial Expert*, Mysore: Indian Thought Publications, 1984.

Goyal, Bhagwat S. "From Picaro to Pilgrim: A Perspective on R.K. Narayan's *The Guide.*" *Indo-English Literature,* ed. K.K. Sharma.

____. "Thematic Patterns in the Early Novels of R.K. Narayan." *R.K. Narayan: A Critical Spectrum.*

____. "Indo-English." *Contemporary Indian Literature and Society.*

Gupta, G.S. Balarama. "A Sinner is a Sinner is a Sinner – A Study of Raju." *Perspectives on R.K. Narayan.*

Gupta, Rameshwar. "The Gandhi in Narayan." *Perspectives on R.K. Narayan.*

Gupta, Santosh. "Jagan's Experiment with Truth in *The Vendor of Sweets*." *The Journal of Indian Writing in English*, no. XVI.

Harrex, S.C. "R.K. Narayan: Malgudi Maestro." *The Fire and the Offering: The English Language Novel of India 1935-1970.*

Harrex, S.C. "*The Guide* as a Guide to Narayan's Art." *R.K. Narayan: A Critical Spectrum.*

Holmstrom, Lakshmi. "Women Characters in R.K. Narayan's Novels." *Perspectives on R.K. Narayan.*

Interview with William Walsh, B.B.C. London, Third Programme, 22 February, 1968. Quoted by Lakshmi Holmstrom, *The Novels of R.K. Narayan.*

Iyengar, K.R. Srinivasa. "R.K. Narayan" *Indian Writing in English.* New Delhi: Sterling, 1985.

Jayantha, R.A. "*The Man-Eater of Malgudi*: Some Aspects of its Narrative Strategy." *Literary Endeavour*, vol. III, nos. 3 & 4, April-June 1982.

____. "Gandhi, *The Gita* and Gayatri in *The Vendor of Sweets*." *Triveni*, April-June 1985.

Kalinnikova, E.J. "Indian Myths and Legends in R.K. Narayan's Interpretation." *Perspectives on R.K. Narayan.*

Kantak, V.Y. "The Achievement of R.K. Narayan." *Indian Literature of the Past Fifty Years 1917-1967.*

Kapadia, Novy. "Middle-class Milieu in R.K. Narayan's Novels." *Commomwealth Fiction.*

Kaul, A.N. "R.K. Narayan and the East-West Theme." *Considerations*, ed. Meenakshi Mukherjee.

Kaul, R.K. "The Comic Vision of R.K. Narayan." *Essays presented to Amy G. Stock.*

Kohli, Suresh. "Views of an Indian Novelist: An Interview with R.K. Narayan." *Indian and Foreign Review*, vol. 7, no. 15, May 15, 1970.

Macdonald, Bruce F. "Humanity and Aesthetic order in *The Vendor of Sweets*." *Perspectives on R.K. Narayan.*

Malhotra, Tara. "Old Places, Old Faces, Old Tunes – A Critical Study of R.K. Narayan's Latest Fiction." *The Banasthali Patrika*, no. 13, 1969.

Malik, Amita. "TV: R.K. Narayan goes sweet and sour." *An Interview. Indian Express*, July 25, 1986.

Mathur, O.P. "The West Wind Blows through Malgudi." *Perspectives on R.K. Narayan.*

Mehta, Ved. "The Train Had Just Arrived at the Malgudi Station." *John is Easy to Please.* London: Secker and Warburg, 1971.

Mukherji, Nirmal. "Some Aspects of the Literary Development of

R.K.Narayan." *The Banasthali Patrika*, no. 13, July 1969.

Murti, K.V.S. "Monkey and Hanuman." *Studies in Contemporary Indian Fiction in English.*

Naik, M.K. "The Theme and Form in R.K.Narayan's: *The Man-Eater of Malgudi.*" *The Journal of Commonwealth Literature.* no. 3, April 1976.

____. "Irony as Stance and as Vision: A Comparative Study of V.S.Naipaul's *The Mystic Masseur* and R.K.Narayan's *The Guide.*" *The Journal of Indian Writing in English,* vol. 6, no. 1, Jan. 1978.

Narasimhaiah, C.D. "Indian Writing in English – An Introduction." *The Journal of Commonwealth Literature*, vol. 5, July 1968.

____. "R.K. Narayan." *The Swan and the Eagle.*

____. "R.K. Narayan's *The Guide.*" *Aspects of Indian Writing in English,* ed. M.K. Naik.

Narasimhan, Raji. "The Inward Glance of Narayan." *R.K. Narayan: A Critical Spectrum.*

Narayan, R.K. "Gods, Demons and the Modern Times." *The Literary Criterion,* Winter 1972.

Narayan, R.K. "English in India: The Process of Transmutation." *Aspects of Indian Writing in English*, ed. M.K. Naik.

Nath, Suresh. "*The Financial Expert*: An Appraisal." *Perspectives on R.K. Narayan.*

Pandit, M.L. "A Note on the Oedipus of Sophocles and Narayan's Raju." *The Journal of English Studies*, November, 1983.

Parvathi, B. "Themes in the Novels of R.K. Narayan." *The Journal of English Studies,* vol. 13, no. 1, November, 1981.

Peters, John D. "Some American Reflections on Indian Literature in English." *The Journal of Indian Writing in English,* November 1985.

Phillip, David Scott. "The Reinvented Traditionalist." *Perceiving India through the Works of R.K. Narayan, Mulk Raj Anand and Raja Rao.*

Prasad, Hari Mohan. "Shades in the Prism – An analysis of *The Dark Room.*" *Perspectives on R.K.Narayan.*

Rao, S.S. "R.K. Narayan's Art and *The Vendor of Sweets.*" *Triveni,* no. 13, January 1969.

Rao, V. Panduranga. "The Art of R.K. Narayan." *The Journal of Commonwealth Literature,* no. 5, July 1968.

____. "Tea with R.K. Narayan." *The Journal of Commonwealth Literature,* no. 1, June 1971.

____. "The Craftsmanship of R.K.Narayan." *Indian Writing in English.* ed. Ramesh Mohan.

Sethi, Sunil. "Interview of the Fortnight. R.K.Narayan." *India Today,* February 15, 1982.

Sharma K.K. "*The English Teacher*: An Evaluation." *Perspectives on R.K. Narayan.*

Sharma, Som P. "*The Vendor of Sweets*." *Perspectives on R.K. Narayan.*

Shepherd, Ron. "The Sublime and the Ridiculous: Allegory and Irony in R.K. Narayan's Fiction." *R.K.Narayan: A Critical Spectrum*.

Shiva M. Pandya. "R.K. Narayan's *Waiting for the Mahatma*: A Study in Structure and Meaning." *Studies in Modern Fiction.*

Shrivastava, Ramesh K. "Portrayal of Children in R.K. Narayan." *Six Indian Novelists in English.*

____. "What is so Great in R.K. Narayan." *Six Indian Novelists in English.*

Srinath, C.N. "R.K. Narayan's Comic Vision: Possibilities and Limitations." *The Literary Landscape: Essays on Indian Fiction and Poetry in English*.

Sundaram, P.S. "Malgudi: The World of R.K. Narayan." *The Indian P.E.N.*, vol. 43, nos. 1-2, 1977.

Taranath, Rajeev. "The Average as the Positive – A Note on R.K. Narayan." *Critical Essays on Indian Writing in English.*

Thwaite, Anthony. "The Painter of Signs." *Times Literary Supplement,* June 20, 1976.

Varma, R.M. "R.K.Narayan's *A Tiger for Malgudi*." *The Journal of Indian Writing in English*, vol. 13, no. 1, January 1985.

Venkatachari, K. "R.K. Narayan's Novels: Acceptance of Life." *Indian Literature,* XIII, 1 March 1970.

Verghese, C. Paul. "Art of R.K. Narayan." *Problems of the Indian Creative Writer in English.*

Viswanathan, K. "Reluctant Guru." *Perspectives on R.K.Narayan.*

Walsh, William. "R.K.Narayan." *A Manifold Voice: Studies in Commonwealth Literature*.

____. "India." *Commonwealth Literature*.

____. "Nataraja and the Packet of Saffron: The Indian Novel in English." *Readings in Commonwealth Literature*.

____. "The Big Three." *Indian Writing in English.* ed. Ramesh Mohan.

____. "Fiction: The Founding Fathers – Mulk Raj Anand, Raja Rao and R.K. Narayan." *Indian Literature in English.*

Westbrook, Perry D. "The Short Stories of R.K. Narayan." *The Journal of Commonwealth Literature*, no. 5, July 1968.

Williams, H.M. "R.K. Narayan: The Saga of Malgudi." *Studies in Modern Indian Fiction in English.* vol. I.

____. "Precarious Innocence: Patterns in the Malgudi Novels of R.K. Narayan." *Perspectives on R.K. Narayan.*

Woodcock, George. "Narayan, R(asipuram) K(rishnaswami)." *Commonwealth Literature.*

Works on Indian-English Novel

Amur, G.S. *Indian Readings in Commonwealth Literature.* New Delhi: Sterling, 1985.

Dhawan, R.K. *Commonwealth Fiction*. New Delhi: Classical, 1988.

Dwivedi, A.N. ed. *Studies in Contemporary Indian Fiction in English*. Allahabad: Kitab Mahal, 1987.

Harrex, S.C. *The Fire and The Offering: The English Language Novel of India 1935-1970*. Calcutta: Writers Workshop, 1978.

Hemenway, Stephen Ignatius. *The Novel of Inida.* 2 Vols. Calcutta: Writers Workshop, 1975.

Mehta, P.P. *Indo-Anglian Fiction: An Assessment*. Bareilly: Prakash, 1983.

Mukherjee, Meenakshi. *The Twice Born Fiction: Themes and Techniques of the Indian Novel in English*. New Delhi: Arnold-Heinemann, 1974.

Naik, M.K. *Dimensions of Indian English Literature.* New Delhi: Sterling, 1984.

Phillips, David Scott. *Perceiving India through the Works of R.K. Narayan, Mulk Raj Anand and Raja Rao.* New Delhi: Sterling, 1986.

Parameswaran, Uma. *A Study of Representative Indo-English Novelists.* New Delhi: Vikas, 1976.

Raizada, H.C. *The Lotus and The Rose: Indian Fiction in English 1850-1947.* Aligarh: Aligarh Muslim University, 1974.

Ramamurti, K.S. *Rose of the Indian Novel in English.* New Delhi: Sterling, 1987.

Rao, A.V. Krishna. *The Indo-Anglian Novel and the Changing Tradition.* Mysore: Rao and Raghavan, 1972.

Sarma, Gobinda Prasad. *Nationalism in Indo-Anglian Fiction*. New Delhi: Sterling, 1978.

Sharma, K.K. *Indo-English Literature*. Ghaziabad: Vimal, 1977.

Shirwadkar, Meena. *Women in Indo-Anglian Fiction*. New Delhi: Sterling, 1978.

Shrivastava, Ramesh K. *Six Indian Novelists in English*. Amritsar: Guru Nanak Dev University 1987.

Verghese, C.Paul. *Problems of the Indian Creative Writer in English.* Bombay: Somaiya, 1979.

Williams, H.M. *Studies in Modern Indian Fiction in English.* Calcutta: Writers Workshop, 1973.

Books on Indian Writing in English

Iyengar, K.R. Srinivasa. *Indian Writing in English.* New Delhi: Sterling, 1985.

Jotwani, Motilal. *Contemporary Indian Literature and Society.* New Delhi:

Heritage, 1970.

Mukherjee, Meenakshi, ed. *Considerations*. New Delhi: Allied, 1977.

Murti, K.V.S. *Kohinoor in the Crown: Critical Studies in Indian-English Literature.* New Delhi: Sterling, 1987.

Naik, M.K., ed. *Critical Essays on Indian Writing in English*. Delhi: Macmillan, 1977.

____. *A History of Indian English Literature.* Delhi: Sahitya, 1982.

Naipaul, V.S. *India: A Wounded Civilization.* New Delhi: Vikas, 1977.

Narasimhaiah, C.D. *The Swan and The Eagle*. Simla: Indian Institute of Advanced Study, 1969.

____. *Indian Literature of the Past Fifty Years 1917-1967.* Mysore: Rao and Raghavan, 1970.

Sinha, Krishna Nandan, ed. *Indian Writing in English.* New Delhi: Heritage, 1979.

Srinath, C.N. *The Literary Landscape: Essays on Indian Fiction and Poetry in English*. Delhi: Mittal, 1986.

Walsh, William. *Indian Literature in English*. London: Longman, 1990.

Williams, H.M. *Indo-Anglian Literature 1800-1970: A Survery*. Madras: Orient Longman, 1976.

Works on Indian Literature

Radhakrishnan, S. *The Hindu View of Life*. London: George Allen and Unwin, 1967.

____. *The Principal Upanishads.* London: George Allen and Unwin, 1974.

Raja, C. Kunhan. *Some Fundamental Problems in Indian Philosophy.* Delhi: Motilal Banarasidas, 1974.

Taimni, I.K. *The Science of Yoga.* Madras: Theosophical Publishing House, 1974.

Books on Fiction

Lodge, David. *Language of Fiction*. London: Routledge and Kegan Paul, 1970.

Welty, Eudora. *Critical Approaches to Fiction*, ed. Shiv K. Kumar and Keith Mackean. New York: McGraw-Hill, 1968.

Books on Mythology

Frye, Northrop. *Fables of Identity: Studies in Poetic Mythology*. New York, 1963.

Books on Poetry

Gardner, Helen, ed. *The Metaphysical Poets*. Calcutta: Rupa, 1980.

Index